ISBN 0-8148-0730-5
© Éditions Fernand Nathan, 1981.
Reprinted with permission by William S. Konecky Associates, Inc.
Typography by Arts & Letters, Inc., Brookline MA.
English translation by Lawrence Lockwood.
Printed and bound in Hong Kong.

Solange de Mailly Nesle

ASTROLOGY

History, Symbols and Signs

LEON AMIEL PUBLISHER

Introduction

*Can astrology
still contribute
to human
knowledge?*

Astrology: to believe or not to believe? Opinions with respect to astrology, in most instances, owe much more to the realm of belief than to knowledge.

Indeed, in the seventeenth century, Sir Isaac Newton remarked to a disparaging astronomer, "the difference between us, Mr. Halley, is that I have investigated this topic, whereas you have not."

In turn, would it be unwarranted for us to try to form an opinion on this matter and attempt to examine the underlying principles of astrology, so that we may determine whether it should be regarded as a pseudo-science?

For the vast majority of us, the predictive aspect of astrology represents the sole attraction, even though prediction is only one corollary of astrology, and it has probably been misused in too many instances. It would seem that those who consult astrologers reveal needs which are not limited merely to acquiring certainty about the future.

The language of astrology

Astrology is a *socio-historical reality* which emerged 5,000 years ago among the Sumerians and was visibly present in Mesopotamia, in ancient Greece, Rome, and Egypt, in the Islamic World, during the Christian Middle Ages, and during the Renaissance in Europe. Astrology is a mode of thought or a frame of reference which played a role in the lives of our forebears, even though Rationalism abruptly detached us from it three centuries ago. In relation to the history of different civilizations, the latter form of knowledge is of comparatively recent origin, whereas our emotional make-up continues to be influenced by the source of astrological expression, namely, its distinct way of interpreting the world. Thus, it appears valid to determine whether astrology can still help expand our knowledge of the world and our capacity to understand ourselves.

Symbols constitute an instrument for investigating astrology, and these symbols reflect the ways in which mankind defined its own position within the universe during the earliest periods of history.

In those times, the unconscious occupied a predominant position in human thought. Just as we now seek to give priority to the conscious through logic, primitive Man felt a similar need: he expressed the power of his unconscious by associating its content with external objects. Primitive man perceived the external world in the same way that he experienced his own internal world. In this way, he became part of the universe and sought his place within it. Primitive Man lived amidst projections because the logic of conceptual thought had not yet arisen; and symbols were the mode of expression which he adopted.

Symbols trace the entire path extending from unconscious experience to the point of projection, or physical representation. A symbol embodies the scale of correlations which extends from darkness to clarity, from the unconscious to conscious concretization. Thus, symbols represent points of reference or guideposts, permitting identification of the impressions which the mind experiences and providing a means of expressing feelings as a part of life.

The earliest origins

Around 3,000 B.C. in Sumer, the birthplace of astrology, a cosmogonic poem, the *Enuma Elish,* or the preface to the *Epic of Gilgamesh,* provided accounts of the origins of the world.

Mesopotamian cosmogony resembles the types of cosmogony which have been encountered on other continents. The only difference is in terms

Fascinated by the wonders of the universe, men dedicated their souls to understanding its mysteries. Worshippers at Tel Asmar, "the square temple of the god Abu," (circa 2750 B.C.).

Opposite page: Could the cosmos reveal the secrets of deities whom Man had worshipped since the earliest times? (Nebula of Orion).

a unified form and felt a fundamental need to attribute order to phenomena, they gradually classified the heterogeneous aspects of reality while envisioning a hidden homogeneity.

In this way, the Sumerians observed nature in all of its various manifestations, seeking to understand their own presence in the world and impose order on their own lives. They concluded that each component of the universe is linked to the whole. Each aspect of nature on our planet exists in harmony with the movements of the heavens. The microcosm is attuned to the macrocosm, and human beings, who have also sprung from nature, are attuned to the cosmos and are, on their own terms, a cosmos.

This unitary vision of nature, or the over-all oneness of life, is governed by destiny. Every event is derived from a conscious power represented by an array of hierarchically arranged divine wills. It is still necessary, however, to grasp the meaning of *destiny* in the Chaldean religion. Destiny is not synonymous with determinism in the sense in which we employ the latter term today, because the gods who shaped destiny did not deign to control minor events. They only established a somewhat general pattern, which continued to offer considerable freedom, and human beings were ultimately responsible for their own destiny, either by fulfilling it on an ordinary scale, or through exemplary feats, as in the case of Gilgamesh. As mortals imitate the exemplary behavior of the gods, and as mortals are compared with them in their accomplishments or daily lives, they draw closer to the gods, thereby transcending the human condition. The gods indicated paths which could be followed, but men were obliged to decipher their messages and choose their own paths.

of its abundant creativity. Of course, it is not compatible with contemporary scientific verification, but one undeniable fact persists: similar myths and types of cosmogony have been observed in various regions of the globe which could not have been in contact with one another.

According to the theories of antiquity, the heavens and the earth had been separated, but the heavens imparted a legacy, an indelible imprint: by understanding the earth, Man could understand the heavens, and conversely, by observing the heavens, he could interpret the terrestrial milieu.

First by intuition, and then empirically, the Sumerians proceeded to develop a scale of correlations between earthly events and celestial phenomena. Since they intuitively perceived the universe in

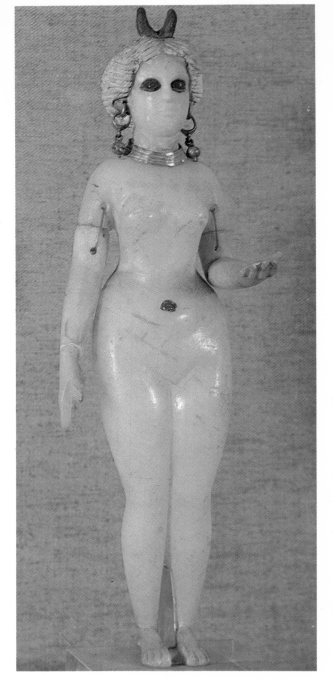

The entire universe was seen as a book of omens through which the divine powers which governed life could communicate with mortals; hence the importance of celestial omens.[1] The Sumerians, who invented cuneiform, which was composed of wedge-shaped characters engraved upon clay tablets, were able to bequeath us the ancient records of their observations from the tops of the *ziggurats:* "heavenly hills" or "towers between the heavens and the earth." These structures have been rediscovered in Babylon, Ur, Erech and Lagash. The *ziggurats* were built with unbaked bricks, in the form of seventy-story pyramids, reaching heights of as much as 84 meters (273 feet). The *ziggurats* were used both as granaries and as temples for observing the heavens.

From the tops of the *ziggurats,* the priests, who were astronomers and astrologers, observed the heavens each night by means of the gnomon (a sun-dial which was invented by the Sumerians and improved in a later era by Anaximander of Miletus) and the clepsydra (a type of water clock).

Amidst the sea of stars scattered throughout the sky, the priests gradually discovered five specific bodies, which, unlike the others, were not stationary. These travelling bodies were called the five wild goats, or the five planets.

Over the centuries, the Sumerians classified the distinctive features of the planets, recording their information on clay tablets. They observed the trajectory of each planet, computed its distance from the earth, and observed the brightness, color, and size of the planets. The external characteristics of

the planets were gradually associated with the gods — the spiritual powers which had created the universe according to Sumerian cosmogony.

The gods represented primordial images of human existence; they were *archetypes,* or, indeed, original models derived from the psyche. By the process of projection, these internal images were rendered coherent and through religion acquired concreteness.

In this way, men associated or linked — hence the term *religo* — the hidden regions of the mind, or the content of the unconscious, with externally visible forms within a mystical framework.

Preceding pages: "Jupiter," the King of the Gods, was associated with the largest and most awe-inspiring planet, which majestically leads its satellites through the heavens (Jupiter and its four satellites: Io, Europa, Ganymede, and Callisto).

1. Instead of being merely a technique for predicting the future, astrology represented a metaphysical vision of the world. "It was like mental music, the consummate symphony of the whole," according to Philo of Alexandria, who was one of the philosophers who most fully understood the Chaldeans.

Thus, earthly phenomena depended directly upon the deities. The god *Sin,* or the Moon, who governed fertility and the life-force, thereby causing vegetation to grow, was associated with trees and plants. The planets represented the gods themselves, or served as their messengers, expressing the activities of the gods and the influence which they wielded over life itself.

The unity of symbols

In various regions of the globe, the same symbols have been associated with the same planets. For example, there are the different representations of *Venus:* whether one speaks of the Amorites' goddess Nana, the Phoenicians' Astarte, Ishtar among the Assyrians, Aphrodite among the Greeks, or Hindu and Chinese equivalents, the morning star, throughout the world, has symbolized love or the force which attracts creatures to one another, as well as beauty. Both Shamash and Apollo are solar deities who were invoked in order to gain enlightenment. And, Apollo, the Greek god of light, whose bow and arrows symbolize the sun and its rays, was invoked when Plato was searching for ways to determine the fundamental laws of the Republic: "Apollo, the Delphic deity, has seen fit to provide the most important, the most beautiful, and the earliest laws (. . .) because this god traditionally interprets religion (. . .) in order to offer guidance to mankind," *(The Republic).*

Symbols are ageless, and they recur throughout the centuries. The Sun, which illuminates, radiates, and enriches, became the God of Justice and Truth, represented by Apollo in Greece and, later, in 1st century Rome (right). This type of symbolism was repeated eleven centuries later in Christian places of worship. For example, the Cathedral of Gerona in Spain contained this decorative tapestry (12th century).

Similarly, the following hymn was sung in Mesopotamia to honor Shamash: "Your rays uncover secrets, continuously revealing their pathways with a burst of light... You guide all living things, without exceptions. In the upper and lower regions, you are our protector..."

Mercury, known as Hermes among the Greeks, was the divine messenger who symbolized Communication and who was equivalent to Nabou, the divine scribe, or the lord of science and the written word in Mesopotamia.

The Greeks' *Ares* and *Nergal* were gods of war.

Saturn and *Ninib* were both envisioned as wise old men, whose intellectual skills outweighed physical prowess. Occupying the highest position in the heavens, Saturn, closest to the upper spheres, or the seat of divine power, elevated the spirit through renunciation of earthly desires.

Similarities in imagery have existed for all of the planets among all civilizations which have observed and worshipped the heavens. The Babylonian lunar deity, *Sin,* constitutes an exception, however, inasmuch as masculine characteristics were attributed to the Moon (in this instance), whereas the Greeks considered the Moon to be feminine.

For this reason, we should not be surprised by the rapidity with which Mesopotamian planetary deities and those of Greek mythology intermingled during the fourth century before Christ, at the time of Alexander the Great's conquests in Asia.

These gods possessed the same essential meaning and reflected identical modes of experience: planetary symbols permeated the Chaldeans' primordial vision of life, and the gods of Greek mythology embodied the vision of the Greeks. There was a shared history, the history of the human soul, and there were the same forms of memory, which, since Jung,[1] have been known as the *collective unconscious.*

---

1. Carl Gustav Jung (1875-1961), a Swiss psychiatrist and psychologist who was the founder of "depth psychology," studied the "collective unconscious" in relation to archetypes" and the "principle of synchronicity."

Iouis.   *Sar nus.*   *cya rs.*

Septem   *planete.*

Sol.

lucifer.   *Mercurius.*

luna.

Situated at the center of our universe and surrounded by planets, the Sun symbolizes an enlightened conscience. Its chariot symbolizes its path through the firmament, as well as the ideals which we strive to attain (13th century manuscript).

The collective unconscious embraces identical patterns and forms of behavior which mankind has developed in response to identical natural phenomena. These elements coalesce into patterns which Jung called *archetypes,* and subsequent explanations will be those which the famous psychologist offered. Archetypes can help us understand the subject of astrology. They condense the earliest forms of human experience into universal and primordial images. It is believed that archetypes are innate and that they were engraved upon our psyches and imprinted within our brains at the earliest stages of development, as a result of Man's earliest experiences; thus, archetypes are transmitted by heredity to every person who comes into the world.

Mythological language expresses these archetypes, portraying them as deities. Mythology is the history of the human psyche or of the expression of the soul. Thus, it is highly logical for psychologists to draw upon Greek mythology in order to explain typical human behavior patterns.

The twelve principal Greek deities are exemplary images which embody eternal characteristics, predominant personality types, and predominant tendencies within the unconscious. In spite of efforts by the conscious to maintain mastery, all of us depend upon the unconscious; for primitive Man, it represented hidden forces which he could not control. Whereas these forces appear to render the vicissitudes of our lives incomprehensible, our ancestors sought to fathom their meaning. Why should the natural phenomenon of human evolution be different from the rest of nature? Why should human beings constitute an exception to the order of the universe?

In seeking to understand nature, primitive Man strove to uncover the hidden meaning of his own destiny. As laws concerning nature and the cosmos

Man within the universe:
Man is not isolated
from the universe. He fully
belongs to the universe and
is a miniature image of it:
a microcosm.

been brought into play. Deep within us, however, like a sediment which has accumulated for hundreds of years, there are the unconscious patterns bequeathed by our ancestors. The primordial way of perceiving the world persists, because our brains are not devoid of imprints: we come into the world with an age-old transcript of the prior experiences of our ancestors. We are born with a collective memory called the *collective unconscious.* Through dreams, unconscious patterns reappear: images of the Sun and Moon, which are present in every person's dreams, acquire the same meanings that were attributed to them during Antiquity. Analysis of dreams shows that the Sun image represents the father, the conscious mind, or society: the Ideal. These meanings are precisely the meanings which have been associated with the Sun by astrological tradition in keeping with the myth of Apollo.

Dreams spontaneously rekindle the multiple factors which, in earlier times, played a role in human experience. Dreams link us to the cosmos, and demonstrate that there is still an unconscious, yet authentic association between man as a microcosm and the universe as a macrocosm. Dreams open a door to the primeval darkness of the cosmos, and permit us to renew our ties with the eternal.

The firmament above may be regarded as infinite space, but our inner firmament, the unconscious is filled with its imprint. The gods of Olympus still reside within us but have acquired other names. Because we are accustomed to seeing their unceasing journeys through the cosmos, we do not readily understand this point. The gods, as primordial images within our unconscious, were concretized in the firmament. Although we no longer perceive these deities in the heavens, the psychic factors which brought them to life have not been abruptly erased.

emerged, there was an intimation of the eternal laws governing the ostensible disorder of human existence. The universe and the planets became a mirror for human beings, who could then comprehend themselves in relation to images derived from nature.

In our own era, however, we have forgotten and even denied our connections with the firmament. We are no longer capable of recognizing our affinity to other components of the universe. Nevertheless, the atoms within our bodies, atoms which are composed of nuclei and particles, strangely resemble a sun with orbiting planets.

The collective unconscious

The universe has been transformed from a spiritual entity into a quantifiable, physical one: logic has

Whereas the firmament has constituted a theatre for our primordial images, our abandoning this theatre has not deleted its essence from our psyche. An author does not cease to exist when his play ceases to be performed. No longer in the public eye, he remains in the shadows. The same is true of astrology. The starry firmament of our birth no longer contains the gods who once appeared upon this stage, but our inner firmament still contains "psychic factors." In this way, it provides an echo of what we are in relation to the universe. "You can find the stars of your destiny within your own heart," (Schiller).

Our inner firmament

Accordingly, it is possible to affirm that astrological symbols reflect the universe of our unconscious and that interpreting these symbols naturally incorporates methods which cannot rely upon purely intellectual processes. An aspect which surprises novices when they first encounter astrological symbols is that these symbols always encompass multiple meanings that appear to lack consistency. The reason is that a symbol can bring together various aspects of existence or the different forms which a given entity may display. As we have seen, symbols express combinations of different tendencies, embracing both the concrete and the abstract, although the various aspects may be interrelated in ways which are not always recognizable through logical inquiry. In order to approach astrological symbols and understand the intrinsic correlations that they offer, it is now sufficient to follow the interplay of analogies intuitively, so that we may permit the images of their concealed harmony to be rekindled within us.

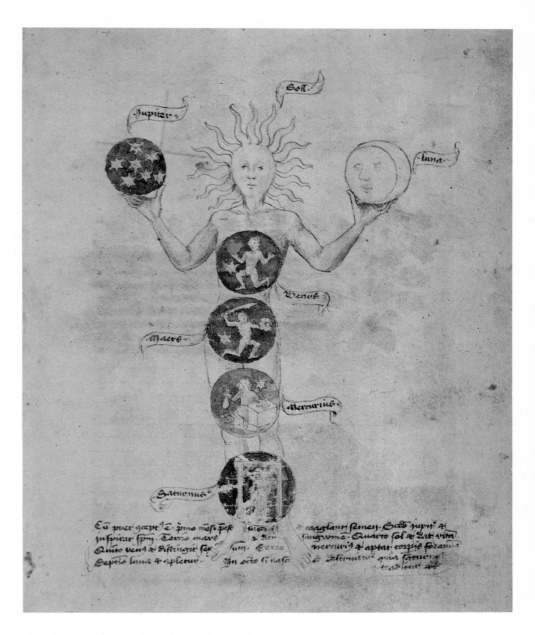

The universe within Man: The planets have been present within us from the beginning; they represent our inner firmament.

For example, the Sun, by analogy with the dialectic which it maintains with the Moon, and which is entirely comparable to the dialectic existing between men and women, represents the masculine pole. Through its role in relation to the movements of the planets, the Sun also represents the father who provides guidance for a child discovering the world. In terms of this same correlation, the Sun becomes the role that one wishes to possess within society, and, just as the Sun is the center of our world, its symbolic form can be interpreted as the center of gravity which human beings seek to attain. Lastly, inasmuch as the Sun provides light for the world, it represents a pole where one encounters conscious thought, as well as the ideals or meaning which we constantly seek to give to our lives.

Looking at Ares or Mars, the warrior archetype, we encounter all of the modes of applying com-

Are we possibly coming close to understanding how forms of energy within the universe are interrelated?

bative, aggressive, impulsive, or defensive energy, varying from the energy of an infant instinctively expressing its presence within the world to the energy of a military leader who fights to defend or conquer a region, or a doctor who attempts to thwart death, or an athlete who struggles to expand the limits of human potential, as André Barbault[1] has explained so appropriately. The Mars symbol is understood and concretely represented in our lives

in various forms derived from a single set of correlations. It is even possible to speculate that its potential has not been exhausted and that, in the future, when our civilization enters another phase where our way of life shall depend even more upon computerized information, the vital energy and the drive to dominate our surroundings which Mars represents may be expressed in other ways. When the instinct to struggle for survival can no longer be expressed by the forms which have existed thus far, it may be expressed by a different type of combat; for example, defense of one's territory may occur in the form of battles between brains, as "para-psychological" warfare, where the energy Mars represents shall be symbolically transferred to "flexing of the brain."

Thus, each symbol represented by the planets em-

The God of War, as he appears here, was associated with the planet Mars, which periodically glows as it approaches the Earth and then quickly moves away.

1. André Barbault, *Connaissance de l'astrologie* (Understanding Astrology) (Seuil, 1975).

braces different levels of existence or different modes of expression, which are unrelated to one another except through patterns of functional similarities. It is only possible to grasp these intrinsic laws with a mental subtlety which is different from logic and could be called "poetry" in the Greek sense of the word: the effort to produce something, or the capacity to create. The plurivalence of symbols can be compared to seemingly different systems which actually represent a single structure, even though, in many instances, the code can only be deciphered by methods which are confined to an intuitive level (all of the systems of biological existence, beginning with the atom and the cell, up to Man himself).

Inch by inch, we are unravelling the invisible symbolic threads which are interlaced throughout the universe and were perceived by our forbears.

Each planet is, above all, the symbol of a collective tendency that is inherent in all human beings, although each of us at the moment of birth manifests these tendencies in our own way in relation to the positions of planets within the heavens.

The planets represent a fundamental source of energy whose different modes of expression correspond to the intrinsic harmony of specific symbols. In turn, the rhythms of the planets and their movements within the cosmos determine the cycles by which energy is to be released.

As a whole, the planets represent mental images of these forms of energy, conveyed to us by the collective unconscious: symbolic patterns are true-to-life testimony. Whereas astrology is no longer placed within a religious framework, it can be situated within a physical and metaphysical perspective of the universe; the natural laws of the universe which we shall rediscover were concealed by divine intention. Thus, if the planets retain all of the qualities which centuries of mythology have attributed to them, they now constitute expressions of natural laws, instead of deities.

The planets represent the different manifestations of our inner reality, on the basis of patterns of unconscious analogies between humanity as a microcosm and the universe as a macrocosm. The planets are our inner cosmos.

Poets have sometimes used the "royal path" of symbols to express unity within the universe. Mozart's "Magic Flute" expressed this quest, and Karl Friedrich Schinkel marvelously evoked it in the decor of the throne room within the palace of the Queen of Night.

19

Bootes aut Ophylax hr stellas i dextera manu .uij. que ñ occidunt i capite .i. i singlis humis .i. mamill sigla i dextro cubito .i. inr genua .i. i singlis pedibz singlas. Bootes post tgum urse maioris uersis pedibz ad uirgine uideris.

Corona hr stellas .uiij. i orbe positas que ñ occidunt clare contra caput serpentis septemtrionalis

Serpentarius sub hcule posit e. Serpenta i capite .ij. i singlis pedibz t humis .i. i sinistra manu .ij. i dextra .iiij. i cubitis singlis t genib; singlas. i crure .i. fiunt .xvj. omis clare. Serpens i ore .ij. t i capite .iiij. usz ad manu se tenentes i flexu corpis .xv.

Scorpione calcat serpentarius.

Scorpius hr stellas in singlis cornib; .ij. i frote .iij. claras. in dorso .iij. i uentre .ij. in cauda .v. in aculeo .ij. fiut .xix. hr i spaciu duox signox partitus.

Virgo hr stellam i capite obscura .i. i singlis humis singlas i sinistra ala .i. i singulis cubitis singlas. in singlis manib; singlas sz i sinistra clariore q uocatur spica. i tunica obscuras .vi. i singlis pedibz singlas. suma .xvij.

virgo ob pedibus boetis e: confan tiores pedes urse maioris.

Leo hr stellas in capite .iij. i collo .ij. i pectore .i. i spina

ry in cauda media .i. i sum mitate caude .i. clau sub uentre .i. sub pec tore .y. i pedibz pon b; claram .i. in me dietate uentris .i. in libz .i. in posteriori genu .i. Summa .xvij. uider alie ad cauda et .vij.

Cancer hr stellas i pecto re .ij. qs appellant asinos inr qs e nubicula candide colois q psepiu appellat i dextris utrisq; pedibz iiij. obscure. in sinistra pte pede priori .ij. i scdo .y. i uno una i qrto .i. i dextro cornu .ij. i sinist .ij. summa .xxvij.

Leo iuxta geminos po sit e. Sed his in dorso psepiu.

Geminox unum qui iuxta cancru e hr stellam i capite .i. claram. i singlis humis singlas cla ras. i dextro pede .i. i singlis genib; singlas. in pedibz singlis sin gulas. Alr hr in ca pite .i. i mamillis singulas. in sinistro cubito .ij. i manu .i. i sinistro genu .i. in pedibz singulas. iuxta sinistrum pedem .i. que uocatur pp. Summa .xviij. Gemini habet a leuo latere agitatorem.

Agitator comitatur sinistrum tangit.

Taur hr stellas in u troq; cornu .i. i utq; oclo .i. i naso .i. hee .v. hyadas uocat. i ungla .ij. i collo .ij. i dorso .ij. sub uentre .i. i pectore .i.

Taurus orione tangit qu sub illo e situs.

Sunt .xvij. stel le athalantides ul' pliades i cau da tauri posite. Sed septima obsca et.

Orion hr stellas i capite .iij. claras. in singlis humis singlas claras. i dext cubiro .i. obscura. i dext manu .i. in balteo .iij. i ech indicu .iij. claras. i genib; singlas. i pedibz singlas. fiut .xvj.

Orion sub tauro e.

Development of the Zodiac

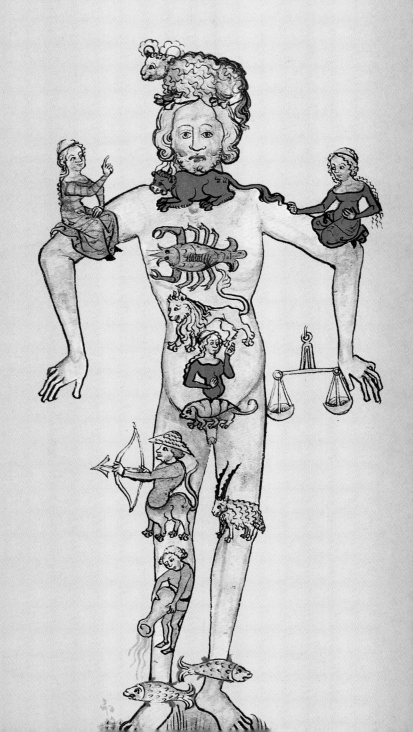

"*Blessed art thou, unfathomable Matter,
stretching in all directions, from our souls
to the Realm of Essences,
making us yearn to rend
the seamless veil
of phenomena.*"

PIERRE THEILARD DE CHARDIN

The Zodiac

The Chaldeans have been recognized as the earliest civilization to observe the planets, but astrology as a mathematical science originated among the Greeks. The intermingling of Mesopotamian and Greek culture gave rise to astrology, or the science of the stars.

When Alexander the Great returned from his conquests during the fourth century before Christ, he was accompanied by Berossus (*circa* 330-? B.C.), a Chaldean astrologer who established a school of astrology on the island of Cos and disseminated Chaldean scientific knowledge.

Right: a manuscript indicating positions of the Sun and Moon in relation to signs of the Zodiac, identified according to months.

Opposite page: Illumination from 15th century French manuscript. Planets are represented by personified images who rule the signs of the Zodiac. Above, Aquarius and Capricorn are ruled by Saturn; Aries and Scorpio by Mars; Taurus and Libra by Venus; and Gemini and Virgo by Mercury. In turn, Cancer is dominated by the Moon, and Leo is governed by the Sun.

Preceding pages: Man encompasses the celestial and the terrestrial. Each sign of the Zodiac is associated with a part of the body.

Chaldean and Greek concepts of the universe were similar in many ways.

Whereas Chaldean concepts were more primitive, the Greeks developed a more refined perspective.

Pythagoras, Plato, Aristotle, and other thinkers had erected a structured interpretation of reality: the universe was a single entity, wherein each component was analogous to the whole. In other words, the microcosm incorporated the image of the macrocosm. "Everything in the heavens resembles everything which exists below, and everything below resembles everything in the heavens." (The "hermetic" doctrine was attributed to the deity *Hermes Trismegistus,* "three times greater," who was the counterpart of the Egyptian deity Thoth.) It follows that since human beings were interconnected with a universe composed of interdependent parts, they were interconnected with the planets.

The Greeks developed a mathematical and geometrical framework for their world-view, relying upon Pythagoras' science of numbers. Hence, the universe was perceived in terms of harmonies and rhythms.

Accordingly, Berossus did not come to a region devoid of expertise in astronomy. Indeed, the Greeks had studied the movements of the Sun and the Moon, as well as the positions of planets, and they had also created a Zodiac, which was developed in a definitive form during the era of Hipparchus (second century before Christ).

The origins of the Zodiac remain obscure.

An almost identical symbol — a wheel divided into twelve equal sections with specific names — has been found in Egypt, Judea, Persia, India, Tibet, China, North and South America, Scandinavia and the Islamic World.

23

From the wheel of life to the zodiac

Zodiac is derived from the Greek word *zôè*, meaning "life," and from *diakos*, which means "wheel." Hence, the word *zodiac* can be translated as "the Wheel of Life."

Nevertheless, *zôè* is etymologically linked to *zôon*, which means "animal," and the Zodiac has often been called "the Path of the Animals." Eight of the twelve signs actually represent animals. The meaning of the signs remains unclear, but they continue to constitute "symbols" in the purest sense.

Through studying hieroglyphic and etymological content we can use the fields of ontogeny ("study of origins") and mythology to explore the pri-mordial meanings of the signs, which may be a summation of universal laws formulated during antiquity.

Names for the signs were not chosen at random; indeed, they reflect gradual development among different civilizations, ever since mankind has studied the heavens, in order to understand his position within the universe.

The Ancient World believed that all energy was identical, producing multiple forms of matter (involution) as it underwent various transformations. At the lowest point in the cycle, energy was redirected toward increasingly intricate forms, where multiplicity was reconciled with oneness (evolution). In this way, the circular structure of the Zodiac may allegorically express the principal categories of vibrations within the universe, or different states of mind.

Nevertheless, human beings, with only a limited awareness of the energy which they absorb or release, are governed by an often incomprehensible destiny. Mythology recounts the battles of heroes against demons who pursue or attack them. A hero's triumph expresses an ascent to a higher level of awareness, indeed absolute awareness: (do the demons represent currents of energy, or as we would say today, "psychological drives" which we must resist?)

Because each sign is dominated by a planet or a deity identified by mythology, the signs represent thresholds which human consciousness must cross in order to attain completeness.

One of the most ancient myths — 3,000 years before the Christian era — is the myth of *Gilgamesh,* which originated in Chaldea. Although it has not yet been possible to detect references to the constellations of the Zodiac, the twelve cantos of the *Epic of Gilgamesh* actually appear to represent the twelve sections of the Zodiac.

Gilgamesh, the son of a goddess and a mortal, was the despotic ruler of Uruk during the phase of the Bull. He ravished women and young girls, and he pursued a life of debauchery in his palace. Enkedu, who is described in a manner linking him to symbols corresponding to Aries, was sent to kill Gilgamesh. In the ensuing battle, Gilgamesh triumphed, and the two men became friends (this situation may symbolize the two twins represented by Gemini). Subsequently, they traveled to a cedar

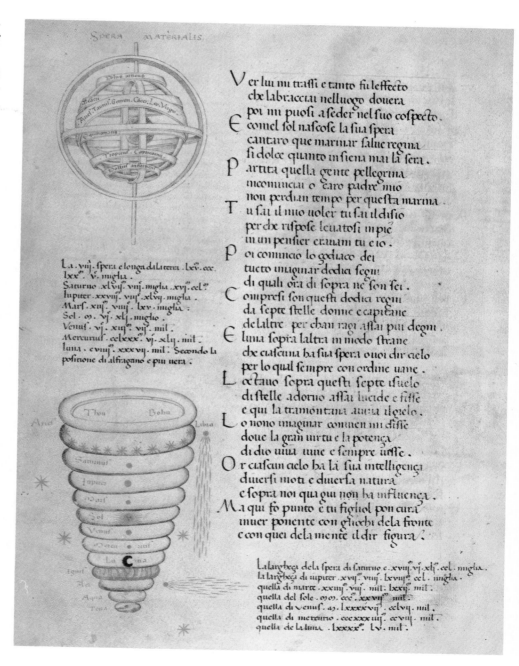

The mystical ascent: representation of forms of planetary energy marking stages of transformation.

The symbolic struggle between Man and his inner demons, represented by struggle between a hero and a lion.

forest, where the two heroes slew a monstrous creature which was a Moon-Demon (a demon from the unconscious, representing a transition to symbols associated with Cancer).

After this victory, Gilgamesh acquired the attributes of a Sun-Hero (the Leo sign), and, later, in the eighth canto, when he sought to descend to the netherworld, he was obliged to fight against scorpion-men, thereby evoking the eighth sign.

The *Epic of Gilgamesh* portraying a man's quest for immortality, may have inspired several myths, including the Labors of Hercules (where it is also possible to identify the twelve signs of the Zodiac). In harmony with the twelve phases of the Sun, this epic recounts the temptations which human beings must confront in pursuing self-awareness. During Antiquity, the quest for self-awareness consisted of entering an inner labyrinth and emerging victoriously. Triumphing over oneself produced a state of mind which, even though it could not be imparted to others, was a level of experience: in other words, wisdom.

From symbols to the twelve constellations: the Path of the Sun

Gradual development

The astrologer-priests who observed the heavens 3,000 years before the Christian era had determined that planetary motion occurs against a background of unmoving stars. Gradually, the stars were classified according to visually identifiable patterns: the constellations. Thus, the constellations became a backdrop, or, to a certain extent, a map for plotting the movements of the Sun, the Moon, and the planets.

The greatest attention was allotted to the Moon, because it is closest to the Earth, and the constellations were initially divided according to the twenty-eight positions within the lunar trajectory. Thus, the earliest zodiacs which have been discovered in Babylonia, India and China are lunar zodiacs.

In a later period, after it had been determined that the principal heavenly body governing our lives is the Sun, the twelve phases of the Sun were added to the Zodiac, and ultimately replaced the phases of the Moon.

The nomenclature for the twelve solar sectors, which was introduced during the era of Hammurabi, is already recognizable on Chaldean tablets produced as early as 1200 B.C. Nevertheless, the Greeks furnished the definitive nomenclature when Greek and Chaldean scientific knowledge merged during the third century before Christ.

Aries ("the Ram") was called *Ku,* and was identified by the epithet "the hired hand."

Taurus ("the Bull") was called "the jaw of the ox."

Gemini was called "the twin giants."

Cancer was represented by a land-crab known as *Nangar,* meaning "wood-worker or carpenter."

Leo was already being named after the lion, but it was also known as "the noble dog," or even "the king."

Virgo was called *Mi,* which means "a cluster of flowers."

Libra was represented by two stars which had been identified in the Northern and Southern Hemispheres, known as "the trays of the scale."

Scorpio was called *Gir,* which means "scorpion."

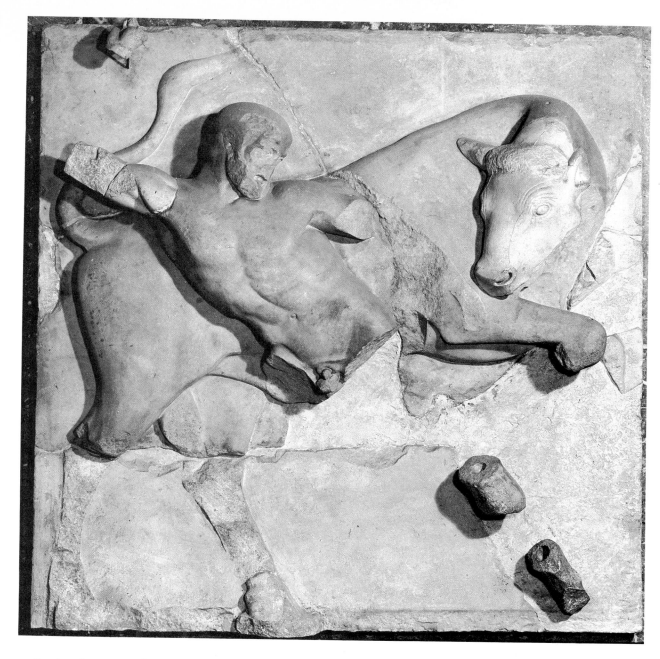

Zodiacal symbolism is expressed within the Twelve Feats of Hercules, representing the triumph of the human soul over its weaknesses, as portrayed within this Greek bas-relief, where Hercules is taming the Cretan bull.

Sagittarius was called *Pal-Bih-Sag,* but this sign had not yet acquired its present-day meaning.

Capricorn was a fish or a goat, and this symbolic association has survived.

Aquarius, known as *Gu,* embodied the concept of "currents of fresh water."

Pisces, known as *Zib-Me,* which means "tails," appeared to symbolize the Tigris and the Euphrates.

It has often been thought that the Zodiac and astrology itself were of Egyptian origin. Indeed, there are texts indicating that frequent contact between Egypt and Chaldea existed as early as 1500 B.C. Nevertheless, comparison of Chaldean and Egyptian mathematical texts which have been preserved demonstrates that the Chaldeans were more scientifically advanced. This factor explains their leading role in astronomy, and it provides a basis for believing that the Egyptians may have acquired much of their knowledge from Chaldea.

The Greeks themselves, for a long time, fostered the misconception of Egyptian superiority. They probably exaggerated Egypt's cultural importance because they had maintained commercial and military ties with Egypt from 700 B.C. to 400 B.C., whereas the Persians were their adversaries. Hence, the Greeks were accustomed to claiming the Egyptians as their precursors in such fields as metaphysics, arithmetic, and geometry, because they sought to honor the Egyptians and, perhaps, to boast of their own ties with Egypt, but also because they were less familiar with Mesopotamian culture.

The Egyptians contributed to development of the Zodiac. The Zodiac of Denderah, discovered during Napoleon's campaigns, is one of the oldest known.

Opposite page: During the Christian Middle Ages, a renewal of Greek knowledge took place under the influence of the Arabs, who copied the earliest manuscripts from Ptolemy's era and bequeathed them to our culture. This is a 9th or 10th century version of a Ptolemaic planisphere.

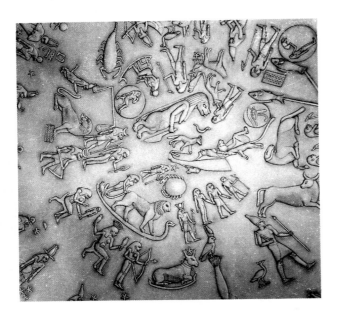

The Egyptians displayed little curiosity in terms of determining the trajectories of planets. They were primarily concerned with the ascent of equatorial constellations because they hoped to predict flooding of the Nile. In Egypt, stellar astronomy was predominant. It is difficult, in any respect, to speak of true astrology among the Egyptians, except insofar as astrology may have been accessible solely to the initiated, royalty, and the priesthood, and may have thus far eluded rediscovery in our era.[1]

During the third century before Christ, after the victories of Alexander the Great, the Greeks disseminated their knowledge in Egypt, and widespread interest in astrology began to develop from then on.

One legacy is the famous Zodiac of Denderah, discovered during Napoleon's campaigns, and it has been the source of many historical conjectures. Initially, this Zodiac was believed to predate the Christian era by 5,000 years or more, although it was later attributed to the Roman period. On the basis of carbon-14 analysis, some persons have revived the earlier viewpoint, or have suggested that the Zodiac of Denderah was created gradually. Which theory is closer to the truth?

Although the Egyptians' contributions to the development of astrology were relatively limited on account of their apparent lack of interest in the planets, they definitely contributed to development of the Zodiac, as did most of the Mediterranean civilizations, along with other civilizations seeking to identify sources of energy within the cosmos.

The Zodiac, which began to be developed in Greece during the fifth century before Christ and was completed during the second century before Christ, is a repository which summarizes and concretizes Mesopotamian, Greek, and Egyptian symbolic traditions within a circular configuration. It traces the observable path of the Sun in relation to the belt of stars surrounding the Earth, thereby permitting identification of planetary positions. During the era of the Stoics, Aristarchus of Samos (*circa* 310-230 B.C.) had already determined that the Earth rotates around the Sun, and not vice versa. Twenty more centuries would elapse before this theory was confirmed by Copernicus.

---

1. I am inclined toward the latter viewpoint: astrological practices definitely existed in Egypt, but astrology was of a mystical nature, beyond the secular sphere, and its lore was only revealed to the initiated, who were seeking a means of salvation and ultimate freedom for the soul. This was an esoteric form of knowledge, instead of being an esoteric science, as it later became among the Greeks. Pythagoras must have been aware of this occult knowledge, which set the stage for dissemination of Chaldean astrology.

ISTA PROPRIO SUDORE NOMINA UNOQUOQUE lepuf
PROPRIA EGO INDIGNUS SACERDOS ET MONA
CHUS HOMINE GERUUIGUS REPPERI AC
SCRIPSI PIXLEGENTIBUS

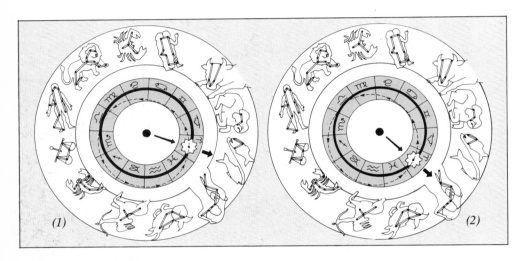

Precession of equinoxes

● *The Earth at the center of the Zodiac*

☼ *The Sun*

⚹ *The ecliptic, or the path of the Sun*

🌑 *The celestial equator (projection in relation to plane of the terrestrial equator).*

● *Vernal point (white area within Zodiac derived from Sun signs).*

Shaded circle: Zodiac with Sun signs.
Unshaded circle: Zodiac according to constellations.

Nevertheless, the usefulness of the Zodiac does not diminish, because it constitutes a frame of reference for determining relative positions of the Sun and the planets with respect to the Earth.

On the other hand, the names formerly given to constellations no longer correspond to the positions defined by astronomy. For example, the Spring equinox, or the point at which the Sun ascends toward the junction between the ecliptic[1] and the equator, no longer coincides with the constellation of Aries. Instead, the Spring equinox coincides with Pisces and shall soon shift to Aquarius.

This change in positions is attributable to a slight tilting of the Earth, caused by solar and lunar gravitational attraction. Accordingly, the celestial poles and the celestial equator have been reoriented to some extent: the vernal location corresponding to 0° with Aries when development of the Zodiac probably began has retrogressed in a clockwise direction. This phenomenon is known as equinoctial precession.

Hipparchus had already discovered equinoctial precession during the second century before Christ, but his observations did not affect astrological interpretations because the signs had traditionally been regarded as points of reference for determining relative positions of the Sun and the Earth. In other words, between March 21 and April 21 (the Spring eqinox), the Sun, as it did in the past, enters a celestial region representing the pattern of forces symbolized by Aries. At this time, the North Pole and the South Pole on our planet remain equidistant from the Sun, and the vibrational relationship between the Sun and the Earth is still the same. These conditions are symbolically represented by Aries.[2]

Thus, it is necessary to avoid confusion between the so-called "Zodiac of signs" and the Zodiac derived from constellations, even though they would be superimposed during the Aries phase. It should be recalled that one type of Zodiac indicates relative positions of the Earth and the Sun, whereas the other type represents the belt of stars surrounding our planet. Astrology has been greatly harmed by confusion between the principles underlying each

---

1. The ecliptic is the outline of the apparent path of the Sun, as observed from the Earth.

2. During the second century before Christ, Ptolemy, whose *Tetrabiblos* offered a definitive codification of astrology, explained how the signs were divided: for example, Libra corresponded to the seventh phase, because "day and night are of equal duration throughout the Earth" during the Autumn equinox. The Crab (Cancer) represented the fourth phase, "because the Sun, upon entering this sign, travels in an opposite latitude," and, "with the Crab governing Summer, the general nature of the signs is consistent with the seasons." This example demonstrates that names had not been adopted in relation to images represented by the celestial constellations, but in relation to the respective positions of the Earth and the Sun.

type of Zodiac. After having provided points of reference within the heavens, the signs of the Zodiac constitute a basis for contemplating the laws which the Ancient World had formulated for the universe, laws which modern science may yet rediscover.

A rational explanation for the Zodiac?

Why were twelve signs chosen for dividing the Zodiac? Was this an arbitrary choice?

Daniel Verney, in *Fondements et Avenir de l'astrologie* (The Origins and Future of Astrology, Fayard, 1974), accepts the belief that "the signs of the Zodiac represent potential modes of existence within terrestrial universality," but he observes that this factor "does not explain how a discontinuous qualitative structure is compatible with a region which remains continuous."

What constitutes a possible scientific basis for dividing the Zodiac into twelve sections?

Michel Auphan offers a hypothesis which has been adopted by Daniel Verney: duodecimal (by twelve) division is derived from the interaction of groups of waves with different axes...and it corresponds to ratios for basic frequencies: 1, 2, and 3.

"Beginning with its intersection with the equator (vernal location), the ecliptic is divisible into twelve sectors, on account of the presence of a system of waves arranged within the Earth like portions of an orange. The trajectory of the Sun and the Earth's rotation upon its axis influence this system of waves. Each of the twelve sectors is the source of a type of vibration with a distinct configuration. It is mathematically possible to discover the specificity and spatial arrangement of signs and to reencounter the principal elements of the astrological tradition." If this hypothesis can be verified, it shall become necessary to reexamine our presence within the uni-

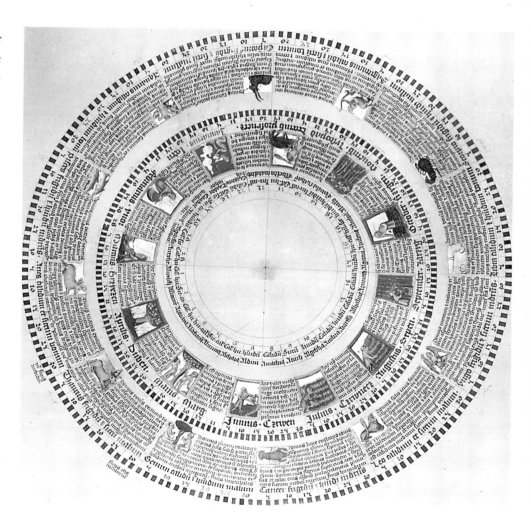

verse: the Zodiac may represent a means of access to our interaction with universality.

Raymond Abellio, in *La Fin de l'esoterisme* (The Purpose of the Occult), has affirmed that "it shall therefore be indispensable for astrology to be elevated from the position of a science, or, indeed, an art, to a 'higher' level where it must then be regarded as a pillar of wisdom."

Signs of the Zodiac are only defined according to relative positions of the Earth and the Sun, and they are therefore associated with natural phenomena: 14th century Zodiac indicating seasonal activities corresponding to each sign.

31

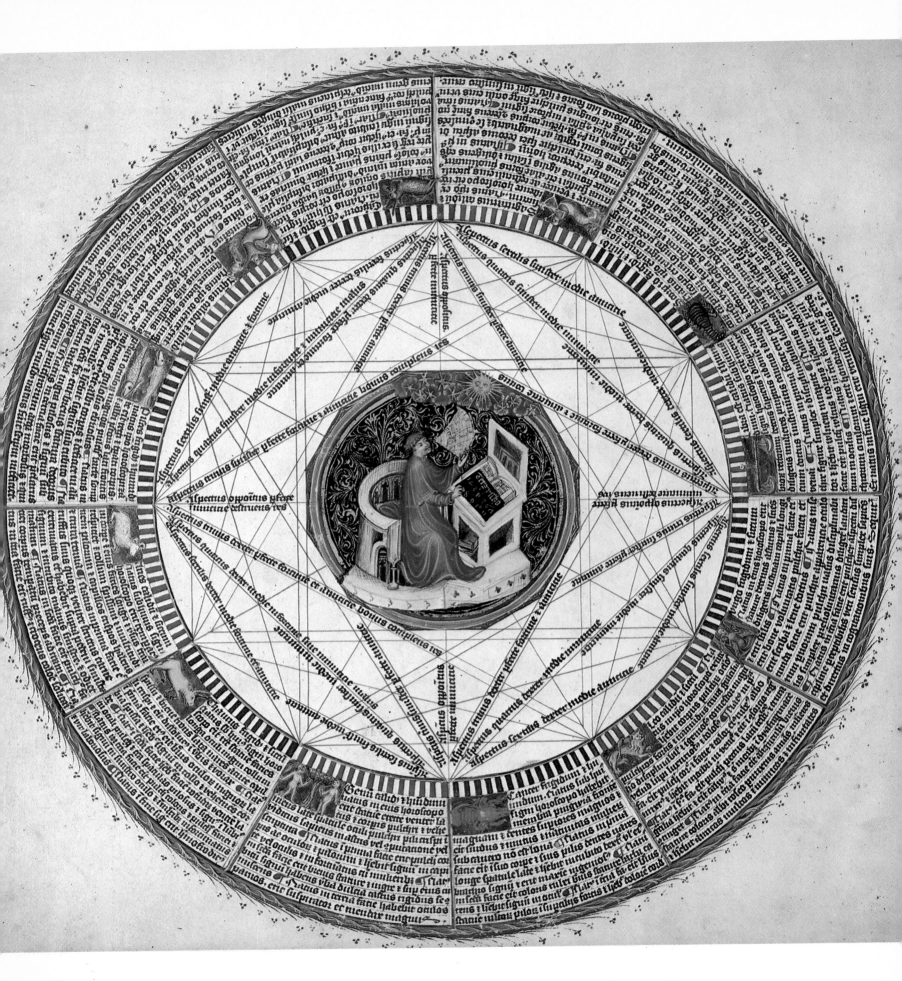

From the twelve constellations to the zodiacal calendar

On the basis of the sections of the Zodiac, the Greeks, as geometers and mathematicians, developed the calendar during the fifth century before Christ, thereby defining how time was to be measured:

— The circumference of the circular path (360°) of the Sun represented a *year;*

— Division of the path of the Sun into twelve sections provided twelve *months;*

— Thirty *days* were obtained from division of each 30° section, whereby the Sun advanced by one degree each day;

— Later, the seven days of the *week* were defined by incorporation of the seven planets;

— The *names* of the *days* were chosen by associating a planetary deity with each day:

- Day of the Moon *(dies Lunae)*   Monday
- Day of Mars *(dies Martis)*   Tuesday
- Day of Mercury
  (dies Mercurii)   Wednesday
- Day of Jupiter *(dies Jovis)*   Thursday
- Day of Venus *(dies Veneris)*   Friday
- Day of Saturn *(dies Saturni)*   Saturday
- Day of the Sun *(dies Dominica*
  or *dies Solis)*   Sunday

In providing names for Saturday and Sunday, the Germanic languages adhered more closely to the names of planets: *Saturday, Sunday (Sontag).*

Left: An astrologer, or "mathematician," studying the laws and language of the Zodiac.

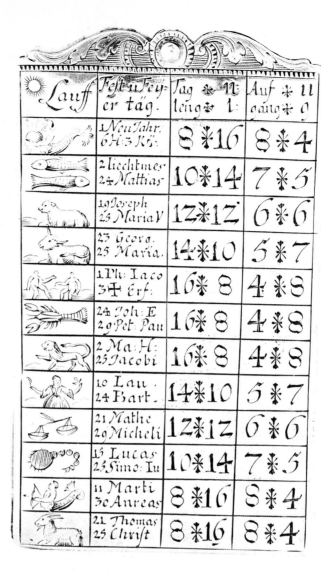

Conventional time correlated with astrological time: a perpetual calendar indicating signs of the Zodiac.

Below: a perpetual calendar with two movable discs for determining days of the week. At the center, lunar time is represented by the second disc, which indicates phases of the Moon. The innermost portion of this instrument contains a calendar for determining holidays, positions of the Sun in relation to the Zodiac, lengths of days, sunrises and sunsets, and lengths of nights.

From the Zodiac to the attributes of signs

Subsequent to the arrival of Berossus in Greece, astrology underwent a transformation; in Mesopotamia, it had been a collective form of knowledge applied to an entire society, but, in Greek science and culture, astrology became individualized, through codification of planetary trajectories, mathematical casting of horoscopes, and association of sets of characteristics with the symbols comprising the Zodiac.

Throughout the Mediterranean region, the Zodiac, during the first twelve centuries of its development, embodied sets of symbols representing natural conditions associated with specific months. This form of symbolism corresponded to a range of meanings existing on a collective level. Hence, the assertive vigor of Aries represented the sprouting of seeds during the Spring, or the vitality of nature during that season. To begin a project during the Spring was synonymous with drawing upon the radiant energy associated with that season.

The Greeks interconnected the principles of physics and psychology with this symbolic keyboard for natural conditions. They were able to impart meaning and logic to concepts which had previously existed solely as intuitions.

The contributions of the Greeks

It is known that the essence of "Greek genius" consisted of having elevated thought to a conceptual level, and having defined interrelations among conditions by developing propositions through deductive processes. Thales of Miletus (*circa* 640-548 B.C.), a geometer, astronomer, and cosmologist who was probably the earliest Greek philosopher, and, in a later era, Pythagoras (400 B.C.) established the foundations of Greek scientific thought.

Thales appears to have traveled frequently to Egypt, Persia, and Crete, just as Pythagoras visited Persia and India. Both thinkers drew upon knowledge developed by other cultures.

Thales offered the first *rational* explanation of the cosmos as a whole — in other words, *cosmology* — and he explicitly affirmed the underlying oneness of the universe. He provided a basis for understanding the scientific principle of physical nature, whereas Chaldean cosmogony prior to that point had explained the structure of the universe in a *mythical* form.

"There is an entity which is the original principle for creation of all other things, and to which all other things must return through decay. It remains unchanged despite the diversity and transmutations of qualities which it may acquire. This is the indestructible essence or substance of all things."[1]

According to Thales, water, as a physical substance, rationally constitutes the Original Principle, which had been represented in a mythical form by the goddess Nammu in Chaldean cosmogony.

Anachimenus, the last representative of the School of Miletus, who regarded air, instead of water, as the Original Principle, advanced a concept which became a fundamental doctrine in astrology: Man resembles the universe as a part resembles a whole.

Development of astrology in mathematical terms is primarily derived from the theory of universal harmony formulated by the noted philosopher *Pythagoras* (*circa* 572-490 B.C.) — who was the first to employ the term "philosopher" (seeker of wisdom). Pythagoras' theory of the universe was based upon harmony and numbers, and it was sum-

---

1. Léon Robin, *La Pensée grecque* (Greek Philosophy) (Albin Michel, 1923), p. 59.

Mars

Mars suis Ung pou rebarbatif
Mais pour bien faire fort actif
En mon teps ie Deulz que tout hôme
Labeure que pas Ung ne chome
Le Vigneron qui houet qui taille
Le faboureur face semaille
Qui bien menploiet a grant plante
Lupsera des biens en este.

Je suis noble mars floussant
Tresgentil et tresgracieux
En moy Vient bien fructifiant
Car ie suis farge et plantureux
Et caresme se glorieux
Est en mon regne. si Vous dis
Que suis en mon temps Vigoreux
Pour auancer mes bons amis.

Far left: Planetary gods and goddesses. Some of these deities, such as Innana (counterpart to Ishtar and Venus), were associated with veneration of the Earth, and they were linked to signs of the Zodiac.

Opposite: This page from the "Shepherd's Calendar" expressed the properties of Aristotle's four elements: Fire is hot and dry; Air is warm and moist; Earth is cold and dry; Water is cold and moist.

marized by two mystical sayings: "What embodies the greatest wisdom? — Numbers. What embodies the greatest beauty? — Harmony." He attributed specific characteristics to certain numbers and geometric forms. This philosophical outlook was a source of the theory of planetary aspects (harmonious aspects and conflicting or dissonant aspects) which predominates in astrology.

Empedocles (*circa* 490-420 B.C.) merits recognition for having replaced the unitary theory of matter with the theory that all substances were derived from *four elements:* fire, earth, air, and water.[2] This concept became a basic principle in developing astrological interpretations and in understanding the Zodiac.

Empedocles also formulated laws concerning mutability in order to explain how different substances interacted with one another in accordance with laws of compatibility or affinity. Movement was explained in terms of "emanations which originate from mixtures or from elementary substances, entering pores or invisible pathways (...), and traveling along these pathways." Affinities between different substances existed when emanations from one substance were congruent with the pores of another; otherwise, substances were incompatible, as in the instance of oil and water.[3]

"Light consists of emanations which only reach us subsequent to their departure from a luminous body"[4] (Léon Robin, *La Pensée grecque*). Thus, Empedocles made it possible to understand the influence of the stars. He foreshadowed the atomic theories developed by Leucippus (*circa* 500 B.C.) and Democritus (460?-370? B.C.), who refined the theory of the elements by introducing the now-familiar term *atoms.*

In medicine, Hippocrates (460-377 B.C.) enriched astrological principles by studying the human body in relation to rhythms which astronomers had observed within the universe as a whole (cycles in illnesses, critical days, et cetera). Hippocrates gave coherence to medical records discovered in Chaldea, where the development of illnesses, as well as remedies, had already been explored in relation to planetary cycles.

The *Timaeus,* written by Plato (428-348 or 347 B.C.), greatly influenced astrological theories and methods. "He demonstrated that myths, instead of being allegories or fables, represent the earliest form of scientific expression. He described a probable sequence for the development and composition of phenomena which are identified through experience (...) This was a necessary stage of knowledge, and it cannot be detached from intermediate or descriptive science, nor from the pure reason represented by the dialectic."[5] Plato explained that the universe is a living entity, created by the demiurge and composed of the four elements, which are distinguished

2. In Chaldea, the names given to the four elements were: *An,* the sky; *Ki,* the earth; *En-Lil,* the atmosphere; and *Nammu,* primordial water.

3. Léon Robin, *La Pensée grecque,* Albin Michel (1923), 1973, page 128.

4. Robin, page 131.

5. Robin, page 256.

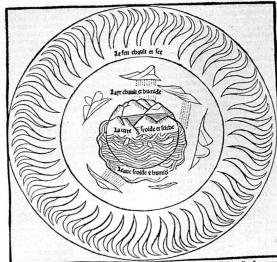

Opposite: Signs of the Zodiac in relation to the four elements.

Right: This page from the "Shepherd's Calendar" identifies types of temperaments according to the four elements.

FEU	TERRE	AIR	EAU

prendent leur estre par generacion. Et est cy a entendre que sont deux manieres de chaleur. L'une si est la chaleur du soleil et du ciel et ceste est cause de generacion et de conservation si comme il appert aulcunesfoys es nues esquelles sont engendrees les raynes par la vertu de la chaleur du soleil. L'aultre chaleur est des elemens et ceste cy est aulcunesfoys cause de corruption si come il appert ou miroir ardant qui art le drap pour cause de la chaleur q vient des rays de l'air qui sont brisies dessus le miroir. De rechief la chaleur si ramaine les choses de sa bas avec celles de lassus si comme il appert quant la chaleur monte de bas en hault elle convertit la terre en eaue et l'eaue en air et l'air au feu p sa vertu. De rechief la chaleur si amolie aulcunesfoys les choses dures si comme il appert de vng oeuf qui est cler et mol de sa nature qui est enduri par la chaleur du feu. De rechief la chaleur si fait aulcunesfoys les choses grosses et espesses devenir tendres et soubtiles si comme il appert en la glace qui est grosse

et soubtile / mais par chaleur elle est convertie en l'eaue q est soubtille. De rechief la chaleur si nettoye et purifie les metaulx de tout rouel et de toute ordure, et se est ou pur et il est mis ou feu il se fuit par la chaleur / mais il ne se degaste ne appetice point et ne pert riens de son pois. De rechief la chaleur est aulcunesfoys cause de corruption et no pas p sa nature mais par accident / si comme il appert en vng cas de ble qui est moille qui se pert et se connoit par la chaleur qui st engendre. De rechief la chaleur est cause de legierete de sa nature si come il appert es grains et es toutes choses qui sont pl' legieres quant elles sont seicehes par chaleur quelles nestoyent devant. De rechief quant la chaleur oeuvre en yne chose moiste elle y engendre vne fumee qui rent le corps dont il est plus legier / et de ce vient que vng corps vif est plus legier que quant il est mort pour la chaleur 7 les perit qui est es voynes et es conduis du corps vif et n'est pas ou corps mort et de ce vient aussi que nous sommes plus legiers aptes mégier

from one another by molecular form, although all of the four elements are interconnected and interrelated in a perfectly harmonious form.[1]

The universe is maintained in ternary motion by a soul, and its motion embodies three essential forms of energy. This theory was applied to the development of astrological signs and to their interaction. Plato also explained that the stars constitute the most effective means of measuring time; he also described the varying rotations of planes in relation to the ecliptic, as well as many other concepts which were adopted in astrology.

Aristotle (384-322 B.C.), who was the tutor of Alexander the Great, developed the theory of elementary properties of matter, which has been incorporated within astrology. Adapting the elements defined by Empedocles, he explained that:

— *Fire* combines warmth and dryness,
— *Earth* combines coldness and dryness,
— *Air* combines moisture and warmth,
— *Water* combines moisture and coldness.

The *Epicureans* summarized the previously cited theories by affirming that human beings encompassed the image of the universe, "because we could not gain knowledge of our environment if we had not been formed in the same way."[2] The principle now known as the Law of Synchronicity was expressed in the following manner: "The universe is a living entity whose parts enter into sympathetic relationships. Because nature does not permit a vacuum, the motion of any portion of this entity must produce an impact throughout the entire universe."[3]

The *Stoics* likewise incorporated astrology within their views, and they contributed to the dissemination of astrology in Greece. They regarded celestial bodies as living deities which governed human destiny through Universal Sympathy.

Initially, these concepts were associated with the symbols comprising the circle of the Zodiac, the circle of life, and they provided fundamental principles for defining attributes, ultimately permitting development of the entire astrological system which would make it possible to prepare horoscopes with precision.

1. See A. Bouché-Leclercq, *L'Astrologie grecque* (Greek Astrology), Paris, Culture et Civilisation, 1899.
2. Bouché-Leclercq *(Ibid.)*
3. *Ibid.*

Attributes according to the Zodiac

The *four elements* identified by Empedocles — namely fire, earth, air, and water — were combined with the twelve signs:

- Aries, Leo, and Sagittarius are *fire* signs;
- Taurus, Virgo, and Capricorn are *earth* signs;
- Gemini, Libra, and Aquarius are *air* signs;
- Cancer, Scorpio, and Pisces are *water* signs.

These associations offer numerous correlations, inasmuch as the meanings expressed by the four elements are both psychological and physical:

Fire is associated with energy, vitality, dynamism, creativity, the need to dominate and to produce changes.

Earth is associated with solidarity, stability, concentration, strength, perseverance and enrichment.

Air is associated with expansion, forming of bonds, exchanges, the need for renewal, mobility, and growth.

Water is associated with the instinctive, the unconscious, memory, expression of emotions, calmness, receptivity, malleability, and flexibility.

Later, the humors defined by Hippocrates were redefined in relation to the four elements:

- *Fire* produced a choleric spirit.
- *Earth* produced a melancholy spirit.
- *Air* produced a sanguine spirit.
- *Water* produced a phlegmatic spirit.

The four elements were also associated with the principles defined by Aristotle, permitting attributes to be determined: for example, Aries, a fire sign, was considered "hot and dry." In other words, such qualities as intensity, excitability, and vivacity, corresponding to warmth, were combined with such qualities as precision, intransigence, and conflict, representing dryness.

Taurus, an earth sign, was considered "cold and dry." Hence, such qualities as forethought, prudence, and self-control, which represented coldness, were combined with qualities representing dryness.

Gemini, an air sign, was considered "hot and moist." Qualities representing moisture, such as pliability, kindness, adaptability, and appreciation for harmony, were combined with qualities associated with warmth.

Cancer, a water sign, was considered "cold and moist." In other words, qualities associated with coldness and moisture were combined.

The principles of *ternary movement* — cardinal, fixed, and mutable — were also integrated with the twelve signs, according to whether they marked the beginning, the peak, or the end of a season (or foreshadowing of the next season). Dynamic qualities were therefore imparted to each sign.

Aries, Cancer, Libra, and Capricorn, which initiate seasons, constitute the *cardinal* triplicity. These signs express a desire for movement and progress.

Taurus, Leo, Scorpio, and Aquarius, representing the peaks of seasons, constitute the *fixed* triplicity. These signs express a desire for accomplishment and equilibrium.

This lavishly decorated Persian manuscript shows that Islamic artists sought to express the fundamental concepts from which astrology developed. Here, Cancer is portrayed in relation to its element — water.

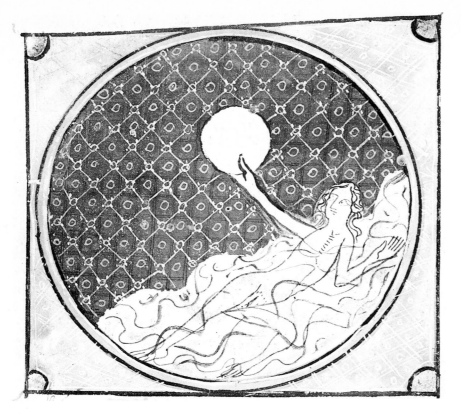

Venus rules Libra and Taurus.

Gemini, Virgo, Sagittarius, and Pisces, marking transitions from one season to the next, form the *mutable* triplicity; they express a desire for change.

Masculine and *feminine* principles have also been interwoven with the signs. Aries, Gemini, Leo, Libra, Sagittarius, and Aquarius (fire and air signs) are associated with the *masculine* principle. Taurus, Cancer, Virgo, Scorpio, Capricorn, and Pisces (earth and water signs) are associated with the *feminine* principle.

It is appropriate to understand masculine and feminine symbolism in relation to the *yang* and the *yin,* namely emissivity and receptivity.

Lastly, the *planets* (or planetary deities and the tendencies which they symbolize) have been linked to astrological signs.

Thus, there are the planetary domains, or houses, which are of Mesopotamian origin, although they underwent further development in Greece, in accordance with affinities among planets and signs.

Associations between planets and signs reflected an extremely ancient theory of "the essence of the universe," as well as incorporating geometric laws, in relation to the positions which planets occupy within the cosmos, whereby:

- Mars governs Aries,
- Venus governs Taurus,
- Mercury governs Gemini,
- The Moon governs Cancer,
- The Sun governs Leo,
- Mercury governs Virgo,
- Mars (along with Pluto, in a later era) governs Scorpio,
- Jupiter governs Sagittarius,
- Saturn governs Capricorn,
- Saturn (along with Uranus, in a later era) governs Aquarius),
- Jupiter (along with Neptune, in a later era) governs Pisces.

In this way, the Greeks combined Mesopotamian planetary astrology with the twelve signs of the Zodiac.

Accordingly, an Aries temperament corresponds to the beginning of Spring, to fire (heat and dryness, a choleric temperament, to the cardinal triplicity (energy, vitality), to the masculine principle, and to the planet Mars. Thus, there is an entire sequence of correlations, composed of interwoven analogies, for distinguishing each sign and each temperament according to the Zodiac.

Multiple correlations emerge, offering an inexhaustible abundance of interpretations and requiring the interplay of emotions, feelings, intuition, and logic.

The Moon, which dominated the night and natural cycles — rainfall, tides, fertility — and reflected light from the Sun, was associated with the inner world of imagination and sensitivity, or the instinctive dreams and impulses which can affect us.

The Horoscope

From four celestial points to the twelve houses

The Zodiac expresses twelve objective modes of existence, analogous to the twelve phases of the Sun. There are twelve types of rhythms or pulsations within the universe, and each represents a universal state of being.

The Chaldeans and, to a much greater extent, the Greeks studied planetary motion within the context of these forms of energy. Thus, a panorama of planetary influences were developed in relation to the signs: a planet's behavior, depending upon its particular nature, was more or less compatible with vibrations travelling through the cosmos.

For example, when Mars coincides with Aries or Scorpio, it appears to spur individuals and nations to action, but does not do so when it shifts to Pisces. Jupiter affirms its authority in Sagittarius and its generosity in Pisces, governing both of these signs because the full extent of its power is attained.

From the tops of their ziggurats, however, the Chaldean priests observed that planets displayed exceptional strength at four celestial locations and they learned to define the influence of planets more precisely: it depends upon the Earth's rotations every twenty-four hours. The dynamism of a given planet does not possess the same intensity at every location on the Earth's surface. Instead, intensity is determined by the precise orientation of any location in relation to the solar system. According to the orientation of the Earth, planetary influences may be expressed in different ways for a specific location, and the orientation can be determined by projecting terrestrial coordinates (the horizon and the meridian for the particular location) celestially.

Thus, the Chaldeans introduced a new aspect of the Earth-cosmos relationship: namely, earthly locations which they projected into celestial space in order to determine modes of vibration. In order to choose auspicious occasions for erecting temples or cities, conducting religious rituals, or declaring war, they selected times corresponding to the ascent or zenith of a favorable planet for starting and pursuing a particular form of activity. The Chaldeans primarily practiced astrology on a collective plane; the entire nation had a stake in choosing terrestrial dates coinciding with the beginning of planetary trajectories.

The Greeks adopted the Chaldeans' knowledge and applied it to individuals when they observed that two persons born on the same date did not necessarily possess completely identical attributes.

For example, the Sun is in conjunction with Leo when two persons are born on August 5. In other words, the Sun's position in relation to the Earth evokes forms of energy which Leo represents. These persons may tend to be ambitious and self-reliant in accordance with the traditional characteristics of the Leo-image. Nevertheless, it is possible for Venus to coincide with Virgo on the same date. Thus, as a result of qualities associated with Virgo, both persons could express sensitivity tempered by a certain degree of shyness, or even timidity. Although planetary indications at the time of birth may be similar, these two persons could lead their lives in entirely different manners.

Therefore, prior methods were inadequate because they did not permit all types of influence to be taken into account. It was not possible to define the manner in which a person's life would specifically reflect a planet's position within a specific sign.

Adopting the Chaldeans' techniques for determining the start of events on a collective plane, the

Certain persons appear to possess special affinities with a given planet. In terms of its position in the natal horoscope, as well as the accompanying aspects, one planet may be more prominent than others and may acquire greater importance. Here, famous men of Antiquity are portrayed in relation to their respective planets.

41

Dürer's "Nemesis" could be used to illustrate La Fontaine's verses: "We often meet our destiny/ along the very paths/ we choose for escaping it." The painting allows us to consider the role of the horoscope, which ought to give us insights about our innermost inclinations, instead of merely expressing unbending predestination.

42

Precise astronomical and mathematical rules must be followed in casting horoscopes.

Greeks projected terrestrial coordinates at the time of birth in relation to the Zodiac; in this way they could identify four points whereby a person would be most strongly affected by the forms of energy represented by individual planets.

The first point to be identified was the *ascendant,* corresponding to the intersection between the terrestrial horizon and the ecliptic. It is still called the "Path of the Sun;" this location represents the strongest relationship with cosmic energy, and becomes visible on the horizon at sunrise. The Greeks called it the *"horoscope,"* which is translated as "determining the hour" (this term is often employed in our era to refer to the entire celestial chart at the time of birth).

The ascendant represents the moment at which the apparent route of the Sun becomes visible on Earth. It is the first Zodiacal location which a person receives, and it represents initiation of the soul into the cosmos, the earliest perception of one's environment, or an entry into astrological time as expressed by the firmament. Thus, this point represents a person's acquisition of self-awareness — his inner personality as it is felt and experienced.

The ascendant can be situated within any sign of the Zodiac (Aries, Gemini), depending upon the place and time of birth. The form of energy which combines with the soul, or the manner in which the ego shall perceive and experience the world, is represented by the sign where the ascendant appears.

If a heavenly body is rising at the time of birth, it will be located close to the ascendant, so that its influence shall be in harmony with the ascendant. The expression "to be born under a lucky star" is derived from this phenomenon.

The next level of importance is attributed to the location where planets reach their zeniths — *the midheaven.* This location is directly overhead, at the intersection between the local meridian and the ecliptic.

In determining symbolic associations for a given location, the midheaven represents a source of energy which guides a person in pursuing fulfillment. It symbolizes a person's perception of his own destiny, or a point toward which he is intuitively drawn. The celestial region which inspires a person can be located within any sign of the Zodiac, depending upon the place and time of birth. It expresses a combination of types of energy which a person strives to develop for self-fulfillment.

For example, if the midheaven is situated within Capricorn, it can be assumed that a person will seek durable and noteworthy success which he might hope to gain through perseverance.

For a considerable period of time, there was uncertainty as to whether the ascendant or the midheaven most fully expressed the importance of planets situated in those locations.

Through experience, the ascendant was recognized as being predominant, because it appears to be most deeply experienced at a psychic level. The personality is perceptible from earliest childhood, whereas the goals which shape individuals' efforts emerge gradually.

For centuries, astrologer-priests developed predictions by scanning the eastern horizon for planets

43

LA MAUVAISE ÉTOILE

descendant symbolizes an individual's way of interacting with his surroundings, or how he feels, experiences, and enjoys the world. Thus, it is concretely expressed through associations (contracts, marriages) and through conflicts (disputes, divorces, lawsuits). The descendant coincides with an opposite sign from the ascendant, and it embodies conflict among forms of energy which are simultaneously contradictory and complementary.

Hence, an Aries "ego" may hope and possibly believe that interactions with others are governed by an approach represented by Libra (the opposite sign), where harmony and equilibrium predominate. As a result of his energetic temperament, however, this individual may inspire reactions which surprise him because they are unexpected.

Lastly, astrologers identified the *nadir,* situated opposite the midheaven, or directly beneath us. The planets travel through the sky to this point without being seen, and it is situated opposite the sign which symbolizes an individual's aspirations. The nadir expresses the complementary forces which a person may require for fulfilling his destiny; it represents a person's deepest roots, or that which is regarded as a source. It concretely represents a person's way of perceiving his family and his birthplace, or the things which he expects (or does not expect) from them. By extension, the nadir can also represent the physical components of a person's home — dwellings and land.

For example, a "Cancer" nadir is situated opposite a "Capricorn" midheaven. In order to acquire the inner strength represented by Capricorn, the individual may need a place where he can find solace and inner warmth provided by forms of energy symbolized by Cancer.

The ascendant, with the descendant as its corollary, and the midheaven, with the nadir as its

ascending through the heavens and for planets which would reach a zenith directly overhead.

In relation to the ascendant and the midheaven, two additional points within the sky were considered important, namely, points which are diametrically opposite to them. Opposite the ascendant where planets rise, there is a point where planets descend, receding and disappearing from the visible portion of the sky, and it is called *the decendant.*

The descendant is the location which counterbalances the ego, but there is also a complementary relationship within the day/night dialectic. The

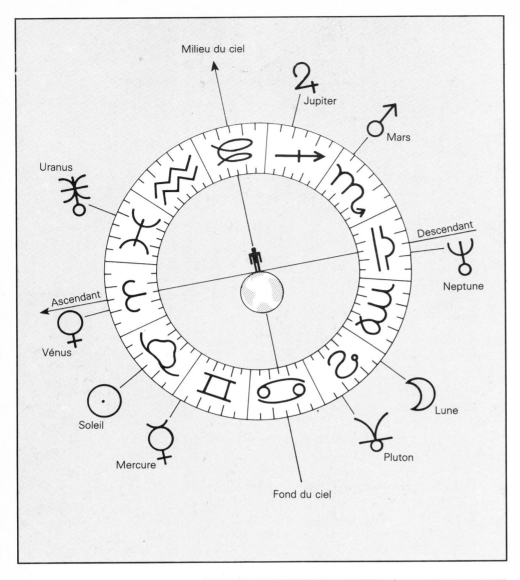

Milieu du ciel

Jupiter

Mars

Uranus

Descendant

Neptune

Ascendant

Vénus

Soleil

Mercure

Lune

Pluton

Fond du ciel

Man surrounded by a planetary configuration, with terrestrial coordinates projected onto the Zodiac. This example represents a person born under Taurus with an Aries ascendant, although Venusian and Neptunian traits can be expected to have great influence, because Venus and Neptune are situated along the horizon line.

Arrangement of the houses, or areas of life, according to the Zodiac. The first house is located beneath the left hand of the person appearing here (his arms represent the plane for the horizon). Other houses appear in a counterclockwise pattern.

corollary, symbolized the touchstones of an individual's life. They formed intersecting lines whereby the terrestrial coordinates for specific locations could be projected onto the Zodiac.

With temporal locations being individualized in this way, human beings were brought into contact with the universe. Man experiences the world in relation to himself (the ascendant), in relation to others (the descendant), in relation to destiny (the midheaven), and in relation to his origins (the nadir). Thus, a planet situated at one of these locations is experienced as a combination of its own symbolic associations and the symbols corresponding to the specific location. The four individualized cardinal points form a cross indicating the set of polarities which exist for an individual and his surroundings. They represent the manner whereby consciousness, which is temporally specified by terrestrial coordinates, will be interconnected with universal consciousness.

Thus, Man is individualized within a universal structure, but, inasmuch as this structure is divided into twelve sections, a person's spatial aspect is only represented by four angles. By analogy, the Greeks, as geometers of human psychology, defined twelve sectors of life within the localized areas which they projected into the firmament within the four angles. Hence, sets of symbols for the twelve domains of existence, computed according to the ascendant, correspond to the sets of symbols for the twelve signs representing phases of the Sun.

These domains were called the *twelve houses:*

Six houses are situated above the horizon, intersecting with the portion of the firmament which is directly overhead;

Six more houses are situated below the horizon, dividing the invisible portion of the firmament beneath us.

At the turn of the century, the French mathematician Paul Choisnard developed a circular format for indicating natal horoscopes. Before that time, a square was used, as shown by this engraving indicating the horoscope of King Henri II.

Therefore, an individual Zodiac resembled the celestial Zodiac, with localized space being divided into twelve equal 30° segments (there were approximately seven methods of computing the houses, but the Placidean method is most frequently employed in our era).

Whereas the signs of the Zodiac appear to travel around the Earth like the hands of a watch measuring pulsations within the universe, the twelve houses constitute stationary divisions of the sky, comparable to the twelve sections representing hours on the dial of a watch.

The twelve celestial sectors (signs) travel through each house every day, one after another: the attributes associated with signs and planets emerge in succession, according to the houses which they enter.

Proceeding from left to right, one encounters the twelve domains of existence which are analogous to the signs of the Zodiac:

Aries, the sign of dynamism, corresponds to the *first house;* it begins beneath the ascendant, representing the world of the ego, as well as potential physical strength and latent capabilities. This house represents a person's innermost personality, as he gains self-awareness and seeks self-expression throughout his life.

Taurus, the sign of stability and a sense of possession, corresponds to the *second house,* which symbolizes a person's attitude toward material items which he may consider necessary in terms of advances and acquisitions leading to self-fulfillment. Instead of representing quantities of possessions, this house more fully represents the satisfaction or lack of satisfaction which a person obtains from possessions, as well as his degree of physical self-sufficiency.

Gemini, the sign of creativity and adaptation, corresponds to the *third house,* representing the elements of communication which, in various forms, are essential for life. It also signifies schooling, interaction among siblings, and, by extension, siblings themselves, as well as intellectual activity (writing, publishing, or even correspondence). The third house is the realm of concrete thought represented by the painter's brushstroke, the musician's score, or the author's use of literary language. It also represents a person's needs for self-expression, and his mode of self-expression.

Cancer, the sign representing gestation, sensitivity, and innermost feelings, corresponds to the *fourth house* (It is also the sign of motherhood and domesticity). The fourth house symbolizes a person's spiritual and material assets, belongings received from his family, inheritances, and family obligations in material terms, such as land and dwellings. It also represents an individual's manner of self-expression within his home and the way in which feelings are expressed.

Leo, the sign of joy and self-reliance, corresponds to the *fifth-house,* and represents fulfillment of wishes, children, love, intimate ties, and financial ties. The fifth house encompasses the joy which a person derives from creative endeavors.

Virgo, the sign of thought and self-control, corresponds to the *sixth house,* symbolizing development of awareness of one's own limits. Within this domain, a person prepares himself for life, through daily work, relationships with subordinates, duties and obligations in professional or private situations, and through minor illnesses. This house represents an individual's way of confronting ordinary hindrances.

Libra, the sign of harmony and justice, corresponds to the *seventh house,* and is situated precisely after the descendant. It symbolizes a person's contact with others and the reactions which he evokes on a social scale. It can also represent sentimental ties, or relationships derived from a person's interests, as well as conflicts. This house reflects the way in which individuals perceive their relationships with external reality.

Scorpio, the sign of destruction as a precursor of renewal, corresponds to the *eighth house.* It symbolizes sexual activity as a means of self-renewal, but also death, possible physical risks (accidents, operations), or spiritual losses (depression, mourning, sadness). By extension, the eighth house represents assets obtained through partnerships, matrimony, or inheritance, as well as liabilities through borrowing or indebtedness. It expresses a person's

What sign and what house will the Moon enter, and what will be the aspects formed with other planets? (Tarot card owned by King Charles VI.)

Aratus Cilix

Ptolemeus Aegyptius

M. Manlius Romanus

Azophi Arabus

Dürer created this celestial map showing the Zodiac and the stars, with numbers and degrees having been provided.

attitude toward death, psychic phenomena, the mysteries of the hereafter, and, in concrete terms, one's attitude toward loss of physical independence (the possible termination of spiritual life).

Sagittarius, the sign of unification of tendencies, corresponds to the *ninth house,* and symbolizes the desire for advancement on a spiritual plane — ideological, philosophical, or political aspirations or endeavors, as well as a person's dreams. This is the domain of abstract thought, and, by extension, it symbolizes foreign travel and foreigners themselves.

Capricorn, the sign of mastery and innermost ambitions, corresponds to the *tenth* house. It is situated precisely after the midheaven and represents a person's capabilities or ambitions. By extension, this house represents accomplishments and social standing, the reputation which a person acquires, or changes in status. It also expresses the means chosen by a person for pursuing his destiny.

Aquarius, the sign of generosity, corresponds to the *eleventh house,* and symbolizes plans, hopes with respect to other persons, and, by extension, other persons who may offer sympathy, aid, and protection. It also represents participation in cultural or social groups. This house reveals an individual's attitude toward his peers.

Pisces, the sign of ties to other persons and sacrifice, corresponds to the *twelfth house,* and symbolizes a person's undisclosed private life. This is the domain of major physical or spiritual torments which lead to personal growth. It represents unavoidable sacrifices and limitations upon personal freedom (illnesses, disappointments). By extension, this house symbolizes captivity, exile, and medical treatment. It can also symbolize secret contradictions, and expresses the soul's deepest aspirations to transcend the material world in order to pursue its own path.

Initially, astrologists were able to recognize the influence of Jupiter upon such attributes as extroversion, friendliness, and optimism. Persons influenced by this planet tend to be self-confident and generous. Later, it was determined that the characteristics associated with Jupiter are compatible with Sagittarius: thus, a warm personality is accompanied by the individual's desire to affirm his authority within his own domain.

By means of the houses, it became possible to determine the areas of life where a person's inclinations may be expressed; when Jupiter coincides with Sagittarius, thereby occupying the tenth house, a person tends to ascend the rungs of the ladder of social and professional success, so as to affirm his ambitions and authority. Whereas the planets represent tendencies within our psychic structure, the signs are filters which refine these tendencies, and the houses represent areas of life for expressing them.

The houses only acquire actual significance when they encompass a planet. Then they permit one of our attributes to be concretely expressed within an area of experience.

Correlations have been observed between planets and handwriting patterns, and may also be possible to determine a person's sun sign from his physiognomy.

The macrocosm and the microcosm

Although the terms "macrocosm" and "microcosm" were first used by the Greeks, these concepts originated in Chaldea and Egypt.

The Ancients, on a scientific level, were already seeking correlations between the infinitely small and the infinitely large. Applying the Law of Interdependence between the heavenly and the earthly, the Chaldeans used celestial phenomena to choose dates for their efforts in chemistry. As complementary fields, alchemy and astrology were applied at the same time, with celestial and terrestrial transformations being interconnected by factors which could be called a system of vital influences. Later, when the Epicureans examined these interchanges, they adopted the term *emanations*.

It is also known that, prior to the Epicureans, interdependence of the heavens and the Earth was envisioned by such leading thinkers as Thales, Anaximenes, Empedocles, Plato, and Aristotle.

Later, the concept of interdependence between the planets and the Earth was strongly emphasized by the Stoics who affirmed that interdependence encompassed "ceaseless exchanging of molecules or propagated motion." Thus, the Greeks developed a framework for the protoscientific concepts of the Chaldeans and for Egyptian knowledge, which had, in fact, been profoundly influenced by Mesopotamian ideas. The world-view which emerged in Ancient Greece was even carried to India where its medical aspect underwent further development (each portion of the human body was associated with a region in the firmament). This world-view was based upon three fundamental postulates which allow us to understand the import of the horoscope or the birth-motif:

(1) *The cosmos is unified:* the cosmos is a single living organism. Like the Earth within the universe, Man, as an inhabitant of the Earth, is a minuscule component of the universe. Man is a microcosm.

(2) *The part resembles the whole:* the world is governed by a single source of energy, and Man, who is surrounded and shaped by the incessant motion of cosmic forces, resembles the world itself. Man contains all of the attributes of the universe because he belongs to the universe. These attributes are concentrated within human beings, just as a cell possesses all of the attributes of an entire organism. Man is a cosmos in miniature, a microcosm, and he resembles the entire cosmos, or the macrocosm. If the part is similar to the whole, it is possible to understand the whole by examining its parts. In

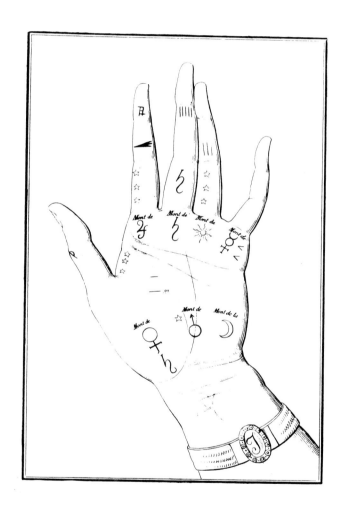

Chart of the Empress Josephine's left hand. In palmistry, certain portions of the hand have been associated with planetary symbols. Indeed, the shape of the palm often reflects the importance of planets which are extremely significant in a person's natal horoscope. For example, a "Saturnian" may have a prominent Mount of Saturn. Analogies between the part and the whole are present at many levels.

our era, this mode of reasoning is the basis of such sciences as morphopsychology (study of facial features), iridology (study of the eye), chirology (study of the shape of the hand), and graphology (study of graphic expression or handwriting), as well as many types of psychological tests (Rohrschach, Szondi, Murray, Jung) derived from the theory that a person unconsciously expresses the structure of his psyche through the symbolic content of ink spots, drawings, phrases, *et cetera* ... Whereas these sciences examine a portion of human morphology or a small-scale projection of the psyche, astrology employs cosmic units of measurement to understand human personality. Nevertheless, the concept of structural analogies between the part and the whole is shared by all of these fields, and it can be observed that differences exist only in terms of levels of investigation or the magnitudes being used: astrology proceeds from the macrocosmic universe to Man as a microcosm, whereas the other sciences view Man as a macrocosm in relation to the specific microcosms which they permit to be studied.

(3) *The part is interdependent with the whole:* "Similar objects which are separated by space instead of being contiguous are in harmony by virtue of their resemblances; even without being in contact, objects are in motion, and their influence is necessarily transmitted." In this passage from the *Enneads,* Plotinus (*circa* 205-270 A.D.) explained the Law of Correlations among objects with similar characteristics. This law is now known as the Law of Synchronicity, and it is the basis for astrological influences. The effects of the stars upon mankind cannot be explored by cause-and-effect reasoning. Because human beings are composed of the same elements as the universe, they naturally exist and function in harmony with the universe. The

"The Raven": illustration for Poe's poem by Gustave Dore. In Edgar Allan Poe's poem, the raven is a personification of the soul or the unconscious, which permits the poet to carry on a simulated dialogue with destiny. Coinciding planetary movements and terrestrial events have often been perceived as predestined.

part and the whole are linked by a general simultaneity, and there is coexistence or concomittance for specific cycles or vibrations within the firmament and within human beings. Both are components of a single entity: the universe.

Astrology is not derived from causalist determinism, but from interdependence between the heavens and Man amidst the oneness of the cosmos. Distances are of little importance, because both are governed by identical emanations flowing between similar entities. Man and the heavens are in harmony.

SYNCHRONICITY

Astrology incorporates the principle of synchronicity, whereby events which are not causally related to one another but do possess identical meanings — at a symbolic level — may occur at the same time. Thus, the natal horoscope reflects the symbolic relationship between a person and the universe, as well as cycles of simultaneous associations. Boilly's "Electrical Spark" suggests these intangible correlations.

When the morning Stars sang together, & all the
Sons of God shouted for joy

London. Published as the Act directs March 8. 1825 by Will Blake N 3 Fountain Court Strand

54

From microcosm
to the natal horoscope

From planetary relationships
to psychic structure

If an individual is, on his own terms, a universe, he contains the Moon, the Sun, and the planets. Astrology regards the human psyche as an internal celestial horizon where it is possible to observe our ideal image, or the Sun, with other characteristics circling it like planets: the Moon (feelings, imagination, sensitivity); Mercury (intelligence, mastery of concrete and abstract relationships); Venus (the source of attachments, the capacity to love); Mars (the source of action and virility); Jupiter (the source of growth, generosity); Saturn (the source of cohesion, consciousness, stability). The planets, according to positions within the Zodiac, form angular relationships which must be analyzed in order to derive an equation for our psychic structure.

The Chaldeans had already investigated conjunction and opposition, and, by using Pythagoras' theories, the Greeks developed improved methods for interpreting geometric relationships within space. When a circle is treated as a whole, it can be divided by four fundamental numbers:
— 1, representing a single point, provides the conjunction relationship: 0°.
— 2, representing a line, provides the opposition relationship: 180°.
— 3, representing a triangle, provides the trine relationship: 120°.
— 4, representing a tetrahedron, provides the square relationship: 90°.

As the planets enter into these angular relationships, there are exchanges of energy which can be either harmonious or discordant: two (or more) planets are said to be in *conjunction* when they are located at the same degree within the Zodiac (an orb, or difference of 10° is allowed). In this instance, the relationship is identical to the relationship between the Sun and the Moon at the time of a new Moon. It represents the merging of two types of energy in a more or less favorable form according to their particular characteristics. For example, a Venus-Jupiter conjunction can provide congruency and reinforcement, expressing emotional openness, and a Saturn-Mars conjunction, whereas a restraining inclination and an inclination toward activity coincide, can express conflict or inhibitions.

Opposition exists when two planets are in a 180°

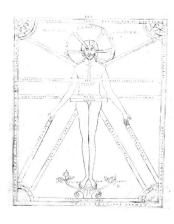

Harmony within the human soul corresponds to harmony among the spheres. If a person does not wish to be a "plaything of destiny," his life must express his horoscope in a way which is consistent with each planetary vibration. (Preceding page: illustration from the Book of Job, by William Blake; above: the microcosm, as shown in a Latin manuscript; below: anonymous engraving from the 17th century.)

Verbi deus potentia lucis creat exordia,   *Cælum vocat, fundat solum et magna pfert lumina*   *Ger. de Iode*

relationship (facing one another, like the Sun and the Moon during the full Moon phase). In this instance, we encounter an aspect embodying tension and conflict which may be resolved, depending upon the particular planets and their possible relationships with other heavenly bodies.

The *trine,* which expresses a difference of 120°, is situated between conjunction and opposition. This relationship is traditionally regarded as facilitating exchanges of energy between planets.

The *square,* corresponding to 90°, or half of a relationship embodying opposition, also represents a state of tension. Nevertheless, this form of conflict is more dynamic and more balanced. It inspires expression of energy, whereas, in a state of full opposition, the effects of forces which are present tend to alternate in a see-saw fashion.

Lastly, the *sextile,* corresponding to 60°, or half of the trine, facilitates releasing of energy, although in a more rapid and more effective form.

Conjunction, opposition, trine, square, sextile — these are elements of a planetary geometry which reveal geometric relationships within the psyche, by expressing capabilities and internal contradictions. The art of astrology consists of interpreting these astral configurations which become an individual's inner firmament at the time of birth.

Psychic structure in relation to the natal horoscope

For a long time, there was disagreement as to whether the heavens at the time of conception or the heavens at the time of birth more fully represented an individual's psyche. Because the conception motif only embodies embryonic energy, the natal horoscope became predominant because it reflects the forms of energy contained within a personality which already exists.

The *natal horoscope* is the specific psychic configuration which emerges in correlation with a given astral configuration at the time of birth. In order to determine or "cast" the natal horoscope, it is necessary to prepare a celestial chart corresponding to the time and place of birth (projection of terrestrial coordinates and the positions of planets in relation to one another, as well as in relation to a person's birthplace). In this way, an individual is viewed as the center of the world, and is surrounded by a specific astral configuration.

How should the scope of a person's chart be understood? When an individual is born, he is affected by a specific planetary configuration: the firmament above becomes an inner firmament. Specific patterns of the collective unconscious are established, and the predominant symbols of humanity are imprinted upon a person's unconscious in a specific arrangement.

"The horoscope corresponds to a certain point in reciprocal interchanges among the gods, namely among psychic archetypes," Jung affirmed. Thus, a person's natal horoscope indicates how he has been "grasped" by the world through archetypes which are common to all mankind, or how a person shall subsequently experience different archetypes as he "grasps" the world. The language of the collective unconscious is personalized, and the entirely individual way in which a person shall reflect ancestral symbols is expressed.

The natal horoscope embodies the symbolic relationship between a newborn child and the universe.

The cosmos is not external; it exists within Man. The Romantics understood that men are not detached from the world: they live and resonate with it, and external storms reflect our inner firmaments ("The Storm," by Fereol de Bonnemaison).

It consists of unconscious correlations which the astrologist must decipher and interpret by using the methods developed by tradition.

The Sun symbol, for example, may be situated within a square or an opposition, relative to the Mars symbol (the source of aggressiveness), so that conflict arises. For this individual, it shall be difficult to reflect the Sun archetype to the fullest extent. Effort will be required, amid certain conflicts, for developing the ideal image existing within the psyche and for expressing this image favorably. By contrast, another person born under a trine between the Sun and Mars shall be able to channel energy derived from Mars so as to achieve internal unity without difficulty.

The maternal image, which is emotional, receptive, and nurturing, as represented by the Moon, may be diminished by a conflict with Saturn, symbolizing suffering and frustration. A child who does not contain the ideal archetype of the mother may repeatedly display restrained or blocked expression of emotions, or, on the other hand, he may insatiably pursue unrequited love.

In this way, an astrologist gradually untangles the skein of astrological factors: the position of each planet in terms of the signs which it enters, the angles formed with other planets, and the principal points of the planetary motif (ascendant, midheaven), as well as the house within which a planet may be situated. The astrologist examines various aspects in terms of their interdependence so as to develop a general over-view of an individual's psyche.

The astrologist refrains from defining planetary motifs as an inescapable form of determinism because these motifs are psychic factors. They are human phenomena which must be examined internally, and not by outward appearance.

Each planet represents a specific symbol as it has been received at birth.

Its role develops throughout a person's life, and it may manifest itself in different forms — favorable or unfavorable — depending upon an individual's ability to gain self-awareness (man's relationship with the planets is unconscious, but, as this relationship is discovered, it can be lived in a different way).

Thus, Mars (the principle of aggressive energy) in an unfavorable configuration may guide a person from the beginning of his life toward unthinking actions, or even violent reactions, exposing him to multiple risks or accidents. So long as this form of energy is unconscious and uncontrolled, the astrologist, by examining the movement of Mars in ephemerids (charts indicating positions of planets), will be able to predict multiple obstacles. Nevertheless, if the native becomes conscious of the multiple influences of Mars, he may gain mastery over the energy derived from Mars and cease to be "governed" by that planet, becoming capable of applying energy in a premeditated manner.

The natal horoscope is an individual symbolic structure existing at the psychic level and representing the source of a certain type of behavior or, as a result, events. Like the symbol which it conveys, it is transmitted to the entire personality, and may therefore become a guide to self-awareness, or merely a pivot for predictions concerning external situations. It could be said that the natal horoscope expresses the symbolic grammar of a person's psyche. To discover its verbs, complements, and specific rules is to discover the individual mode of expression, as it exists within the vast book of the collective unconscious. All of these concepts which we have outlined in present-day terms were codified in Alexandria by Ptolemy.

The bible of astrology: Ptolemy's contributions

It is not coincidental that consolidation of astrological traditions was achieved in Alexandria. This Egyptian city, during the second century A.D., was not only a center for Hellenistic astrology, but a cultural magnet for the entire Mediterranean; it was a crucible where Mesopotamian, Greek, and Egyptian culture intermingled, and, in 140 A.D., a compilation of astrological principles known as the *Tetrabiblos* (literally "four books" in Greek) was created by a learned Greek, Claudius Ptolemaeus.

Ptolemy (*circa* 90-168 A.D.), who spent his entire life in Alexandria, was not only an astrologer, but a widely renowned mathematician and astronomer. The Greek astronomical principles which he transmitted to the Western World predominated throughout Europe until the twelfth century. In turn, his contributions in astrology are noteworthy for two reasons.

First, Ptolemy's compilation was primarily didactic, embodying a different mode of astrological writing: whereas astrological concepts had previously been expressed in a fragmentary and laconic form (for example, in tablets describing Mesopotamian prophetic observations), or poetically, as in Manilius' works in Rome, Ptolemy provided clear definitions which constituted a rational structure.

Ptolemy also summarized prior knowledge. He cataloged successive trends in astrology which had developed into accepted traditions. He explained the doctrine of the four elements (air, earth, fire, and water) and the ways in which energy is exchanged among them, as well as how the four fundamental attributes (warmth, coldness, dryness, and moisture) are classified. In particular, Ptolemy described the necessary steps for casting natal horoscopes. Although the earliest horoscope (419 B.C.)

Ptolemy projecting terrestrial coordinates within the sky (16th century manuscript).

was of Babylonian origin, it was still extremely rudimentary, and Greek science, as represented by Ptolemy, had developed more complete methods for preparing horoscopes, along with procedures for interpreting them.

Thus, the *Tetrabiblos* became the Bible of astrology. It was a fundamental source for Arab and European astrologers, who, until the seventeenth century, merely prepared commentaries on Ptolemy's work, thereby rendering tribute to the three thousand years of astrological knowledge which had been developed from the time of the Sumerians to the beginning of the Christian era.

59

Sctm philosophoy deliram̄ta notant̄ duo deci signata abaricie incipiam̄?

hec om̄a signa sunt corpo ris hōns. & signa solis ince lo apparentis.

How Astrology Was Applied

"... Science without conscience
is merely a debasement of the soul."

RABELAIS

The journey

The movements of heavenly bodies have attracted the interest of numerous civilizations. There are even carved bones from the Ice Age, suggesting that our forbears had become aware of the phases of the Moon.

Somewhat closer to our own era, the observatories at Stonehenge (2750-1870 A.D.) and Carnac confirm that the Celts were capable of predicting eclipses, as well as the different declinations and phases of the Sun and the Moon, but our understanding of the religious and practical interpretations developed by the Celts is extremely limited, inasmuch as they had no means of recording their knowledge.

With our current level of knowledge, Mesopotamian culture can be identified as the first civilization to develop and apply an entire body of precepts derived from observations, and its discoveries were preserved by means of cuneiform tablets.

The basic precepts were disseminated among many other cultures. Insofar as "history began in Sumer," it was a form of history saturated with planetary metaphysics. It appears that knowledge acquired along the Tigris and the Euphrates spread to Egypt during the sixth century before Christ, and later to India and China, as a result of Alexander

The ziggurats were built in the form of gigantic pyramids with steps. The ziggurats of Babylon, Uruk, and Ur (left) were approximately 280 feet high. They permitted the Chaldean priests to observe the sky in relation to a vast horizon.

Preceding pages: astrology mingled with existing religious beliefs. The Sun, appearing in the form of "Our Lord, Jesus Christ" (9th century) is surrounded by signs of the Zodiac. Maran, "Our Lord," was the name used for the deity of the Sun city, Hatra-Shamash, during the 2nd century B.C.

the Great's conquests during the fourth century before Christ. The fundamental perspective of the universe which astrology provided was carried from one continent to another, with each civilization contributing specific ideas by combining this perspective with preexisting doctrines and by applying it in terms of specific ways of life and specific attitudes toward destiny.

Although the influence of astrology cannot be evaluated without difficulty, it has occupied a distinct position within the history of civilizations and human thought; preponderant in some instances, or woven into vital decisions affecting the course of events, astrology inspired or shaped many philosophical and religious currents, it also guided the hands of artists and left its mark upon creations which were regarded as evidence of Man's presence on Earth.

Mesopotamia: an astrological religion

How old were the earliest Chaldean observations? Berossus had indicated 490,000 years, whereas Pliny and Cicero spoke of 480,000 years, and Diodorus of Sicily (first century B.C.) had indicated 473,000 years. Today, it is difficult to accept these claims. Thus, it is sufficient to examine the history of astrology by approximations and to begin with the sites or texts which have been preserved.

The earliest *ziggurats,* or "towers between heaven and earth," were erected 4,000 years before Christ. The *ziggurats* allowed the priests to seek communication with the eternal or partake of the sacred image of celestial space which was the only entity

One of the few Babylonian pillars showing a priest and a ziggurat (before 2000 B.C.).

In Mesopotamian writing, a single ideogram, consisting of a star, expressed assimilation of the celestial and the divine (Fragment of astronomical tablet. Early elements of the Zodiac, namely a raven and the Virgin with a cluster of wheat, appear beside the star).

Next page: Neo-Babylonian pillar showing a priest venerating the Sun and the Moon in their symbolic forms.

capable of rendering human existence meaningful. The priests reported their observations to their kings, who were the earthly custodians of divine power in order for the kings to shape the lives of their subjects. All activities, from the most important to the most commonplace, were imbued with aspiration associated with the cosmos: customs or social structures and existence itself were only meaningful insofar as it was possible to emulate the deeds of the gods or to incorporate sacred elements.

In Chaldea and in Assyria, each city contained several observatories, which were usually erected adjacent to the temple or the royal palace. The priests led an extremely secluded life, not unlike monks, and they recorded sun-spots, phases of the moon, movements of planets, and wind currents. Ultimately, they began to forecast eclipses. In approximately 2750 B.C., the tablets of Sargon of Akkad confirmed that the priests had identified omens of solar eclipses. Nevertheless, they possessed greater skill in predicting lunar eclipses, and contemporary verification through astronomy demonstrates that, in some instances, the priests' computations were accurate within several minutes.

At Nineveh, there were fragments which may have come from an enormous glass lens. Is it possible that the priests made use of optical instruments? They developed an agricultural calendar which permitted selection of sowing periods. After dividing the ecliptic into twelve equal segments derived from the twelve phases of the Moon, they subdivided it into 360 degrees, corresponding to the 360 days of their year. Each day consisted of twelve equal portions, or twelve pairs of hours, which the Greeks called "Babylonian hours." Each hour was divided into sixty minutes, each minute into sixty seconds, and each second into sixty units. Because it was known that the 360-day year was not identical to the actual solar year, a thirteenth month was added every six years.

On account of the Sumerians' system of computing time, it is possible to determine and verify important dates in their history. The year began during the month of Nisan, corresponding to the beginning of Spring, as in the calendar used by most of the Christian World during the Middle Ages. Months were divided into four equal segments which ended with days of rest on the seventh, fourteenth, twenty-first, and twenty-eighth days. This calendar permitted precise regulation of private and public life in accordance with celestial instructions. According to omens which the priests derived from astral configurations, the King issued decisions concerning all activities which were vital to a city's inhabitants. Secular time existed only insofar as it coincided with ecclesiastical time, or cosmic time. A temple intended to provide communications with the heavens would only be erected after protracted scrutiny of planetary configurations in order to select the most appropriate date. The same practices were carried out in order to choose auspicious times for erecting cities, which were built in relation to a square corresponding to division of the

This scene may portray new year ceremonies where the sun god, Shamash, is shown emerging from between two mountains. He is accompanied by other Mesopotamian deities (seal of the scribe Adda, circa 2250 B.C.).

universe into four horizons or four cardinal points (like the celestial Jerusalem). No activity could be undertaken without consulting the planets in order to ensure that earthly life would benefit from celestial forces. Thus, at the archeological sites where temples had existed, one finds carved inscriptions: "As King of Assur and Chaldea, I have erected this temple at an auspicious time, in honor of my Lord..."

Mesopotamian art, in all its forms, attests the influence of astrology—temples and *ziggurats*, as well as bas-reliefs, clay urns, and painted pottery, where dialogues among planetary deities, kings, and planets are portrayed. Some scenes in enameled brick depict religious ceremonies where the astrologer-priests interwove earthly life with the movements of planets. Considerable importance was given to these ceremonies because they precisely echoed celestial rhythms on earth. The most important festival tòok place when a new year began, as the Sun resumed its path. This renewal was commemorated by reminding men of their origins, in order to make them aware of their positions within the structure of the cosmos. The methods were not strikingly different from present-day therapies based upon psychoanalysis, where there is an effort to recreate through catharsis (gaining of consciousness) the unconscious "dramas" experienced during early childhood.

Whereas agricultural activities and events pertaining to temples and cities were recorded in the great holy book, the wars which created and destroyed civilizations marked its chapters. In turn, battles were governed by the positions of the planets and prophecies. One account states that when Assurbanipal (668 B.C.), went to war against Teumman, the King of Susiana, he postponed his attack for three days because a solar eclipse had just occurred. In this way, he obeyed the omens for the battle where a victory had been foretold. Assurbanipal confirmed these omens by putting his enemies to rout.

Sargon the Elder (*circa* 2750 B.C.), the monarch of Akkad, has gained recognition for providing seventy tablets summarizing all of the elements of astrological knowledge from his era. This compilation, which was continued by his heirs, was known as the *Namman-Bel*. According to Seneca, Berossus probably translated this text for the Greeks, who were entranced by the knowledge of the Chaldeans.

Greece:
Astrology becomes personalized

It would be misleading to assume that Berossus found Hellenistic Greece to be extremely different from his own cultural milieu. There had been contact between Greece and Chaldea long before Alexander's conquests, represented by the journeys undertaken by some Greek thinkers. Berossus encountered a philosophical climate which, since the sixth century B.C., had relied upon the Law of Analogies between the microcosm and the macrocosm to explain the influence of planetary movements upon human activities. By the fifth century before Christ, the Greeks had begun to adopt a mosaic of doctrines, including some beliefs of Persian origin. For example, there was Mithraism which affirmed that the soul must pass through seven levels of initiation, comparable to the seven planetary modes. Thus, during initiation ceremonies, worshippers wore masks symbolizing the signs of the Zodiac.

The initiatory legend of Hercules' labors was of a more specifically Greek origin, and it is possible to recognize the twelve labors as symbolically embodying the twelve phases of the Sun, or stages which the soul must complete in its quest for freedom. The two pillars represent Gemini; the Lernean Hydra evokes Cancer; the Amazons, Virgo; the centaurs, Sagittarius; and the doe with iron hooves, Capricorn.

Even before astrological signs were combined within the circle of the Zodiac, they had abounded in Greek art for a considerable period of time; thus, Leo was represented by the Gate of the Lions at Mycenae, by the Avenue of the Lions at Delos, or by the funerary lions of Corfu. It is also possible to observe rams, bulls, and other astrological symbols in temple friezes.

During the third century before Christ, it was not difficult for astrology to become interwoven with long-established beliefs and philosophies; it was compatible with contemporaneous doctrines, merging with religious sentiments and even attracting the interest of non-believers.

Mesopotamian and Greek culture coalesced as a result of Alexander's conquests; while Greek schools emerged throughout Mesopotamia, Berossus established his school on the island of Cos. With the support of the Stoics, he disseminated Chaldean knowledge, and astrology acquired a role in Greek thought.

The religious astrology of the Chaldeans underwent a transformation when it was brought to Greece. Science and religion were not separate domains in Chaldea; the Chaldean was similar to a Christian who would pursue scientific research on the basis of Biblical precepts. Religion represented the highest level of reality among the Chaldeans, and astrology, which linked mankind to the cosmos,

Apollo, the Sun God, who appears here with Diana, is one of the most striking symbols of humanity's quest. His motto was "Understand yourself, and you will understand the universe."

Astrology and religion in Greece: bas-relief from the 4th century B.C., showing a sow being sacrificed to the goddesses Demeter and Chore. Demeter's attributes were included within the Zodiac.

to the revered universe, was a component of religion. In Greece, during the third century before Christ, a separation emerged between reality and religion; objective modes of thought were beginning to develop, and the cocoon of dogma was gradually abandoned. A similar change occurred in astrology, as it became detached from a religious context, thereby becoming personalized and acquiring elements of logic. In Chaldea, astrology had been religious, as well as being collectively oriented; it was reserved for the rulers, and it explored the destiny of the entire society, through the ruler. After being introduced in Greece, astrology was dispersed among different religions, losing its official status and becoming oriented toward individual destinies on account of widespread interest in natal horoscopes. As astrology spread to the masses, it became intertwined with the most mundane aspects of life. This transformation, which was perhaps lamentable, probably facilitated the development of astrology on a scientific plane. During the second century before Christ, the Greeks began to apply their instinct for precision, expanding and clarifying arithmetical and geometric principles derived from the Chaldeans to such an extent that it has been possible to affirm that "astrology was the highest expression of science during the Hellenistic period." (Cf. F. Cumont.)

In astronomy, Hipparchus (second century B.C.) was prominent in reshaping the Chaldeans' con-

tributions. He developed a method of computing celestial coordinates according to rectilinear ascents and declinations in order to determine the positions of heavenly bodies. Hipparchus also invented an astrolab for tracing celestial movements, and, using his knowledge of trigonometry, he developed a method of computing the length of a day if the declination of the sun and the latitude of a given location have been determined. Hipparchus contributed many of the astronomical principles which permitted Ptolemy (140 A.D.) to define irrefutable principles for casting horoscopes so that astrology could therefore become a comprehensible form of scientific knowledge. With Ptolemy's *Tetrabiblos,* there was a definitive change in the orientation of astrology; Babylonian prophetic observations, derived from celestial omens, were transformed into interpretation of natal horoscopes in accordance with logical propositions. Of course, the status of astrologers also changed; the Babylonian astrologers had been priests, occupying the summit of the hierarchy and possessing a monopoly upon knowledge, but, in Athens, astrologers became learned men who practiced a respected profession (they were called "Chaldeans," instead of astrologers, and their knowledge was regarded as more authoritative because it had originated in the Orient).

Nevertheless, the secularization of astrology primarily involved outward manifestations; although astrology lost the collective religious content which had existed in Chaldea and therefore became a fully recognized science, it retained a religious sub-stratum which is strongly reflected in Greek art. The attributes of the planets were identical to those of the Olympian deities portrayed in painted pottery, mosaics, sculpture, and in all forms of architecture. Whereas logical interpretations for celestial phenomena were being provided, these in-

Zeus, the Greek god of thunder, rules the divine and human realms.

terpretations were situated within the artistic and religious context of Greek culture, where the gods of Olympus embodied the symbolic characteristics of the planets.

Furthermore, it is possible to affirm that astrology resolved a fundamental ambiguity within Greek civilization. Religious thought and scientific progress which were in conflict in other spheres were brought into harmony through interpreting horoscopes. Although astrological methods had acquired an extremely logical structure, astrology, for the vast majority of its adherents, nevertheless, acquired recognizable religious qualities as it mingled with existing religions. Is it not true that the worshippers who venerated Apollo at Delphi were also praying to a Sun which had occupied an unfavorable position in their natal horoscopes (i.e., receiving discordant aspects from other planets)?

Throughout its development in Greece, astrology coalesced with other philosophical currents. Ptolemy, who codified astrological knowledge, believed that the array of forces defined by astrological computation could only be fully attained if other natural forces failed to come into play. Many present-day practitioners of astrology could benefit from the advice given in the Tetrabiblos: "It should not be assumed that everything which happens to Man is determined by divine edicts at every moment, nor can it be believed that events emanate from an inescapable destiny which is unaffected by any other factors. Such an opinion would be absolutely indefensible." Ptolemy believed that it was necessary to examine significant phenomena, such as plagues, wars, or other collective misfortunes, in relation to celestial configurations, and then to determine whether individual horoscopes indicated influences which could neutralize the effects of these phenomena.

Ptolemy restored a measure of responsibility to human beings, and he endowed astrology with the characteristics of an applied science. Although astrology could uncover the intentions of divine powers, Man was responsible for drawing upon "intersecting" forces, namely the pre-existing forces embodied by natal horoscopes in order to modify his fate. Despite Ptolemy's advice, the content of natal horoscopes is often interpreted as an edict instead of a source of self-awareness which can permit wise decisions. A fatalistic perspective emerged, however, under the influence of the Stoics, who affirmed that knowledge of the future would permit individuals to prepare for adversities with a calm and dignified outlook. According to Stoic beliefs, the only free men were wise men whose aims were in harmony with the intentions of celestial wisdom.

Thus, astrology was not universally accepted by Greek thinkers. During the second century B.C., Carneades (*circa* 215-130 B.C.) challenged the astrological determinism of certain practitioners with arguments which, for centuries, represented the most powerful objections to reliance upon astrology. How can it be explained that different destinies may emerge for two twins born at the same time? How can it be explained why all of the soldiers killed within a given battle were not born under the same sign?

In many instances, Greek logic imposed limits upon the somewhat misleading by-products of astrological interpretations, but, in other instances, it challenged fundamental principles. At certain points, the debate at the summit of the intellectual hierarchy acquired the intensity of a confrontation between rival attorneys, but the ultimate course of events was not altered. Astrology became a fundamental element of Greek culture, and it was carried to other parts of the world from Greece.

" 'Tis Thee we hail, a disc appearing in the sky..." This hymn honored the Sun, represented by the god Aton, to whom the pharaoh Akhnaton is offering a sacrifice.

70

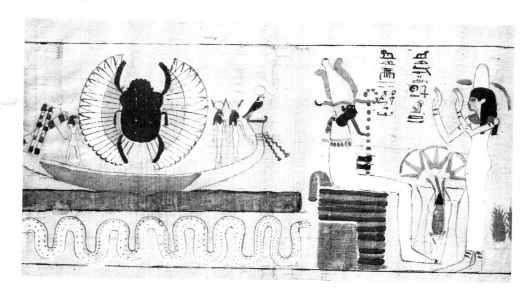

Egypt: an esoteric form of knowledge

There were two distinct periods in the development of astrology in Egypt.

The first period appears to have begun during the fifth century before Christ, at the time of the Persian invasions, when astrology merged with prior religious traditions. At that time, it would have been incorporated within esoteric doctrines reserved for the initiated: kings, priests, and a small elite. This aspect was reflected in a later era, between 150 B.C. and 50 B.C., in the *Vision of Hermes,* which was attributed to Hermes Trismegistos, a deity traditionally indentified as the scribe of the gods. As a counterpart to this priestly form of astrology, stellar astrology was practiced among the masses, and its basis was the sunset ascent of Sirius, which defined the calendar and permitted forecasting of flooding of the Nile.

The second period in Egyptian astrology emerged at the time of Alexander's conquests, when Greek scientific knowledge was introduced. Later, Ptolemy's *Tetrabiblos* permitted Egyptian mysticism to mingle with scientific principles by introducing Greek logic. It is probable that Greek influence gave the entire population access to priestly (planetary) astrology in a form similar to that of our own era.

The Egyptian had won renown for creating a Zodiac, with each sign divided into three ten-degree units—*decanates*—which were governed by specific planets. Moreover, the Egyptian Zodiac included a hawk representing the equator, an ibis symbolizing the ecliptic, and a dog-faced baboon for the two equinoxes.

Until the Greek conquest, however, exoteric religious themes were interwoven with veneration of the Nile: "Egypt is a gift from the Nile." Like the regular movements of the river, the Egyptian ideal embodied permanence. Flooding occurred at a predictable date, and the Egyptians did not consider it necessary to foretell celestial movements with great accuracy.

Predictions concerning eclipses did not appear in Egyptian texts until after the Greek conquest, whereas the Chaldeans had studied eclipses for a considerable period of time, as well as having developed symbolic interpretations of planetary movements. The Egyptians' religion was essentially dominated by the sun, and their doctrines expressed the death and rebirth of the Sun, with night changing to day as the death and rebirth of plants, or as the death of immortalization of monarchs, represented by Ra and Osiris.

Although the preceding description of Egyptian beliefs is perhaps overly brief, a detailed description would depart from the context of the history of astrology. Egypt was primarily a region which inherited astrology, instead of constituting a point of origin. The mental archetypes which may have originally been shared by Chaldea and Egypt were molded according to the specific experiences of each region. It is clear that the type of symbolic thought which emerged in Chaldea is derived from a form of inquiry shaped by living conditions which did not exist in Egypt. Nevertheless, this symbolic perspective was a point of departure for scientific progress of that period.

The boat of Ra, the Sun God, carries the dead toward eternity along underground streams. It is piloted by the god Anubis, who has the head of a jackal.

Rome:
political power at stake

While astrology was gaining acceptance in Egypt, it was also being introduced in Rome during the second century before Christ, subsequent to the Punic Wars. By that time, the Romans had enslaved the Greeks, who revealed the celestial art to their masters.

For six centuries (from the second century B.C. to the fourth century A.D.), and especially after the reign of Augustus, astrology occupied a prominent position in Roman customs and thought, although there were periodic attempts at suppression.

In Rome, astrology lost the religious, metaphysical, and esoteric aspects which had been present in Chaldea, Greece and Egypt. It became one of the many forms of soothsaying, sometimes rivalling other "arts of prognostication," and sometimes supplanting them. Astrology entered an arena where many other doctrinal currents and beliefs existed, and it was a propitious time for new concepts to take root.

Before recorded history, the Romans believed in the omnipotence of mysterious forces identified as benevolent and malevolent spirits. The early Romans practiced an animist religion, without any form of theology or ethical precepts, and without anthropomorphic images of deities. They did not strive to interpret the manifestations of nature as the Chaldeans or Greeks had done. Ancient Rome merely sought to appease and propitiate these superhuman forces during ceremonies where incantations were repeated.

Gradually, these forces (the *numina*) were given identities and names as a result of Etruscan influence: Jupiter, Janus, Mars, Juno, and Vesta. Under their auspices, the Romans began to develop ways of foretelling the future, such as augury, involving examination of the entrails of animals, notably the liver. Priestly orders arose in order to oversee these rituals.

Later, when Rome came into contact with Greece, Africa, and Asia during the fourth and third centuries before Christ, it encountered symbolic associations among its own deities and those of other cultures. Poseidon was recognized as Neptune, Hermes as Mercury, and Aphrodite as Venus. The Greek pantheon was merged with the Roman one, but, to a certain extent, this seemingly natural and instinctive synchretism fostered a religious crisis: a significant disparity existed between actual forms of worship, consisting entirely of invocatory rituals and incantations intended to gain the favor of the gods, and the Greeks' mystical bonds with their deities. Greek religious beliefs were derived from a vast body of secular thought whose moral codes and forms of discipline were interwoven with mythology, but no counterpart existed among the Romans. The Romans became somewhat disoriented, and lost faith in everything which had pre-

viously permitted them to explain their own existence and the role of supernatural forces.

During the third century before Christ, many beliefs imported from Asia Minor began to flourish alongside the Greek deities; the Egyptian cult of Isis and Osiris coexisted with the Persian cult of Mithra. In Rome, with its cosmopolitan population, multiple visions of the universe were present, without a sense of unity and without furnishing reassurance.

It is not unusual for a nation vanquished in warfare to triumph in the realm of ideas: although the Chaldeans had been conquered by the Greeks, they taught the Greeks the principles of astrological science and were their mentors in many fields. This type of phenomenon is even more fully understandable in relation to the turbulence of Rome during the second and third centuries before Christ: the Greeks acquired intellectual prestige, not only in literature and art, but as a result of astrology. During that era, as in Athens, Greek astrologers who had studied in Babylonia were called "mathematicians" or "Chaldeans."

Astrology gained great influence in Rome, not only in religion, but in the arts and politics, although it did not always win unanimous approval. During the first century before Christ, Cicero denounced astrologers who prepared horoscopes: "To my knowledge, the Chaldeans made so many prophecies to Pompey, Crassus, and, indeed, to Caesar, to the effect that each of them would die at an advanced age, at home, and with great honor! It is astounding to me that there would still be anyone who is willing to believe in men whose predictions are disproved every day by actual events." (*De Divinatione*—"On Soothsaying.")

All of the emperors, from Augustus, Tiberius, and Nero, to Vespasian and Marcus Aurelius, consulted astrologers, and, although astrologers were sometimes repudiated or expelled from Rome for involvement in political intrigues, they were among the most carefully heeded advisers.

The first astrologer whose name has endured was a sage known as Nigidius Figulus (99-45 B.C.). When the father of Augustus Caesar was late in arriving at the Senate on account of the birth of his son, this astrologer predicted that "because of the positions of the planets your son shall be a leader."

Under the influence of the Etruscans, the Romans adopted methods of prediction, such as augury, where they examined the entrails of sacrificial animals.

73

Nevertheless, Julius Caesar's legions had previously adopted the sign of the Bull as an emblem, and, when astrologers warned Caesar of the likelihood of death during the Ides of March (44 B.C.), he refrained from adopting precautions because he believed that his fate was inescapably preordained.

The reign of Augustus (27 B.C. to 14 A.D.) marked the definitive merging of astrological concepts with Roman customs and daily life. The Roman *fatum* dominated attitudes about life, and astrology became the guide for superstitious acceptance of destiny. During this period, Manilius, in the *Astronomica* (*circa* 9-14 A.D.), a poem which is one of the masterpieces of Roman astrology, affirmed: "Destiny governs the world, and the universe is ruled by an unbending law."

Roman astrological globe.

When he was still a young man, Augustus was deeply affected by the glorious future which the astrologer Theagenes had predicted for him. Thus, he arranged for publication of his horoscope and for preparation of a silver medal bearing the image of Capricorn, his birth sign.

Having entered the political arena, as a means of justifying rulers' authority, astrology also became a theme for dramatists and acquired a prominent role in literature. While Horace (68-8 B.C.) took pride in having been born under the auspices of Mercury, Propertius (*circa* 48-15 B.C.) depicted an astrologer in his *Elegies*. In turn, the tragedies of Seneca (4 B.C.-65 A.D.) are laden with astrological discourses: in *Thyestes,* the chorus enumerated the twelve signs of the Zodiac, from the ram to the final *sidera pisces* ("star of the fish"), and it described a world which had been cast into disorder because the Sun was retracing its path. Likewise, the *Georgics* by Virgil (70-19 B.C.) constitute one of the earliest astrological almanacs.

Anticipating his death, Augustus expelled all of the astrologers, fearing that they would foretell his demise, because astrology had become more deeply intertwined with political intrigues. If a person wished to pursue a career as an astrologer — or simply remain alive — it was wiser to conceal certain prognostications which would possibly inspire optimism among an emperor's adversaries.

Tiberius (14-37 A.D.), who succeeded Augustus, ordered the execution of any person whose horoscope foretold a bright destiny. Tacitus (*circa* 55-120 A.D.) recounted that Agrippina was informed that her son would become emperor and would slay his mother; that son was Nero, who waited to proclaim himself emperor "at a favorable time predicted by the Chaldeans."

During Nero's reign, the *Satyricon* was written by Petronius (?-67 A.D.), and, in one scene, the menu at a feast included a series of twelve dishes corresponding to the twelve signs of the Zodiac, so that guests would be able to dine according to their birth signs.

There were numerous anecdotes about astrologers who erred in their predictions:

When Asceletarion was arrested for having foretold the imminent death of Domitian, the emperor asked him how his own death would occur. Asceletarion affirmed that he would soon be torn to pieces by dogs. Domitian then commanded the execution of the astrologer, and, in order to demonstrate the falseness of astrology, he requested that Asceletarion be buried with the greatest care. "Although the emperor's instructions were followed, a sudden windstorm destroyed the pyre, and dogs devoured the half-burned body." (Suetonius.)

According to a less dramatic account, Septimus Severus (193-211 A.D.), when he was still a legate, ordered that horoscopes be prepared for several young women, so that he could marry one whose future would be like the future of an empress. Severus married a woman designated by the astrologers, and Commodus, the emperor, sought to punish this audacious act, which he perceived as a betrayal. Just before Commodus could carry out his intentions, however, he was assassinated and Severus became emperor.

Roman statue in bronze (1st century), representing the Queen of the Night, or the moon-goddess, wrapped in a cloak of stars.

Roman altar containing the twelve gods. Some of the twelve gods in the Roman pantheon ruled signs of the Zodiac.

These Roman tales reveal the image which astrology had acquired: although it was omnipotent for predicting the future, the future remained unclear, or symbolic understanding was absent and only one facet of the future was interpreted. The gods had become "consumer products," and the capabilities of astrology were exaggerated in order to render it more marketable. The horrible death of Asceletarion, devoured by dogs, suggested that astrology could not reveal events in a detailed form; it required the assistance of other forms of prognostication, such as augury, which continued to be practiced extensively. It is probable, however, that the persons who recounted this tale to Suetonius were passionate defenders of the science of the stars, believing that, by attributing the correctness of Asceletarion's prediction to the capabilities of astrology, they could increase its prestige and ensure proper historical recognition. Nevertheless, exaggerations of this type brought disfavor upon astrology to some extent.

Alexander Severus (222-235 A.D.) sought to transform astrology into a science which would be accessible to everyone: he established teaching positions in astrology which were subsidized by the imperial budget.

Later, astrology was applied in medicine, and the field of iatromathematics, or application of astrological principles to medicine (*iatros:* doctor, in Greek), arose as a means of providing diagnoses and prognoses for illnesses.

In art, astrology was interwoven with reverence for the gods, and temples were erected in honor of Saturn, Venus, Jupiter, Apollo, and others, although Mars was most widely venerated. According to myths, Mars was the father of Romulus and Remus, and the Campus Martii was used for military ceremonies. Effigies of Mars are found in sculpture, in the murals of Pompeii and mosaics of Herculaneum. Astrologers sought to determine the astrological theme which would correspond to the establishment of Rome (753 B.C.) by Romulus, in order to determine the destiny of the Eternal City.

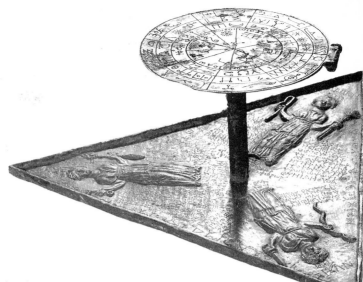

During the third century before Christ, *septizonia,* wherein the seven floors corresponded to the seven planets, were erected. These structures were somewhat reminiscent of the Chaldean *ziggurats.* Moreover, the design of Roman theaters appears to have been inspired by the twelve sections of the Zodiacal circle.

Astrology reigned without rivals, even though edicts by Augustus, Tiberius, or Claudius may have condemned some of its adepts. In many instances, these measures produced the opposite consequence: when astrology receded into the shadows, it inspired vigorous debates among the intelligentsia.

Gnosticism had already drawn upon astrology when it gained a following in Rome during the first century A.D. Gnosticism is a doctrine oriented toward higher knowledge (*gnosis* is a Greek term for knowledge) of divine power, and it embodies a pronounced dualism. This doctrine won the support of several sects which pursued different ways of acquiring higher knowledge, although all of them adhered to cosmological and theological principles which were influenced by astrological beliefs.

In one of the best known Gnostic texts, the *Pistis Sophia,* it is possible to encounter Jesus explaining to his disciples how the creator had arranged the planets:

"He appointed 1,800 governors per 'eon,'[1] and placed 360 other governors in command of the first group (the 360 degrees of the Zodiac). Then he chose five sovereigns to oversee all the governors, and in the world of men, these sovereigns are known by the the following names: the first is called Kronos; the second, Ares; the third, Hermes; the fourth, Aphrodite; and the fifth, Zeus."[2]

Gnostic thought was deeply impregnated with astrological symbolism, but it remained hostile to astrological prognostication. If Gnosticism had not been rejected by orthodox Christianity, would Christian beliefs have possibly incorporated astrological elements? It should be recalled, however, that, during this period, the fundamental principles of astrological metaphysics had long since given way to denial of free will, so that there was usually an extremely passive attitude toward the edicts of destiny.

During the third century, theologians and neo-Platonists challenged this fatalistic outlook, because it was an obstacle to maintenance of morality: "Fatalism is blasphemous because it deprives Man of responsibility, leading him to attribute all responsibility to God, who then becomes the creator of both Evil and Good."

Neo-Platonism, which was of Greek origin, arose during the third century with Plotinus (*circa* 205-270 A.D.), first in Alexandria and then in Rome. Retaining the Pythagorean tradition which had exalted the harmony, equilibrium, and cohesiveness of the universe, neo-Platonism affirmed that each entity within the universe was capable of seeking contact with other parts of the universe. Thus, Plotinus declared that "the movements of the stars announce the future for all things, but they do not shape the future...celestial movements are indications, but not causes."

Plotinus' doctrine was adopted by many thinkers. It resurrected the tradition of perfect harmony and obliterated the deterministic deviations and errors of the Roman world. Because of the authority of this doctrine, it remained possible for the Christian world to tolerate astrology.

---

1. Within the Gnostics' system, the *eons,* or spirits emanating from the Eternal Spirit, were entities representing a transition between God and the physical world.
2. Cited by Christopher McIntosh, *L'Astrologie dévoilée* (Astrology Unveiled), Fayard, 1974, p. 66.

Astrology was often associated with divining techniques. An instrument of this type (discovered in Pergamum at the turn of the century) may have been used for both purposes (3rd century A.D.).

Saint Augustine's "City of God". During the Middle Ages, astrology was fully recognized as a science.

Opposite page: Latin manuscript portraying Christ, surrounded by the Sun and the Moon, as well as the four evangelists, who represent the four fixed signs of the Zodiac.

Early Christianity: a conflict between omens and causes

Between the third and fourth centuries of Christian era, opinions differed as to whether astrology was a science or a form of religious belief. For early Christianity, astrology was merely an offshoot of pagan superstitions, but it was difficult to reject astrology in its entirety. The *Book of Enoch* spoke of seven skies containing seven moving planets, and affirmed that Man had been created by the wisdom of seven substances reflecting the image of the universe. Indeed, Adam's name was a Greek anagram for the four cardinal points. Even the Bible evoked astrological beliefs: the star which guided the Chaldean astrologers, or the Magi, toward Bethlehem, or the solar eclipse which occurred on the day of the crucifixion. Like the twelve Apostles, the twelve sons of Jacob appeared to represent the twelve signs of the Zodiac. Finally, the birth of Christ had occurred on the day of the Winter solstice, and, in many churches, one encounters a rose at the center, surrounded by stained glass images of the Apostles, whereas, outside, one encounters the twelve signs of the Zodiac carved upon the doorway itself.

Even more frequently, it is possible to observe that the four evangelists are represented by an angel (Aquarius) for Saint Matthew, a bull for Saint Luke, a lion for Saint Mark, and an eagle (Scorpio) for Saint John. Furthermore, Constantine, when he inaugurated the Nicean Council, symbolically linked the Sun to Christ, and the twelve Apostles, or pillars of the Church, to the twelve signs of the Zodiac[1]. Numerous disagreements arose, especially with respect to the Magi. If the star were to be regarded as having caused the birth of Christ, divine supremacy would have been refuted. Origen revived Platonic and Plotinian ideas in order to defend astrology, defining it as "a way of deciphering symbolic messages wherein the stars are an alphabet" (Bouché Leclercq). In this sense, the star seen by the shepherds was merely an omen of Christ's arrival on earth.

Various theologians and, indeed, the entire Church zealously sought to deprive astrology of any religious implications, so that it would only exist on a scientific plane. Saint Augustine (354-430) had practiced astrology, and, after several changes of opinion, adopted the views of Plotinus and Origen (Cf. *The City of God*). The Church never officially proscribed astrology, except insofar as fatalist and deterministic interpretations were concerned.

After the fourth century, Christianity gained coherence, and interest in astrology waned because it was no longer in harmony with the aspirations of the dominant religion.

Astrology did not emerge again in Europe until the Middle Ages, when it was reintroduced by the Arabs.

---

1. For those who are interested in correlations between the Bible and astrology, *Christ et Zodiaque* (Christ and the Zodiac) (La Colombe) by André Petitbon provides a helpful summary of the esoteric perspective. Within the Bible itself, astrological references appear in: Deuteronomy, XXXIII, 14; Judges, V, 20; Psalms, XIX, 3; Daniel, IV, 26; Daniel, V, 4; Mt., II, 2; Mt; XXIV, 29; and also in the Apocrypha (*passim*).

The Arab world:
astrology with a penchant for detail

Islamic culture was marked by an exceptional interest in astrology. As the Arabs conquered regions bordering the Mediterranean, they rediscovered astrology through Greek and Chaldean culture, translating fundamental treatises and improving techniques for casting and interpreting horoscopes. After 1000 A.D., their knowledge was transmitted to Christian Europe.

It has been claimed that one astrological manual, *The Book of the Secrets of the Sun and the Moon,* was translated from manuscripts prepared in 1300 B.C. and rediscovered among family records in the tenth century of our era by a Babylonian who had sought refuge in Iraq. This scholar, known as "the Chaldean," devoted his entire life to translating the ancient manuscripts, which comprised an incomparable library.

Nevertheless, the Arabs' interest in astrology can be traced to approximately 750 A.D., when they had encountered Ptolemy's *Tetrabiblos,* as well as the works of Firmicus Maternus, a prominent Roman astrologer during the fourth century before Christ. Among the Arabs, Ptolemy and Firmicus Maternus were regarded as the principal classical authorities in astrology.

The accuracy of Ptolemy's work was enhanced by use of Arabic numerals and the zero, because the Arabs practiced an extremely detailed form of astrology, requiring considerable precision. The adopted concepts known as the doctrine of general or individual "timeliness." The underlying principle was to seek celestial answers for specific questions—which could be of a financial or personal nature, pertaining to any domain of daily life in a general sense—by determining planetary configurations for the particular times when questions were being asked. The Arabs believed that the resulting chart could reflect events or circumstances associated with a given question (This procedure is known today as determining an "horary theme"). The Arabs made use of this technique for selecting the most favorable times for undertaking certain projects, or even for completing certain household tasks. According to an extremely precise set of rules, it was also possible to seek celestial assistance in detecting thieves or recovering lost objects.

Although the Koran forbade any form of veneration of the Sun and the Moon, Islamic astrology was entirely compatible with the belief in predestination. Thus, it flourished for eight centuries, from 750 A.D. to 1550 A.D., amidst a thriving civilization.

10th century Arab astrolabe for computing positions of the planets.

Opposite page: the sign of Aries, as portrayed in the "Treatise on Horoscopes," attributed to Albumazar.

80

Astrology initially gained acceptance in the capitals of the caliphates between the Nile and the Euphrates: primarily in Damascus; in Baghdad, where a renowned school of astrology was established; and in Cairo during the ninth century, under the protection of the famous Harun-al-Rashid, a contemporary of Charlemagne. Later, as Islam continued to expand, Greco-Babylonian astrology in an Arabized form spread throughout a vast territorial expanse extending from India to the Mediterranean: Turkestan, Persia, Turkey, Egypt, North Africa and Spain.

The Arabs built numerous observatories and reshaped the astronomical foundations of astrology. They indentified and named such stars as Rigel and Betelgeuse, and precisely explained the zenith and the nadir. They developed their own Zodiac and adopted names of weapons for the twelve signs: the Knife, the Dagger, the Lance and the Sling, with attributes corresponding to those of Virgo, Aries, Capricorn and Aquarius.

As skillful metal-workers, they were able to produce sophisticated astrolabs for determining altitudes of stars in relation to the horizon, as well as times and latitudes. Particular attention was given to making division of the Zodiac beginning with

The Arabs studied relationships between signs and planetary archetypes, which they "Arabized." The sign of Sagittarius (left) was placed adjacent to the Moon and Jupiter. Saturn, the Moon, Jupiter, Mars, and Mercury are also shown in Oriental forms. The sign of Leo (opposite page) was placed adjacent to Jupiter.

the Spring equinox on the basis of precise identification of equinoxes. Usually, the Arabic Zodiac, instead of reproducing astral configurations, expressed the purely symbolic qualities of individual signs. With the Leo sign, for example, it is possible to observe Helios-Apollo placed astride the solar animal (Helios-Apollo symbolized the Sun, which dominated Leo).

The Arabs also achieved advances in alchemy by relying upon astrology, and they derived numerous medical principles from it. Many authors have associated astrology with Sufism, an Islamic form of mysticism. As in other cultures, however, astrology was not always unanimously accepted by philosophers, particularly insofar as rigidly deterministic applications were concerned. Nevertheless, astrology was not condemned as it had been in Rome. It continued to be a basic element of Islamic civilization, permitting the Arabs to develop a coherent worldview and to shape their actions accordingly.

This harmony is repeated in art, which was strongly influenced by astrology. Such an observation is especially true of miniatures, which became extraordinarily popular during the thirteenth and fourteenth centuries. Miniatures were used to illustrate the most well known astrological texts, such as the treatises of Albategnus, Abu Mashir, and, most famous of all, *The Flowers of Astrology,* by Albumazar (796-873). A Latin translation of this treatise was one of the first works to be printed by Gutenberg.

On account of the need to uphold Islamic strictures against imitation of nature, the astrological miniatures represented a "closed" esthetic outlook, similar to that of modern art. Mosaics and painted ceramic art also revealed the sense of detail governing the Arabs' approach to astrology, which would be bequeathed to medieval Europe.

The psaltery of Blanche of Castile (13th century) shows "astronomers" who are also astrologists.

The Middle Ages:
"Astra inclinant, non necessitant[1]"

The revival of astrology during the Middle Ages is not attributable to a sudden rebirth of deities within men's minds, as if by magic, but to the fact that these deities had not been forgotten. Early Christianity rejected astrology solely on account of the fatalism which it had fostered and the manner in which astrology had been practiced, especially by the Romans. Fatalism denied free will and individual responsibility; it did not allow for divine intervention. Beginning with the eleventh century, however, divine revelation was no longer enough to satisfy Christian Europe's thirst for knowledge. An intellectual elite soon emerged, defining itself as having inherited Greco-Roman civilization and regarding learned men as an aristocracy: the authority of knowledge was derived from Homeric legends, as well as from Plato and Aristotle. Being a Christian did not oblige a person to be ignorant; entirely to the contrary, was it not Saint Augustine who affirmed that knowledge of natural history and astronomy was necessary for reading the Scriptures and understanding sacred concepts? Thus, eminent Christian thinkers began to imbibe Greek doctrines and Islamic scientific knowledge through many texts which were translated into Latin.[2]

As a result of contact with other cultures during the Crusades and through the cultural centers of Islamic Spain (Cordoba, Toledo), Medieval Man rediscovered the science of astrology. He learned that the Aristotelean concept of the universe could

be rendered compatible with the Christian perspective. During the tenth century, Pope Sylvester II became a precursor of this reconciliation by affirming that the Earth constituted the center of the universe and was surrounded by nine concentric circles consisting of the seven planetary spheres, the sphere of stationary stars, and the *primum mobile* defined by Aristotle—a source which Christians could associate with God.

Greece was perceived as having provided a scientific verification of traditional Christian revelations, and, in this way, spiritual needs and the intellec-

"Astronomy in Concordance with Theology," (1490), a treatise by Cardinal Pierre d'Ailly, the Archbishop of Cambrai, shows an astronomer instructing a theologian.

---

1. "The stars dispose, but they do not determine."
2. Many texts were translated by Johannes Toletanus, known as "John of the Moon," who disseminated the earliest astrological manuscripts between 1135 and 1163.

tual rigor of the Scholastics could both be satisfied. During the Middle Ages, conflicts did not arise between religion and scientific knowledge, which included astrology and alchemy.

This was perhaps one of the epochs in European history where individuals' inner lives were most intimately interwoven with external life: internal experience was concretely reflected by external experience. "The heavens and the earth are present within mankind," declared Saint Hildegarde of Bingen (1098-1179), a noted Rhenish mystic, in *Sci vias,* at the beginning of the twelfth century. Just as it has been possible to understand the development of Chaldean symbolic thought, fundamental concepts can be transposed to the Christian World of the Middle Ages, if one allows, of course, for the change from polytheism to monotheism and for a more fully developed comprehension of the world. Astrology was Christianized during the Middle Ages.

Saint Thomas Aquinas (1226-1274), a disciple of Albertus Magnus, definitively incorporated astrology within Christian thought. He regarded human beings as possessing a dual nature: a physical aspect, or our bodies, which, like plants and animals, are governed by the planets; and a higher aspect, the soul, which communicates directly with God and possesses free will.

In the *Summa Theologica,* Saint Thomas stated: "In many instances, astrologers foretell events accurately. This fact may arise from two conditions: firstly, because most men follow their bodily urges, their actions shall usually be subject to the influence of heavenly bodies. There are but a few men who can tame these influences through reason, and they are the only men possessing wisdom. This is why, for many events, astrologers can foretell the truth..."

Astra inclinant, non necessitant ("The stars dispose, but they do not determine") is the famous Thomist adage which prevailed during the Middle Ages and is still cited today by the most knowledgeable astrologists.

Albertus Magnus (*circa* 1193-1280), the mentor of Thomas Aquinas, was one of the most prominent Dominican theologians of the thirteenth century. He associated the medicinal properties of plants with planetary and zodiacal influences. In *Naturalia,* for example, Albertus Magnus explained that martagon was "sympathetic" to Saturn, which governed Capricorn and Aquarius, whereas chicory corresponded to the Sun which governed Leo.

During the twelfth century, the famous predictions of 1186 concerning notable natural disasters (cyclones, windstorms, cataclysms) resulting from a conjunction of seven planets with Libra, which are believed to represent an erroneous interpretation (perhaps these calamities were represented by Saladin's invasion of the Holy Land, or Genghis Khan's conquest of Asia), did not undermine the intellectual prestige of astrology to any extent.

After having been incorporated within religious doctrines, astrology was subsequently accepted by

The Christian world is combined with the astrological universe: the Earth is surrounded by planetary spheres, the Zodiac, and the **primum mobile.**

Left: in this manuscript prepared by Lambert de Saint-Omer (circa 1260), Christ becomes the **Sol Salutis** *("Sun of Salvation") or the* **Sol Justitiae** *("Sun of Justice"), governing the Zodiac and its influence upon human destiny.*

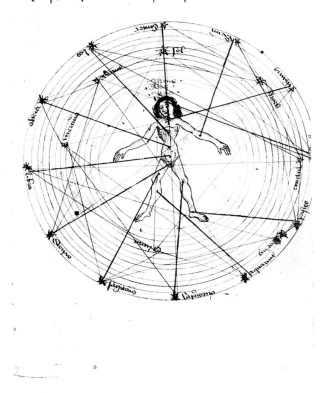

Is Man a prisoner of celestial forces? ("Man and the Heavens," a 16th century woodcut).

the universities. At the School of Medicine in Bologna, where a professorship in astrology was established, as in Padua and Milan, the following *dictum* was in vogue: "Medical studies without astrology are like an eye which cannot see."

There had already been instances of physicians' curing patients by applying the Greek principle of astrological melothesia[1], whereby each sign of the Zodiac governed a part of the body and each planet dominated one of its organs. Surgeons planned operations according to planetary positions in relation to signs governing afflicted parts of the body.

In Paris, or at Oxford, the ancient concept that Man was a microcosm analogous to the macrocosm was taught according to a Christian world-view: astrology was a respected field of knowledge, and rulers were patrons to its practitioners.

Michael Scot was an astrologer to Frederick II of Hohenstaufen, (1220-1250), the German emperor whose court was located in Sicily, at Palermo.

Piero Di Abano (1257-1315), or Peter of Padua, was an adviser to Philip the Fair, but his theories acquired a deterministic orientation, and he was burned in effigy after his death. Nevertheless, the following inscription was carved at the base of his statue in Padua: "He was, indeed, such a master of astrology that he was suspected of witchcraft. Falsely accused of heresy, he was found innocent."

The Inquisition also prosecuted other astrologers, such as the Florentine Cecco di Ascoli, who was accused of heresy for having attempted to compute the date of Christ's birth. He was burned alive in 1327, but his fate represented an exception. During the same period, Guido Bonatti (died *circa* 1300) became famous for assisting the Ghibelline leader Guido di Montefeltro. It is claimed that Bonatti precisely computed favorable dates and times for beginning battles, and that he would climb a belltower to toll the appointed hour. His treatise, the *Liber astronomicus,* was translated into English in 1676 by the famous English astrologer William Lilly.

In Spain, Alphonse X, known as "the Wise," who died in 1284, sponsored publication of astrological manuscripts, including the famous astrological tables which he commissioned in 1262. These have since been known as the *Alphonsine Tables,* and, with the year being divided into 365 days, five hours, forty-nine minutes, and sixteen seconds, they offered far greater precision than Ptolemy's computations. In order to prepare the *Tables,* Alphonse X had assembled the most eminent Christian, Moorish, and Jewish astrologers, who labored for four years.

---

1. This was a form of astrology based upon correlations between signs or planets and the human body.

In 1377, Nicolas Oresme prepared a French commentary for Aristotle's **De Coelo**, a treatise on astronomy and astrology, for Charles V. The title was **Le Livre du ciel et du monde** ("Book of Heaven and Earth").

Below: **Le Livre du ciel et du monde** — Nicolas Oresme using an armillary sphere.

In France, Charles V (1422-1461) himself was an astrologer, and Jacques Coeur (circa 1395-1456), the famous treasurer of Charles VII, practiced astrology and alchemy. Like Pope Sylvester II (999-1003), who had converted one of the towers of the Lateran Palace into an observatory for studying the stars, Jacques Coeur ordered the erection of an "astrologer's tower" within his mansion in Bourges.

During the fourteenth and fifteenth centuries, in France and the British Isles, astrological illustrations were included within books of hours dedicated to "the princes of the aristocracy." Books of hours, such as those created by the Limburg Brothers (Pol, Hermont, Jeannequin), truly constitute treasure-chests of astrological iconography. With abundant illumination, they depict the agricultural tasks of each month and the attributes of the planets governing each sign. The most famous is the *Très Riches Heures* prepared for the Duke of Berri by the Limburg Brothers (1403-1413), which is on display at the Musée Condé in Chantilly. The same museum contains the famous *Livre d'Heures* of Etienne Chevalier (illustrated by Jean Fouquet), as well as books of hours created for the Duchess of Burgundy, the Duke of Rohan, and Jean d'Achey. In England, the Duke of Bedford's book of hours has been preserved.

How Man sees the universe: The Earth is surrounded by the seven planets and the Zodiac (16th century manuscript).

Even in places of worship, our medieval forbears were surrounded by zodiacal symbols. The signs of the Zodiac and the trades which they govern were carved within the facade of the Cathedral of Amiens. In bas-reliefs or in stained-glass windows, astrological symbols appear in a stylized form in the basilica of Vezelay, in the Cathedrals of Senlis and Laon. In turn, a Sun-tower and a Moon-tower were erected for the Cathedral of Chartres. In Italy, astrological imagery was given even greater importance in religious architecture and in public buildings. In Padua, one of the rooms of the Ragione is decorated by an enormous fresco divided into horizontal sections: it portrays the planets and "their children," as well as the signs of the Zodiac, the twelve Apostles, and the tasks corresponding to each month. At sunrise, the rays of the Sun strike the sign with which it coincides during each month. This fresco, however, already represents the beginning of the Italian Renaissance.

During the Middle Ages, only those who knew the secrets of astrology were considered truly educated. In the prologue to the well-known *Canterbury Tales,* Geoffrey Chaucer (*circa* 1340-1400), just after mentioning his training in medicine, refers to his knowledge of astrology. In one of the *Tales,*

Satur nus
Jup ter
Mars
Sol
Ve nus
Mer curius
Lu na

the Wife of Bath explains her temperament in these terms:

"Venus gave me my appetites, my lechery, and Mars granted me my intense ardency. My ascendant was Taurus, and Mars, in this way . . ."

Dante, however, was an illustrious forerunner of Chaucer. *The Divine Comedy* (1302-1321) and several other works by Dante demonstrate the influence of the stars. His poetry so perfectly expresses the Thomist universe and the conventional medieval world-view that I have chosen it as a final illustration of the epoch known as the Middle Ages: in the sixteenth canto of the "Purgatory," Dante questions a suffering soul about the causes of sin and receives the following reply:

"The Heavens determine the movement of our energies, but. . .there is a light to distinguish Good from Evil, and free will, though it endures hardships during its first struggles with the Heavens, ultimately achieves its triumph. . . . Though we are free, we are subject to a greater force and a higher nature, and this power creates within us a spirit which the Heavens cannot master."

How God sees the universe: divine will controls the orbit of each planet (16th century manuscript).

91

The Renaissance: astrology reigns supreme

The Renaissance did not suddenly appear upon the horizon of civilization like the aurora borealis. It was a revival of Antiquity, brightened by a majestic beacon, although the Middle Ages had already illuminated the past to a certain extent. Hence, it is difficult to define chronological boundaries for the Renaissance: whereas its dominant trends had fully developed in Italy by the end of the fourteenth century and began to fade during the mid-sixteenth, the Renaissance did not shed its strongest light upon other regions of Europe until the mid-fifteenth century. Indeed, its vitality extended, especially in England, beyond the sixteenth century.

The "intellectual aristocracy" which had imbibed the rudiments of knowledge during the Middle Ages, evoking the divine prestige of Greco-Roman Antiquity, consolidated its power during the Renaissance. Having sought spiritual nourishment under the aegis of Christianity and the Church during the Middle Ages, this aristocracy pursued higher levels of awareness during the Renaissance, while seeking esthetic and sensual pleasure. In its quest for knowledge, humanism sought emancipation from religious inhibitions: were not the words of Homer comparable to those of the prophets?

"Perhaps more can be gained from reading fables by seeking the allegorical meaning rather than by reading from the Holy Scriptures and merely grasping the literal meaning," Erasmus affirmed.

Myths were re-examined, and they were compared with Biblical precepts: was it possible for eternal knowledge to exist with different external forms? Amid significant discoveries (the New World in 1492) and economic and political convulsions (the fall of Constantinople in 1453), the humanists wanted to rediscover the past in order to define their own origin. They drank from the fountain of ancient wisdom, and the deities of Antiquity were given positions within the cultural pantheon.

Whereas medieval man was a product of divine will — a cipher —, the Renaissance defined Man as a molder of events, responsible for himself and for the universe. The theory of the microcosm and the macrocosm held sway, and astrology, which met the needs of a new world-view, reigned undisputed.

With the invention of printing and as a result of improved means of communication, astrological

During the Renaissance, Atlas was portrayed supporting an astrological universe (Woodcut, 1559).

Opposite page: an astrologer is determining the position of the Sun with an astrolabe (an instrument used for determining positions of stars in relation to the horizon, as well as time and latitudes).

The extent to which astrology influenced the famous predictions of Michel de Nostredame or Nostradamus (1503-1566), has not been determined.

records and manuscripts stored in monasteries, libraries, or royal palaces were printed, and distributed throughout Europe.

Although astrology was still the domain of a handful of scholars, traditions which had been preserved in manuscripts were now disseminated in manuals and by universities which offered instruction in astrology: in addition to Bologna, Paris, Padua, Milan, and Oxford, the list of universities promoting research in astrology now included Florence, Parma, Pavia, Naples, Mainz, Erfurt, Cracow, and Prague.

Rulers and their astrologers

Astrological coteries arose in the royal palaces of France, England, Bohemia, Austria, and Italy, as in the instance of the courts of the Viscontis and Sforzas in Milan, or the Medicis in Florence.

Not only temporal, but ecclesiastical potentates frequently consulted the stars before making important decisions. Luc Gauric (1476-1558) served as an astrologer to Popes Julius II, Leo X, Clement VII, and Paul III, before Catherine de Medici became his patron. He had won renown for having predicted that Alessandro Farnese would become Pope Paul III (1534-1549), and it is said that this Pope did not convene councils without seeking favorable omens beforehand. It is likewise claimed that Julius II chose the date for his investiture according to an astrologer's advice.

Under Leo X, the Vatican acquired means of promoting research and instruction in astrology. Leo X established a chair of astrology in Sapienza, hoping that it would rival those of Bologna, Padua, and Paris.

During this period, horary astrology, or horary questions, introduced by the Arabs, became widespread.

What was the most favorable time to begin a given project?

Astrologers defined ideal celestial configurations for specific ventures, thereby making it possible to determine the most favorable dates for crowning kings or consecrating Popes, but also for erecting cities. In this way, an ancient tradition was being perpetuated, inasmuch as Alexander had adopted the same method for establishing his capital, Alexandria, at 4:30 P.M., on April 16, in 333 B.C. while Constantine had later selected November 3, in 324 A.D. for erecting Constantinople.

Indeed, the time to lay the first stone for a building was not chosen at random; the time had to be right, according to the intended function of the building. Thus, fortresses were erected when the Sun coincided with Aries, royal palaces when it entered Leo, and court buildings when it entered Capricorn. Construction of the Escorial (in Madrid) began when the Sun and the Moon coincided with Aries, occupying the tenth house, in order to foster a mood of boldness and martial prowess.

Moreover, many generals waited to obtain astrologers' opinions before going into battles, and diplomats during the Renaissance refrained from signing treaties if the Moon had entered Aries (because, in this position, the peace-making power of the Moon would not be reinforced by Aries.)

In France, Louis XI (1423-1483) sought the advice of the astrologer Galeotti, and Catherine de

Medici (1519-1589) ruled with the aid of the astrologers Luc Gauric and Cosme Ruggieri, who were also Italians. Later, she relied upon the famous Michel de Nostredame (1503-1566), known as Nostradamus. In England, Elizabeth I sought the opinions of John Dee, but she approached astrology pragmatically in contrast to the superstitious Catherine de Medici.

Nostradamus was a physician of Jewish descent who had completed his studies at Montpellier. After the death of his wife and two of his children, he travelled throughout Languedoc, Roussillon, and Italy, gaining as much fame for healing skills as for his prophetic powers, when he sought to cure the victims of an outbreak of the plague in Lyon. In 1555, Nostradamus published a book of predictions known as the seven *Centuries,* which acquired exceptional popularity. Catherine de Medici, who was devoted not only to astrology, but to the occult, invited Nostradamus to join her court, where he foretold the death of Catherine's husband, Henri II, in a famous quatrain:

The young lion will vanquish the old,
Fighting one to one on the jousting field.
He will pierce his eye within a cage of gold,
Dealing two blows as one, and causing a cruel death.

During the joust which took place between Henri II and the Earl of Montgomery in 1559, the King did indeed meet his death. Both combattants had chosen a lion as an emblem, and the "cage of gold" represented the King's golden helmet, which was shattered by the Earl's lance. "Two blows as one" meant that this misfortune was the first of two calamities expected to befall the House of Valois.[1]

Although Nostradamus was a renowned astrologer, it is difficult to separate purely prophetic elements of his *Centuries* from elements which truly embody astrological principles. The *Centuries* originated with the prophetic visions of the "*magus,*" whose concern with precision induced him to render these visions consistent with astrological cycles.

Catherine de Medici consulting the seer Nostradamus, who appears to be employing divining techniques.

1. Indeed, the King's heir, Henri III, was assassinated, and the House of Navarre acquired the throne.

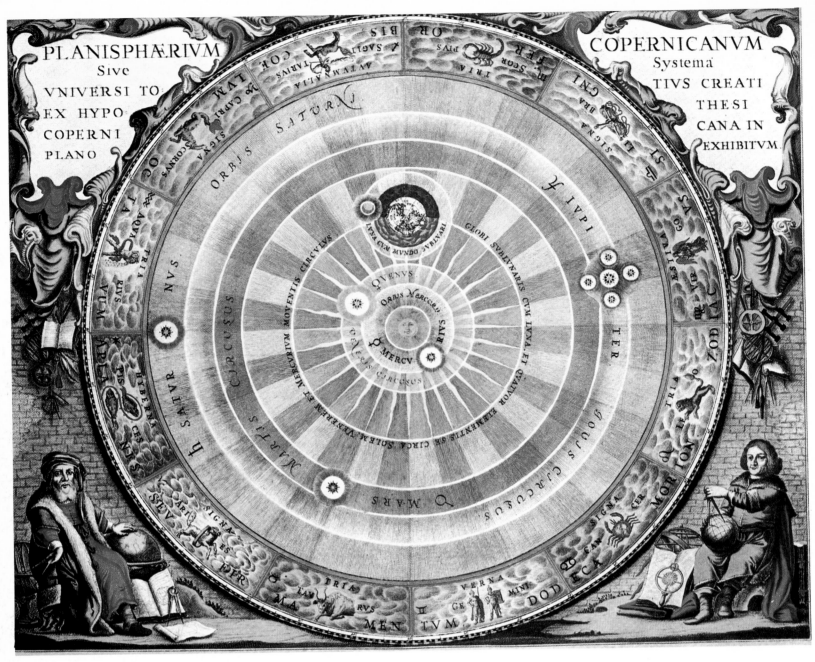

The Copernican revolution: the Sun is the center of the universe, and it is surrounded by the orbits of the seven planets (Jupiter is shown with its satellites) and by the sphere of stationary stars. Nevertheless, Copernicus, believed in astrology and practiced astrology (engraving by Cellarius, 16th century).

Nostradamus was an occultist summoned by the House of Valois to wield the levers of traditional secret powers. Catherine de Medici was exceptionally interested in his knowledge, and she did not exclude the occult as an instrument for governing her domains. A few remnants of an observatory which she erected in the grain exchange are still standing, and this is where the queen observed the stars with Nostradamus or, after his death, with (Cosme) Ruggieri. Nostradamus precisely foretold the date of his own death: July 2, 1566.

After the reign of Catherine de Medici, the royal family of France continued to seek the advice of the most famous astrologers, giving them the title of royal physician and astrologer. (Jean Baptiste)

Morin de Villefranche (1583-1656), regarded as the most noted astrologer of his era, served as an adviser to Cardinal Richelieu, who concealed him in the royal apartments to witness the consummation of the marriage of Louis XIII and Anne of Austria, in order for Morin to cast a horoscope for the conception of the future dauphin. Morin later informed Anne of Austria that her son, who became Louis XIV, would have a splendid future, and Richelieu recommended him to Cardinal Mazarin, who granted him an annuity of 2,000 pounds in 1645.

Morin de Villefranche's prediction for the death of Richelieu was inaccurate by only ten hours, and his prediction for the death of Louis XIII embodied a precision of approximately six days. He also made noteworthy discoveries in astronomy, although these were overshadowed by his success as an astrologer.

Nevertheless, a new vision of the universe began to emerge during the seventeenth century: the Earth was no longer the center of the universe; instead of being the center of a solar orbit, the Earth rotated around the Sun. This concept, however, did not truly transform attitudes toward astrology until the eighteenth century. All of the great astronomers—Copernicus, Tycho Brahe, Kepler, and Galileo—were practitioners of astrology.

Nicholas Copernicus (1473-1543) entrusted his friend, the astrologer Rheticus, with publication of a treatise entitled *De revolutionibus orbis coelestium libri VI*[1], which enunciated the heliocentric theory. Copernicus' introduction stated:

"Hence, if the dignity of different arts were to be evaluated according to the fields which they scrutinize, the art known by some as astrology and by others as astronomy, which the Ancients regarded as the culmination of mathematics, would clearly be the noblest of arts."

Galileo (1564-1642), for his services as an astrologer, earned fees as high as 50,000 pounds. While maintaining that "the heliocentric theory cannot negate the fundamental principles of astrology," (Johann) Kepler (1571-1630), who, as an astrologer to the German Emperor Rudolph II, boasted of "having learned this fact: that, at the time of birth, men. . .receive the imprint of planetary influences and retain it until they die. . . . I can, with few regrets and in all sincerity, take pride in my personal experiences over thirty years."

---

1. Treatise on *Revolutions of Heavenly Bodies*.

Tycho Brahe (1546-1601), who continued Copernicus' investigations, was one of the greatest astronomers of the Renaissance, but he also practiced astrology. Astronomy and astrology had not yet been set apart from one another.

Compendium of astronomy (Germany, 16th century): celestial coordinates for thirty cities in Spain and Italy. (The second cover, in addition to containing a compass and a sundial, provides a list of latitudes for the thirty cities).

Page from shepherds' almanac indicating times for planting crops according to positions of the planets.

Page from shepherds' almanac indicating times for planting crops according to positions of the planets.

Kepler wrote extensively about astrology, seeking to improve its techniques.[2] In a brief treatise entitled "On Improving the Rudiments of Astrology," he summarized his beliefs concerning the natural influence of celestial bodies upon terrestrial phenomena. Kepler believed that "the soul of the Earth" and men's souls were guided by planetary movements, although these movements were omens instead of causes. Thus, Kepler wrote in terms of conjectures, and not predictions. Whereas he upheld the heliocentric system—defining planets' positions in relation to the Sun—he believed that it was necessary to determine horoscopes from a geocentric perspective—since the influence of the solar system upon the Earth was being examined. Hence, it was necessary to improve upon the computations of the Ancient World, instead of merely discounting them so as to discard certain astrological concepts which were unverifiable by mathematical and geometric means.

Throughout the Renaissance, scientific discoveries did not transform prevailing modes of thought: although the physical world became Galilean, Ptolemaic metaphysical concepts survived. The actual transformation occurred in a later era, under the influence of a certain humanistic pride which sought to free mankind from the influence of the stars.

Astrology in rural life

Dissemination of astrological knowledge was no longer confined to the elite, because printing rendered astrology accessible to all layers of society.

2. Gerard Simon, in *Kepler astronome-astrologue* (Kepler: Astronomer and Astrologer) (Gallimard, 1979), has provided a summary of Kepler's ideas.

For example, astrological almanacs primarily oriented toward bucolic activities began to appear. The first of these almanacs, *Le Calendrier et Compost des bergers* (The Shepherd's Calendar and Guide), was printed in France in 1493, and it was so successful that similar almanacs were soon published in Germany, England, and Poland. The almanacs applied the "elections" of horary astrology to rural life. They included tables indicating favorable dates and times for planting (sowing of a given crop should take place during a particular phase of the Moon), harvesting, cutting timber, and herding livestock into pens. Thus, the almanacs regulated many aspects of daily life, by designating proper times for bathing, administering purgatives, bloodletting, and falling in love.... There was a propitious time for each activity, and it was necessary to ensure favorable celestial conditions before proceeding with a given venture.

The concept of adapting life to the rhythms of nature (which has reappeared today with the concept of biological clocks) was so widely applied that it soon degenerated into exaggerated determinism, thereby contributing to the decline of astrology.

Medical astrology

Astrology became a cornerstone of medicine, and many noted astrologists began their careers as physicians: for example, Avicenna (980-1037) in medieval Baghdad, and, closer to our own era, Girolamo Cardano, in Italy.

Girolamo Cardano (1501-1576) was one of the most renowned Italian astrologers of his era: as a physician, philosopher, mathematical genius, and astrologer, he sought to combine aspects of various doctrines and formulate therapeutic principles which were enormously successful. Cardano wrote exten-

Paracelsus: "What can a doctor accomplish if he knows nothing of cosmography?" (16th century engraving).

sively—including a commentary upon Ptolemy's *Tetrabiblos*—and he proposed establishment of an "erudite aristocracy" which would counsel rulers through astrology, science, and technology.

The most illustrious physician-astrologer was Paracelsus (1493-1541), a Swiss who emigrated to Germany. Some authors have regarded him as the founder of homeopathy, because he applied the Law of Similarity, whereby similar forces act upon similar objects—on a universal scale—a fundamental concept in homeopathy. Paracelsus emphasized analogies between the external universe and various parts of the human body, or analogies between the macrocosm and the microcosm.

"Zodiacal man" — 15th century engraving. The parts of the body are associated with signs of the Zodiac: the head is ruled by Aries, the neck by Taurus, the kidneys by Libra...

"In their properties, nature, and categories, as in their positions and movements, Man's innermost stars are similar to the stars above, differing from them only in form and substance. Their nature is the same within the heavens and within the microcosm...for the Sun, the Moon, and all the planets, as well as the stars and everything within the heavens, can be found in Man...the body attracts the heavens...and this occurs in accordance with divine will."

Paracelsus believed that the physician should know the patient's horoscope in order to cure illnesses. It would not be possible to determine proper proportions for remedies without taking into account patterns of celestial influences.

"Consider this carefully: what can a remedy for women's wombs accomplish if you are not guided by Venus? What can your remedy for the brain accomplish without the guidance of the Moon... If the heavens are not favorable and do not permit your remedy to achieve its purpose, nothing can be accomplished."

Paracelsus likewise appears to have discovered the principle of psychosomatic illnesses, insofar as he regarded human beings as possessing three bodies: a physical or animal body, a sideral or planetary body, and a luminous or spiritual body. Thus, it was possible to explain illnesses in terms of deep emotions (conveyed by the planetary body) which engulfed the luminous body and, in many instances, only represented elimination of poisons from the soul through the physical body.

After analysis of the patient's horoscope, whereby the signs were associated with respective parts of the body—the head is governed by Aries, the neck by Taurus, the heart by Leo—the physician completed his diagnosis according to positions of planets and signs which they occupied, always keeping in mind that each planet is likewise associated with an organ of the body. It was also possible to define the patient's proclivities: illnesses affecting the heart were attributable to the presence of Mars in Leo, those affecting the kidneys arose from the presence of Saturn in Libra, *et cetera*.

Jean Ganivet's text, the *Amicus medicorum,* published in 1431 and widely used for two centuries thereafter, explained techniques for curing illnesses according to their astrological origins and for predicting susceptibilities according to a person's horoscope.

In 1437, at the University of Paris, astrological principles for selecting the most suitable time for letting blood were debated; it was decided that bleedings should be performed at times when the ascending sign corresponded to the sign occupied by the Moon. Therefore, it was essential for physicians to keep on hand an astrolab, to determine the altitudes of celestial bodies in relation to the horizon.

Indeed, during the Renaissance, not only physical, but mental illnesses were studied from an astrological perspective.

In England, Richard Burton (1576-1640), the author of the famous *Anatomy of Melancholy by Democritus Junior,* developed a system for classifying mental illnesses: thus, he explained that the pathological counterpart to Leo was megalomania, that rejection of external reality likewise originated with Cancer, *et cetera.* Burton explained, for example, that a conjunction of Mars and the Moon in opposition to Saturn and Mercury could produce an alternating manic state, resulting from the fact that the aggressiveness of Mars and the excitability of Mercury, as well as the receptivity of the Moon, overwhelm the restraint associated with Saturn. For Burton, there were no favorable or un-

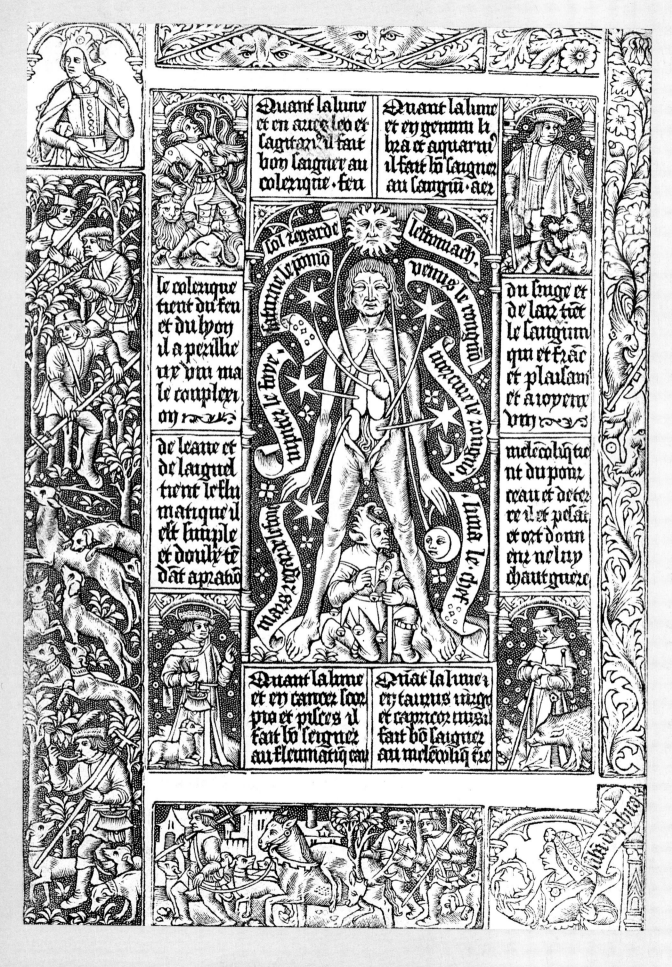

This engraving provides another example of the theory of sympathy: the organs are identified in relation to the planets.

Mercury, as he appears in Mantegna's "Tarots," a series of fifty symbolic figures, or "pieces on the divine chessboard" extending between Heaven and Earth. Mantegna created these images during the Council of Mantua (1459-1460), for the entertainment of those who participated.

favorable horoscopes, as fatalist versions of astrology affirmed; there were only favorable and unfavorable choices. Two persons with the same nativity could lead different lives, according to whether they "decided" to dominate or be dominated by their predicted futures. Similarly, two individuals may possess two different attitudes in identical situations. The remedy for psychological disorders depended upon development of consciousness, inasmuch as the psyche is the point of origin. "The health of one's soul is a matter of choice," but this principle was only applicable, of course, if illnesses had not yet entered a chronic stage.

When Burton was buried at Christ Church, his horoscope was carved upon his tomb.

During the seventeenth century, (Nicholas) Culpeper continued the work of Paracelsus, by methodically classifying plants governed by signs and associated with planets and then by examining their medico-astrological properties. He prescribed an herb associated with a given planet in order to treat an illness caused by an opposite planet. Thus, certain liver ailments governed by Jupiter, the master of Sagittarius, could be alleviated by plants associated with Mercury, the master of Gemini, which is the opposite sign.

Medicine is probably the field where applications of astrology were most fully developed, and numerous paintings portraying the "Zodiacal Man" of Antiquity represent this fact.

Astrology and art

The echoes of astrology are present in all forms of art: through fundamental themes, such as the planetary deities, the cycles of the Zodiac, or the four elements, or direct evocation of such concepts as the Zodiacal Man, the Renaissance combined celestial arts with plastic and decorative arts.

During the Middle Ages, only the Zodiac was portrayed in religious architecture (except in Italy), but, during the Renaissance, not only the Zodiac, but the planetary deities, proliferated in religious and civil monuments. Through the stunning gracefulness of stylized gods and goddesses, the most profound thoughts were expressed: the eternal themes of mythology and astrology permitted Renaissance art to symbolize the multiple facets of spiritual conflicts. Examples include the "Struggle between Reason and Desire" by Baccio Bandinelli (1487-1559), or the "Triumph of Virtue over the Vices" by Andrea Mantegna (1431-1506), or especially the cupola of the Chigi Chapel by Raphael (1483-1520). Here, the Creator is portrayed amidst planetary

deities, possibly expressing harmony between Providence (God) and Necessity (planetary forces), or reconciliation of theology and science.

Venus, the symbol of perfect beauty, fickle Venus who causes men to forget their moral strengths, was tamed by Botticelli (1445-1510) in the "Birth of Venus" and "Venus and Mars," by Titian (1490-1567) in the "Tribute to Venus," by (Paolo) Veronese (1528-1588) in "Venus and Adonis" and "Mars and Venus," or by Perugino (1445-1523), Bronzino (1503-1572) and Simon Vouet (1590-1649). Jupiter, Saturn, and the other planetary deities were portrayed in their mythological conflicts by the greatest painters of the era.

The theme of the zodiacal cycle of months and seasons inspired Botticelli's "Primavera," as well as the "Haying in June" and the "Return from the Hunt in February" by Pieter Brueghel (1568-1625). Similarly, Arcimboldo (*circa* 1527-1593) created truculent portraits where Man and Nature are combined, with the seasons being represented by faces composed of plants symbolizing a given season. Murals and tapestries also abounded with seasonal allegories: the frescoes of Francesco Cossa (*circa* 1438-1477) at the Schifanoia Palace in Ferrara evoke the zodiacal references for each month, combining mythology and the rhythms of Nature: for April, Mars surrenders to Venus, the goddess of the Bull, while vegetation flourishes and lovers join one another... In turn, Tribulzio de Benedetto da Milano portrayed the months in tapestries. Lastly, the four elements — fire, earth, water, and air, con-

"The Triumph of Wisdom over the Vices," created for Isabella d'Este by Mantegna. Mythological deities express the eternal conflict within the human soul. Wisdom is portrayed as Minerva, who wears a helmet and carries a spear. Accompanied by Diana and by Chastity, she has defeated Venus, who is portrayed as the mother of all of the Vices: Pride, Sloth, Suspicion, Hatred, and Greed, who are retreating into a stagnant pool.

stituting the cornerstone of astrology — were presented in a personified form by Arcimboldo, or displayed in the frescoes of Francesco le Poppi at the Palazzo Vecchio, in Florence.

Whereas "Renaissance art" was frequently inspired by the fundamental themes of astrology, technical concepts are also expressed in numerous paintings, engravings, and illuminated manuscripts. Leonardo da Vinci (1452-1519) combined the precision of geometry with artistic expression in representing man as a microcosm. Books often depicted the attributes of each of the twelve symbols by associating signs with parts of the body, portraying the Zodiac-Man. In the Sphaera manuscripts, a detailed chart illustrates the influence of the planets upon terrestrial life.

In Germany, Beham (1500-1550) produced engravings depicting the functions of planets, and Dürer (1471-1528) described the symptoms of illnesses attributed to planetary aspects, such as syphilis. In "Melancholy," he depicted the contemplative life of "children of Saturn." Nevertheless, this was also the era of a new vision of the universe and, whereas Dürer portrayed the celestial constellations, Cellarius (1638-1707), a German geographer, reproduced various images of the world, from ancient Greece to Copernicus.

Astrological motifs abounded not only in the plastic arts, but in items used in daily life: Benevenuto Cellini (1500-1571) portrayed Neptune and the four seasons on a golden salt-cellar for François I. Watches and clocks were adorned with the twelve signs of the Zodiac, and town clocks tolled the hours according to Aries, Leo, *et cetera,* as in the instance of the cupolas of Cremona, or Hampton Court in London, or the belfry of Prague. Life appeared to have become astrological...

"...Everywhere and in everything, men's lives are ruled by the destinies which the Heavens weave through the stars. Those who first dared to comprehend the stars Cast upon the heavens the names which they saw fit."
— Ronsard wrote in the *Hymn to the Stars.*

In France, Italy, and Britain, the stars were evoked in poetry and on the stage. Even William Shakespeare, who gave little credence to astrological doctrines, echoed the beliefs of his era in *King Lear:* "It is the stars, the stars above us, which determine our condition."

As in ancient Rome, astrology was undermined by excesses during the Renaissance. The physical world acquired a new appearance, but Sir Isaac Newton himself rebuked an astronomer who had denounced astrology: "...Mr. Halley, I have investigated this topic, whereas you have not." Newton's words meant: "Do not express opinions about something which you do not understand!"

Newton's warning was uttered in 1687, but, as early as 1666, Colbert, in establishing the *Académie des Sciences,* had excluded astrology from the official curriculum. Astrology ceased to be recognized as a sector of knowledge, even though it had dominated education and had been a pillar of royal power under Catherine de Medici or Elizabeth I of England. Were the foundations of astrology shaking under the weight of new discoveries, or, instead, was the *hybris* of rationalism seeking to diminish the influence of the stars? Confident of being able to dominate the world, men sought to loosen their ties with Nature, to dissociate themselves from the universe in order to reduce it to an arena of objective investigation. The subjective values of the inner mind, which had previously been integrated with the external world in human thought, were abandoned in behalf of an objective conquest of the environment.

One form of excess gave way to another, and an equilibrium between objective knowledge and the unconscious never emerged. This cleavage between the seventeenth and eighteenth centuries led to the modern battle between adherents and foes of astrology.

"Melancholy," an engraving by Dürer, symbolizes the contemplative life of "Saturnians," who meditate upon the secrets of wisdom.

The Quest for Verification

"Astrology is a science in itself and
contains an illuminating body of knowledge.
It taught me many things,
and I am greatly indebted to it.
Geophysical evidence reveals the power
of the stars and the planets
in relation to the terrestrial.
In turn, astrology reinforces this power
to some extent. This is why astrology
is like a life-giving elixir for mankind."

ALBERT EINSTEIN

"Why is there not a world...," a world whose structure is not yet known to us? (Odilon Redon, engraving, 1887).

Preceding pages: Left — "Temple of Flora," by Thornton, 19th century. Flowers which only bloom at midnight represented a fascinating mystery for the 19th century Symbolists, but today's biologists have developed explanations. Right — "The Tree of Life," a 19th century British engraving. Have the intuitions which nourished traditional concepts only produced withered flowers?

ty? Did the light of knowledge only enter the human mind when men recognized that they could understand the world by detaching themselves from it?

For three centuries, Science has conveyed an objective aura, having separated itself from traditional perspectives. Until the seventeenth century, science in Chaldea, Egypt, Greece and among the Scholastics depended upon spiritual or metaphysical principles. Science consisted of intuitions which gave coherence to different levels of reality, and all observations were interwoven with indisputable, supreme, and absolute truths.

The eighteenth century heralded a cleavage between the essence of things and human knowledge: Science ceased to be a reflection of higher powers, and was fragmented into various specialized fields which were usually divorced from one another.

Dante's vision, where knowledge had been compared to a ladder with rungs corresponding to different sciences, as well as to separate levels of self-awareness, or stages in the pursuit of wisdom, was relegated to the distant past.

To examine astrology with the methods of modern science is to examine its underlying principles by means of objective experimentation, as if the domain of intuitions could be explored with a microscope.

It is also necessary to ask this question: today, as in the past, can there be a single source for the various categories of knowledge and also for astrological principles? Did the intuitions which nourished traditional modes of thought only yield withered flowers?

It is appropriate to begin with extremely simple observations, in order to determine whether fundamental astrological principles can be corroborated. Then, at a later point, it will be possible to consider explanations furnished by basic sciences.

Is it possible that astrology was merely a means for Man, confronted by a boundless universe, to overcome his deep fears by projecting his own image onto the universe? If so, would astrology therefore belong to bygone eras, where primitive modes of thought could only "grasp the world" by projecting a human shadow, clothed in an archaic identi-

Correlations between the celestial and the terrestrial

The Sun and the Moon

For centuries, men molded their lives according to the behavior of the Sun and the Moon and their influence upon our planet. There were even Chaldean agricultural calendars presented in the form of advice given by a farmer to his son, for selecting sowing and harvesting times according to the brightness of the Sun.

In Europe, an agricultural tradition disseminated by the medieval almanacs recommended planting of different crops according to specific phases of the Moon. Even in our era, peasants have retained this ancient custom, considering it necessary to plant crops which bear fruit above the ground during a new Moon, whereas a waning Moon is favorable to root crops. Charts were prepared for precisely determining the beginning and completion of different phases of the Moon, so that the peasants could perfectly regulate their sowing times.

Today, some of these traditions have been examined in laboratories, and it has been discovered that in many plants and animals — varying from potatoes, carrots, and algae to salamanders — the metabolism and oxygen consumption are actually influenced by phases of the Moon.

The Greeks, who were skilled mariners, planned their voyages in relation to high tides during the new Moon and the full Moon.

Today, speleologists have discovered that tides also exist within the core of the earth; these tides are taken into account in selecting dates for expedition, and well-drillers do likewise in planning drilling operations.

The Earth is also affected by the eleven-year cycle of sunspots, which was carefully observed by the Chaldeans; this cycle can affect the quality of wine, and its traces are observable in tree-rings. Further-

Mesopotamian cylinder (circa 3200 B.C.) showing a religious scene associated with agriculture. The king, or priest, is followed by a person carrying a cluster of grain.

more, human beings also appear to be affected by its influence: physicians know that illnesses and cardiac crises (the Sun has traditionally been associated with the heart) can recur when sunspots appear. Through laboratory observation of principles which our ancestors had applied instinctively, the influence of the Sun and the Moon upon our planet (especially in terms of meteorological forecasting) is gradually being examined.

Scientific interest in these phenomena has increased, and it has been recognized that the life cycles of many organisms, where terrestrial factors, influenced by lunar and solar patterns, of course, were formerly considered predominant are indeed interconnected with celestial phenomena. It appears that solar and lunar time also regulates the lives of these organisms, and, twenty years ago, a new field began to emerge: namely the field of biological clocks.

In the United States, Professor Brown and his colleagues observed that when some species — such as oysters, *paolo viridis* worms, flatworms, or crabs — are transported to locations other than their natural habitats, these species live in accordance with solar or lunar time. Thus, it was concluded that our two primary sources of light transmit mysterious messages to these species. Research has also been conducted with chicken embryos, which appear to receive data from responses by the geophysical environment to the Sun, with the result that hatching times can be determined precisely.[1]

At this point, it is known that natural phenomena are, to some measure, governed by internal clocks attuned to the Sun and the Moon. At the turn of the century, Professor G. Piccardi in Florence observed that certain reactions occurring in test tubes were significantly affected by cosmic phenomena. More specifically, he observed that precipitation rates are influenced by sunspots, and he also discovered that blood coagulation is associated with phases of the Moon. Thus, he introduced a new field, namely organic chemistry, and biologists have expressed high esteem for his contributions (Today, the research of Professor Piccardi is being continued by Mme. Capel-Boute).

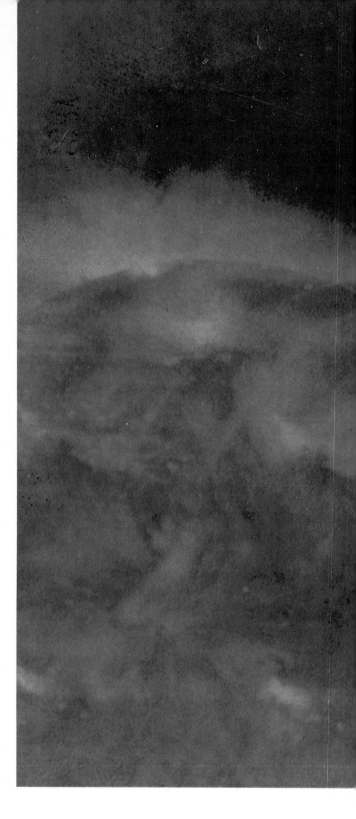

Like Professor M. Takata in Japan, a Soviet biologist, N. Schultz, has observed striking correlations between solar activity and the behavior of human blood.

Proceeding from observations by Dr. William Peterson in Chicago in 1940, whereby it had been recognized that the acidity or alkalinity of blood

1. Cf. Michel Gauquelin, *Le Dossier des influences cosmiques* (The Record with respect to Cosmic Influences), J'ai Lu, 1973.

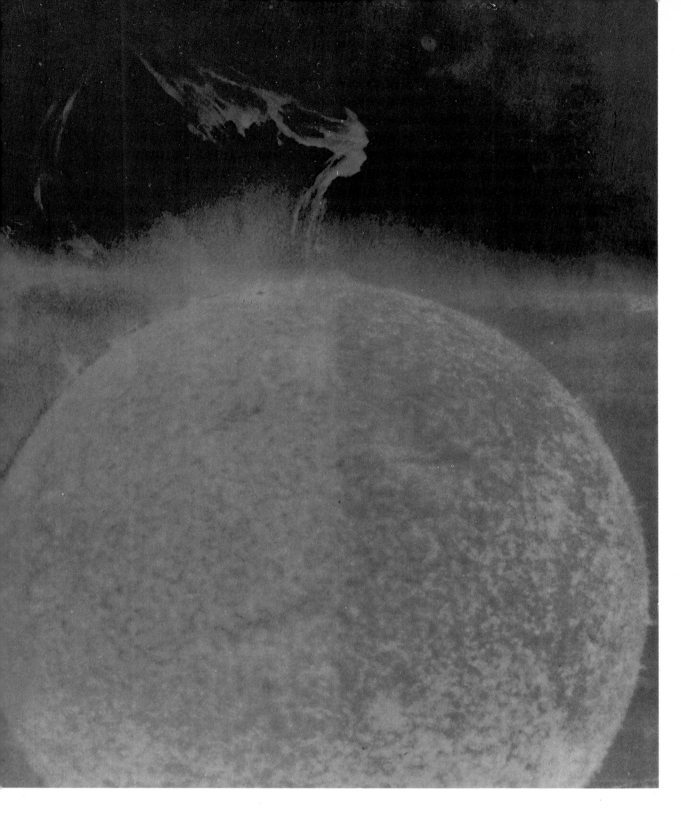

Solar eruption: physicians have observed that cardiac problems occur more frequently when sunspots exist.

can vary in relation to lunar magnetism, Dr. Jonas in Czechoslovakia and Dr. Miavec in Yugoslavia have developed a method of determining the sex of children at the time of conception, on the basis of lunar cycles. On the basis of their research, it has been possible to develop an individualized method of contraception, whereby the angular relationship between the Sun and the Moon at the time of a woman's birth can indicate fertile phases throughout her life.

Do celestial bodies other than the Sun and the Moon actually influence natural phenomena, as the Ancient World affirmed? Do living things possess clocks regulated by planetary rhythms? Today, there are observations which would appear to support such a viewpoint.

"Insane Man," by Gustave Courbet. Particularly sensitive persons may be more deeply affected by planetary movements (or by the onset of a new thousand-year period). Nevertheless, the desperation which they feel is often excessive in relation to actual conditions.

The planets

The research of Dr. Maag in Germany has demonstrated that relationships between celestial configurations and the weather do exist. Studies conducted between 1883 and 1941 showed that temperatures on Earth varied in proportion to the distance between Mercury and our planet. Furthermore, there are statistics appearing to indicate that earthquakes are associated with the position of Uranus within the heavens.

More recently, in Switzerland, Germany, and France (Professor Faussurier), biologists have observed that certain chemical solutions (alkaloids) are influenced by planetary correlations. By examining relationships among the Moon, Mercury, Venus, Mars, and Saturn, studied in pairs, they determined that the composition of certain solutions suddenly changed when specific relationships (square, opposition, conjunction) emerged among these planets.

Furthermore, Mme. Kolisko's research with solutions composed of metallic salts, such as auric chloride, silver nitrate, or stannous chloride, demonstrated that planetary interactions may influence capillary migration of metals through a sheet of paper. Indeed, the behavior of each metal suggested the same correlations which have traditionally been established between the planets and certain metals: relationships were identified between the Sun and gold, the Moon and silver, Mars and iron, and Jupiter and lead. These discoveries are exceptionally important. Prior to that point, it had not been possible to confirm simultaneity between planetary movements and chemical tests, but it appears that specific arrays of celestial forces can be correlated with certain fields of terrestrial forces.

Experimental corroboration for the law of interdependence between the celestial and the terrestrial is gradually being established, but sufficient evidence for formulating theories has not yet been acquired. Although research is still in an embryonic stage, a vast area of exploration has emerged: What is the nature of the "internal clocks" which are attuned to the rhythm of the master clock? Where are they located? Of course, there is also a more important question: do all living things — or all human beings — possess their own internal clocks from birth, clocks which only mark the proper planetary time?

Our knowledge is becoming more detailed, and an affirmative response to the latter question would confirm the theory of natal horoscopes. If most chemical solutions, as well as certain plants, crustaceans, and animals are influenced by biological clocks, and if human blood also reacts to planetary phenomena, is it possible to demonstrate that human behavior is also associated with celestial configurations?

Many authors have concentrated upon correlations between historical trends and solar phenomena. As early as 1918, Doctor A.L. Tchijevski, in a thesis submitted to the School of History and Philosophy at the University of Moscow, observed that, since the fifth century before Christ, political and military events during each century and within every nation on earth were characterized by peak levels coinciding with the sunspot cycles which occur every eleven years.

More recently, André Barbault, on the basis of research completed by Henri Gouchon, has discovered a cyclical pattern corresponding to momentous events, wherein the descending phase emerges every 498 years. The basic indicator is the magnitude of distances between the slowest planets, from Saturn to Pluto. Planetary proximity is greatest for the lowest level, and planets most dispersed within the cosmos when the indicator is at its highest level. With computers, it has been possible to reconstruct the past positions of such recently discovered planets as Uranus, Neptune, and Pluto, in order to examine their mutual interaction with other planets.[1] When planetary proximities are correlated with the history of civilization, according to periods of approximately five centuries, the latter periods, according to Barbault, are marked by significant historical changes.

On this basis, André Barbault believed that the years 1982-1984, when the previously cited indicator is due to recur, shall likewise represent a significant transformation.

In this type of research, however, it is difficult to determine the nature of changes: are these economic, political, or "psychological" changes, or changes affecting the crust of the Earth? ... Few recurrent characteristics can be identified for prior phases. This observation applies to development of highly significant philosophical trends, from the sixth century before Christ, with Zarathustra (Persia), the second book of Isaiah, Pythagoras (Greece), Buddha (India), and Confucius (China), or to barbarian invasions (the Huns led by Attila, the Vandals, and the Goths) during the first century after Christ, which initiated the collapse of the Roman Empire in the West, and likewise to other invasions during the ninth century (Normans, Moslems, Magyars, and Vikings), or, finally, to the fifteenth century, when the indicator emerged once again, before 1482-1484, and was associated with the Renaissance expeditions in search of the New World.

Under these circumstances, it is difficult to "offer predictions." At the present time, it is sufficient to observe that there is a high probability of correlations between celestial phenomena and transformations of civilization. It is possible to "anticipate" changes, but it is extremely risky to define these changes on a global scale, inasmuch as numerous factors of a collective nature (and probably a capability of classifying them by importance), as well as an in-depth analysis of the origins and development of specific civilizations, would be involved. The situation can be compared with natal horoscopes, where it would not be possible to interpret planetary factors precisely without also considering heredity and the environment where a person's formative years are spent.

André Cormier[2] has recently employed a binary system for examining planetary positions according to pairs of planets, from 4,000 B.C. up to the present era. Cormier selected the most significant cyclical phases and adopted the language of the "Yi king," which is a binary language, for interpreting phases. He arrived at astounding correlations, thereby introducing a vast field for research.

In terms of individuals, Michel Gauquelin,[3] a statistician who is an explicit adversary of astrology, studied the ascents and zeniths of different planets in relation to the birth dates of famous persons, in order to determine whether these planetary cor-

The serenity of the wise counterbalances the torments of the insane. This worshipper of Mazda, during the 6th century, which was one of the most tumultuous historical periods, is seeking another path, the path of wisdom. Human free will must be taken into account in all predictions.

1. In *Astrologie mondiale* (Universal Astrology, Fayard, 1979), André Barbault provides an explanation of this research and of the results which have been obtained.

2. André Cormier, *Après le temps des prophètes* (After the Era of the Prophets), Paris, Arcturus, 1980.

3. This study is discussed in Michel Gauquelin's *Le Dossier des influences cosmiques, op. cit.*

relations were in harmony with astrological theories. Gauquelin selected men who had pursued various occupations (actors, athletes, authors), and he later expanded his survey to France, Italy, West Germany, Belgium, and the Netherlands. Gauquelin's results were evaluated by the "Para Committee" (Belgian Committee for Scientific Investigation of Apparently Paranormal Phenomena), which confirmed their validity.

Gauquelin's survey indicated that:

— 5,438 important European military leaders were born during the ascent or zenith of Mars (probability of 1/1,000,000);

— 3,305 members of Academies of Science and Medicine were born during the ascent or zenith of Saturn (probability of 1/100,000);

— 993 statesmen and political leaders were born during the ascent or zenith of Jupiter (probability of 1/5,000);

— 1,485 sports champions were born during the ascent or zenith of Mars (probability of 1/5,000,000); and the over-all result for the 25,000 persons who were studied was five times greater than the expected deviation.

Gauquelin's conclusions do not differ radically from the hypotheses advanced by Ptolemy, who believed that individuals' occupations depended significantly upon the ascents and zeniths of planets. In Gauquelin's opinion, the planets do not dictate selection of occupations, but they are the source of personality traits which may be required for specific occupations. For example, Saturn favors methodical thought, and it can orient an individual toward a scientific career, even though many persons born during the ascent or zenith of Saturn who are "deep thinkers" have not pursued careers in Science. Nevertheless, a higher proportion of Saturn natives has pursued scientific activities.

Keppler affirmed that "similar stars for close relatives are more frequent than for persons who are not related." Michel Gauquelin sought to determine whether astral heredity truly exists, and he compared 25,000 dates and times of birth for parents and children (births between 1850 and 1945). This new survey demonstrated that when a parent is born during the ascent or zenith of a given planet, his or her children "preferentially" enter the world during the ascent or zenith of the same planet.

Finally, another statistical survey demonstrated that the number of "hereditary similarities between children and parents is two and one-half times greater when children are born on magnetically turbulent days than when they are born on calm days." This observation suggests a possible physical substratum for astrological phenomena: the Sun is the power-plant of our solar system, and the planets serve as "transformers" for its energy. According to Michel Gauquelin's hypothesis, a fully developed fetus is a resonator for solar energy. Nevertheless, a significant decline in correlations was observed for Caesarean births or births where medications had been administered: astral heredity ceased to be observable. Gauquelin concluded that there may be a fetal selection process permitting identification of influences corresponding to astral inclinations, although, in births where medical intervention takes place, the designated time for birth can no longer be identified. This experiment is of great importance: it would confirm the fact that the planets are signs, instead of causes, namely that they are associated with biological reactions. It is possible that clocks which are interrelated with our innermost inclinations may produce a signal for birth, when they are synchronized with celestial clocks. Indeed, Plotinus wrote of "sympathetic interaction" among different parts of the universe, where, by seeing "how the parts of the whole correspond to one another, we can consider the existence of one part as a *sign* of the existence of another, even in the absence of the slightest mechanical or physical influence of one of these parts upon another."[1]

Michel Gauquelin's meticulous research constitutes a step toward confirming astrological phenomena. It demonstrates the influence of the planets upon human beings and provides statistical verification. Nevertheless, research governed by the law of causality (whereby a cause exists for every phenomenon) can only provide partial confirmation for astrological principles. Indeed, if one only considers the law of causality, most astrological phenomena are accompanied by exceptions to this law because they embody the principle of *synchronicity* enunciated by Jung.

Synchronicity plays the role of a missing link for understanding the phenomena which we observe and their heterogeneous causes. Synchronicity encompasses events which occur simultaneously and are characterized by similar phases, even though the causes may not be the same. Hence, statistical verification is not yet possible. In contrast, *causality* explains interrelations among events arising from identical causes which are governed by statistical principles. Whereas synchronicity pertains to coincidences, it is concerned with sequences of events; different concepts of time are involved, and synchronicity is a form of causality within a non-linear time frame.

Nevertheless, causality and synchronicity are not mutually exclusive. Each contributes coherence to

"Children of the Planets," from a manuscript (circa 1480) identifying occupations associated with the Sun.

existence. Hence, examination of the ascent or the zenith of a single planet in terms of influence upon natal horoscopes would appear inadequate for examining the vast range of influences upon them, or the ways in which interactions among influences may coincide. Even if an extremely important planetary factor is selected, other simultaneous factors may shape its effects, neutralizing or intensifying them within the context of simultaneity.

In order to pursue fuller verification of astrological principles, it is necessary, it seems, to broaden the field of observation by studying coinciding planetary factors as a whole, while maintaining a non-linear time frame.

In addition, astrological methods have been employed for studying the horoscopes of patients in psychiatric institutions, and diagnoses furnished by astrologers have often been corroborated by the attending physicians (of course, the information initially given to the astrologer only consisted of the patient's sex, birthplace, and time of birth). The celestial charts prepared for patients clearly indicated pathological potentialities, as well as the onset of mental illness and its phases. Perhaps it shall be necessary to maintain a similar outlook in pursu-

1. Cited by A. Barbault in *Connaissance de l'astrologie* (Seuil, 1975).

115

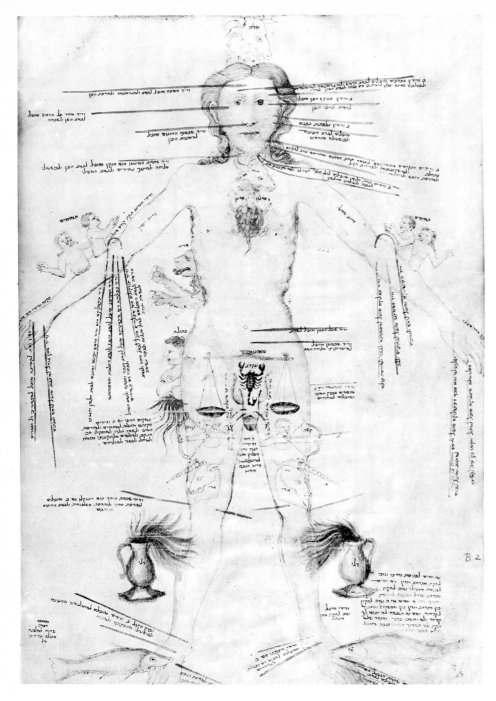

How can we understand the bonds between the macrocosm and the microcosm, where "similar forces act upon similar things?" This Hebrew manuscript identifies affinities between the Zodiac and the human body.

horoscopes for births facilitated by medications (and this has frequently been true since the 1950s) furnish correlations?

It is probable that relationships between the planets and human genetics, or similarities between planetary patterns and adaptations in biological structure, constitute a vast area for future research. The studies cited heretofore do provide a basis for affirming that there is a form of resonance between Nature and the Cosmos. Although it is not yet possible to furnish precise definitions for modes of interaction among correlations, experimental results have brought to light the astrological foundations of bonds between the terrestrial and the celestial, or between the microcosm and the macrocosm.

These results, however, cannot yet constitute proof of the validity of general interpretations of astrological principles. To proclaim theories would constitute misuse of available data. It has been shown that there are still many correlations which must be established by scientific means before it can ultimately be affirmed that "the universe is astrological." It is necessary to verify the fundamental principles of the traditional science which constituted a common source for all other sciences until the Middle Ages and to proceed empirically toward the consequences offered by astrology.

In our era, what fundamental explanations of the oneness of the universe are provided by biology, physics, and astronomy?

ing research concerning correlations between Man and the cosmos.

Research which has been undertaken thus far has not yet furnished indications that the planets "imprint" our inclinations at the time of birth, or that they modify genetic patterns in newborn children. The problem is to determine the point at which the heavens become a reflection of a person's genetic composition. If the indications (primarily the positions of the Moon and the ascendant) which would correspond to a person whose birth occurred naturally are slightly modified by medically induced birth, why do personality studies based upon

An explanation?

Biology

Differences between the inanimate world and the world of living things exist not only in terms of composition but complexity. Systems are interconnected with one another by increasingly intricate combinations of components. François Jacob[1] has written: "There is an entire series of links, levels, and discontinuities from particles to human beings, although there is no change in the composition of matter nor in the reactions which occur. The 'essence' does not change... Any component which biology investigates represents a group of systems and is, by itself, a component within more advanced systems. In other words, it is necessary to examine each structural level in relation to other juxtaposed levels." Is it not true that this view of modern biology evokes the old adage of astrology and traditional thought: "The whole is present within the part?" Perhaps it is possible to extend the conceptual analogy by comparing levels of complexity in living things with various categories of symbols or different modes of expression.

Each part, or component, of the universe is powered by the same type of energy propagated from one system to another, according to modes of transmission which are consistent with the inner order of each component, so that different frequency cycles arise. Within the chain extending from the macroscopic level — lunar and solar cycles which produce light, tides, and the alternation between day and night — to the microscopic or cellular level, the human body is governed by cycles which regulate respiration, perception and reproduction. Neurons within the brain which transmit information throughout the body function with a frequency of 1,000 periods per second. Beta rhythms originating in the frontal lobe, where the highest decision-making and personality functions are located, operate according to a 1,822 periods-per-second cycle. Proceeding from the brain to other organs, we know that the lungs dilate and contract approximately once every three seconds, that the heart beats seventy-six times per minute, that the stomach contracts approximately three times per minute, that the ovaries release an egg every twenty-eight days, and that the life span of red corpuscles is 128 days...

At every level — cosmic, biological, and molecular — the universe is governed by a complex of cycles whose durations vary from nanoseconds to millions of years.

It is difficult, however, to determine how energy is propagated from one transmitting system to another. How can we comprehend the "sympathetic effects" described by the Ancient World, or Paracelsus' principle of "similar entities acting upon similar entities?"

The discoveries of Professor Guillé and his colleagues have begun to lift the veil: it is possible for a DNA molecule to contain the seven metals traditionally associated with the seven visible planets.[2] Indeed, it has been demonstrated that these metals are capable of receiving messages from the environment and transmitting them to genetic functions... This phenomenon occurs because of the presence of a second genetic code functioning as

---

1. François Jacob, *La logique du vivant* (The Logic of Living Things) (Gallimard).

2. The following associations between metals and celestial bodies have been established: gold — the Sun; silver — the Moon; lead — Saturn; mercury — Mercury; iron — Mars; copper — Venus; tin — Jupiter.

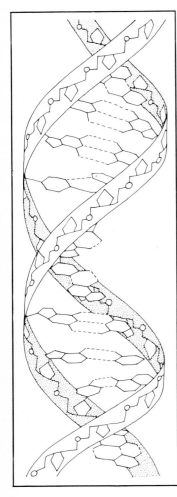

A DNA molecule, which transmits hereditary determinants, is capable of containing the seven metals associated with the seven visible planets. Its spiral shape suggests many images used to express the soul's journey through the planetary spheres in Antiquity, or during the Middle Ages and the Renaissance.

a receptor for variations in the environment and, in particular, for cosmic (gravitational, electro-magnetic...) influences emanating from the planets. These influences would appear to vary in relation to the different aspects of the planets. Hence, it is possible to consider whether the second code transmits this type of data to the conventional genetic code (the sequence of ATGC nucleotid components), which has been understood for many years, thereby producing changes in molecular configurations.

Messages, which may be "disseminated" by means of the three major categories of metals to which the seven traditional metals belong,[1] produce changes in the bonding between these metals and DNA molecules. This phenomenon could produce characteristic molecular patterns, giving rise to quantifiable variations in energy which may transform genetic information. Thus, research continues. It has not yet been possible, for example, to determine whether the movements of Venus, traditionally associated with copper, are accompanied at the same time by (quantitatively and/or qualitatively) observable changes in the copper content of DNA molecules. It is clear, however, that the system of forces acting upon Venus is analogous to the forces associated with copper atoms: the various relationships among elementary forces are of the same nature. It is no longer possible to discount biological evidence of affinities between the macrocosm and the microcosm. Is it possible that the inner cosmos, a replica of the external cosmos, — or this biological clock which echoes the seconds, minutes, and hours of a cosmic master clock — is, quite simply, situated within every cell?

Physics

Heisenberg[2] has expressed the opinion that "the principal difference between the ideas of the Ancients and modern theories is that the former were of an intuitive nature, whereas the latter originate from an empirical attitude: they have been tested and experimentally confirmed — in other words, demonstrated — and are therefore given a far more serious meaning." The theories of modern physics are linked to the fundamental concepts of the Ancient World: the universe was regarded as an organic whole, where all parts were interrelated and interdependent, with the infinitely small reflecting the image of the infinitely large. Today, the complete mutability of matter has been experimentally confirmed. "Consequently, this represents the ultimate demonstration of the unity of matter. All elementary particles are composed of the same substance, which we can call universal energy or matter. These particles are merely different forms in which matter may exist," Heisenberg has affirmed.

Moreover, Bernard d'Espagnat has demonstrated the principle of "non-separability of matter" in his book,[3] by explaining that the concept of independent reality is a concept developed by Man for understanding the world. Thus, a "vacuum" could

1. The three major categories consist of: Category 1, metals which close the molecule; Category 2, metals which may either open or close the molecule; and Category 3, metals which only open the molecule. The seven metals which have been cited belong to the latter two categories.
2. Heisenberg, *Physique et Metaphysique* (Physics and Metaphysics).
3. Bernard d'Espagnat, *A la recherche du réel* (In Search of Reality), Gauthier-Villars, 1979.

not exist within the universe, and particles within our universe must "be in contact" with one another. "The elementary particles comprising all forms of matter should not be considered as isolated from the rest of the cosmos, but as objects which are co-extensive with the entire universe, especially in terms of their so-called 'fields' (gravitational, electromagnetic, or nuclear fields). Naturally, Man, like all other matter, is also 'composed' of particles which are co-extensive with the entire universe. Therefore, Man is, to some extent, joined to the entire surrounding cosmos. He is in constant contact with that which can be called the 'cosmic' environment, a cosmic environment which definitively represents the essential aspects of existence and must also "shape" and influence the individual's conscious self in some form. The influence of this environment, however, is less apparent, for it is situated within the more or less conscious levels of human thought."[1]

Physicists have not yet developed a fundamental law for the movement of matter whereby it would be possible to determine the behavior and properties of all particles by mathematical means. There has been a movement away from causalist theories, with new emphasis upon the law of synchronicity (the law of simultaneity of events) cited by Jung and incorporated within astrology: the celestial resembles the terrestrial — every phenomenon within the heavens triggers an earthly phenomenon.

Thus, it is possible that the intuitive methods of astrology may one day be introduced into the experimental sciences.

---

1. Jean Charron, "L'homme et le cosmos," (Man and the Cosmos), *Planète*, No. 6.

Astronomy

During the seventeenth century, Copernicus' discoveries led to the separation of astronomy from astrology: the planets and the Earth rotate around the Sun. Hence, the Earth is not the center of the galaxy, and the gravitational field is defined in relation to the Sun.

For three centuries, astronomers concluded that other planets did not influence the Earth in any way, and the ancient concept of a universe whose components exchanged "signs" was abandoned: there was only "intersidereal space" between celestial bodies.

In 1955, however, Burke and Franklin detected a "stray" emission originating from Jupiter: indeed, Jupiter transmits long and short waves. Subsequently, using reception equipment which was increasingly more sophisticated, astronomers (or radioastronomers) were able to identify radio waves emitted by all of the planets, from Mercury to Saturn, and these waves became known as "superthermals."

Experimentation continued, and it was determined that, on Earth, the quality of reception is affected by two principal factors:

Every eleven years, the activity of the Sun becomes more intense, producing the phenomenon known as sunspots. This effervescence produces a magnetic screen which interferes with emissions from Jupiter. Between cycles, when the Sun returns to a "normal" level of activity, reception improves.

In addition, the position of Jupiter and its satellites (primarily Io, which is the largest, but also Ganymede and Europa) in relation to the Earth, or the angle which they form when observed from the Earth, modulate these emissions in different

ways.[1] Thus, astronomers have concluded that the solar system is an organic whole, wherein matter and energy are constantly being exchanged among the Sun, the planets, and the satellites. They have confirmed physicists' beliefs concerning the non-existence of intersidereal space, and have likewise confirmed traditional concepts of the interdependence of parts within the oneness of the universe. While astrologists only consider the planets, it appears that it would also be necessary to take satellites into account. In addition, these conclusions are reminiscent of the astrological theory of planetary aspects, whereby the influence of planets varies in relation to their respective positions. It appears that heliocentrism is not incompatible with geocentrism. If the Sun is indeed the center of the solar system, earthly reception of propagated energy is affected by every part of the universe.

The logic of the universe no longer corresponds to the beliefs which had prevailed for the past three centuries. Biology concentrates upon living tissue, while physics responds in terms of co-extensivity, and astronomy introduces corpuscular waves. The intuitive thrust of astrology is being echoed by scientific language. Now, it is possible that a niche exists for astrology within an interdisciplinary context, as an aid to research, but also in order for conclusions to be refined and clarified.

Perhaps it is now possible to understand the attitude of primitive Man, who projected his own image onto the universe in order to explore it and himself. If our cells reflect the image of the universe and constitute systems within other systems,

1. Cf. Michel Gauquelin, *Le Dossier des influences cosmiques, op. cit.*

it appears even more obvious that Man may have been able to discover his own image within the universe.

Moreover, our corpuscles contain all of the data collected by the universe. Are they not a concrete representation of something which could be termed the memory of the collective unconscious?

Lastly, it is appropriate to ponder whether this common source for all of the sciences — the essence of knowledge — could ultimately be the order which governs each system (*cosmos* also means "order"). At whatever level we may observe the

cosmos — planets, parts of the body, cells, molecules, atoms — there is a fundamental order which may correspond to the principle of harmony. This order has not yet been rationally explained in a definitive form, but advances in scientific research permit us to anticipate that it may be understood in the future, and that the various levels of symbols shall be confirmed by indisputable experimental results. For example, it is possible, by analogy, to compare the four DNA nucleotids with the traditional four elements, and to compare the three forms of bonding of metals with the ternary prin-

As mankind has gained greater knowledge of the infinitely large (above: red spot on Jupiter) and the infinitely small (left page: photograph taken with an electron microscope), the calm certainties of logical methods have been questioned.

121

ciple (the three types of movement). Moreover, it has been recognized that, among these categories of metals, seven correspond to those which were formerly attributed to the seven visible planets. Other phenomena, such as ultra-violet radiation, have been associated with the three more recently discovered planets, Uranus, Neptune, and Pluto.

If the levels of complexity of living matter are compared with various levels of symbolism, it is significant to observe that more than one point of contact exists. Employing the three principles and the four elements, the Egyptian tradition (inspired by the Chaldeans) had demonstrated that it was possible to derive the seven visible planets, as well as the seven colors, the seven musical notes, seven metals, and seven scents. Today, the number seven reappears in the seven types of observable crystallization: seven was once a sacred number.

Knowledge embodies multiple modes of perception, but it increasingly appears that rational and intuitive thought are joining hands to explore the "order" within which we exist. And in this context, the astrological approach cannot be excluded. Indeed, it has been observed that metals play a bonding role in relation to planets, as well as chemical solutions or molecules. On the one hand, the discoveries of Professors Piccardi and Faussurier, of Mesdames Kolisko and Capel Boute (as well as other authors) have demonstrated the influence of the planets upon various metal salts and colloids. On the other hand, recent research in molecular biology by Professor Guillé demonstrates the presence of metals, capable of becoming attached to specific DNA chains that play an important role in activating and regulating genetic information. Metals may represent the heretofore unavailable *key to understanding,* in terms of explaining the phenomenon of correlations between the macrocosm and the microcosm, or in terms of grasping the law of synchronicity as a means of expressing coincidental events among different types of phenomena. Metals may provide a physical and chemical basis (through bonding between metals and organic molecules) for the possible modes of influence of planets upon living things.

With this recent data, it now seems possible to envision the development of a true astro-biology, which would no longer be condemned as an irrational pseudo-science, as it is at the present time.

La symbolique zodiacale, expression de notre langage affectif, a marqué l'art de nombreuses époques et de nombreuses civilisations. Ces pages des « Grandes Heures de Rohan », célèbre manuscrit du XVe siècle qui rythmait tous les moments de la vie quotidienne, témoignent de la présence du Zodiaque dans l'existence de chaque être humain.

The Symbols of the Zodiac:

The term "signs" is probably misused insofar as the twelve sections of the Zodiac are concerned: it would be more consistent with their role to speak of *symbols*. The concept of a "sign" denotes something which is known and defined, whereas a "symbol" suggests. Although a symbol does, indeed, originate with the known, it offers, by analogy and correlation, a panorama of previously unknown interpretations, which may have to be developed by guesswork, and are not always fully accessible. A street sign showing a cross means that a crossroads is nearby, and nothing more, but, for a practicing Christian, a cross embodies a series of meanings which only the symbol of the cross can encompass.

A sign "is" — nothing more, and nothing less —, whereas a symbol would be, could be, or becomes. There is a comparable distinction between musical signs and musical notes. One is a form of written expression, whereas the other acquires all of the tones of the instrument for which it is intended. It is necessary to approach zodiacal symbols from the same perspective. In my opinion, for example, being "an Aries" or "a Gemini" is not defined by one precise feature or another; instead, it embodies a group of converging tendencies which can only be expressed by the symbols for Aries or for Gemini (which could be called "signs" if we knew precisely what they mean).

Signs of the Zodiac:
symbols which have been transmitted
from the earliest times through tradition and manuscripts
(16th century manuscript).

An eternal language

Thus, the two-column (myth and symbol/character and behavior) format which has been adopted does not indicate equivalency between the two levels in the strictest sense. I have only attempted to link symbolic expression to psychological expression,[1] as they are manifested within us. I have offered these concepts to the reader for contemplation, and it is unlikely that the reader's own reflections would always lead to the same correlations, even though it may become possible for the reader to develop ties with something which was previously outside his sphere of knowledge. In this instance, my intentions would be fulfilled: to proceed from the Aries or Gemini sign toward rediscovery of their full symbolic richness, as the Ancient World had presented it, and to recognize to what extent these symbols can still reverberate within us.

Fundamental concepts were presented in the beginning in order to explain succinctly the associations underlying zodiacal attributes. In this instance, intuition was granted primacy over logic. Now it is possible to return to the sources, to the initial symbols, with the contributions of mythology and philosophy (ontology) being taken into account. When we describe a spontaneously expressed symbolic image, we know that we are only providing an initial approximation, because the image itself springs from extremely distant origins which are often intermingled with ancient religious concepts. For example, is it not true that Aries was an embodiment of Amon Ra (the Egyptian solar deity), as well as the *Agnus Dei* (or Easter among the Christians), or *Agni* (a fire deity) in the Upanishads (Hindu sacred texts)? Was not the Bull

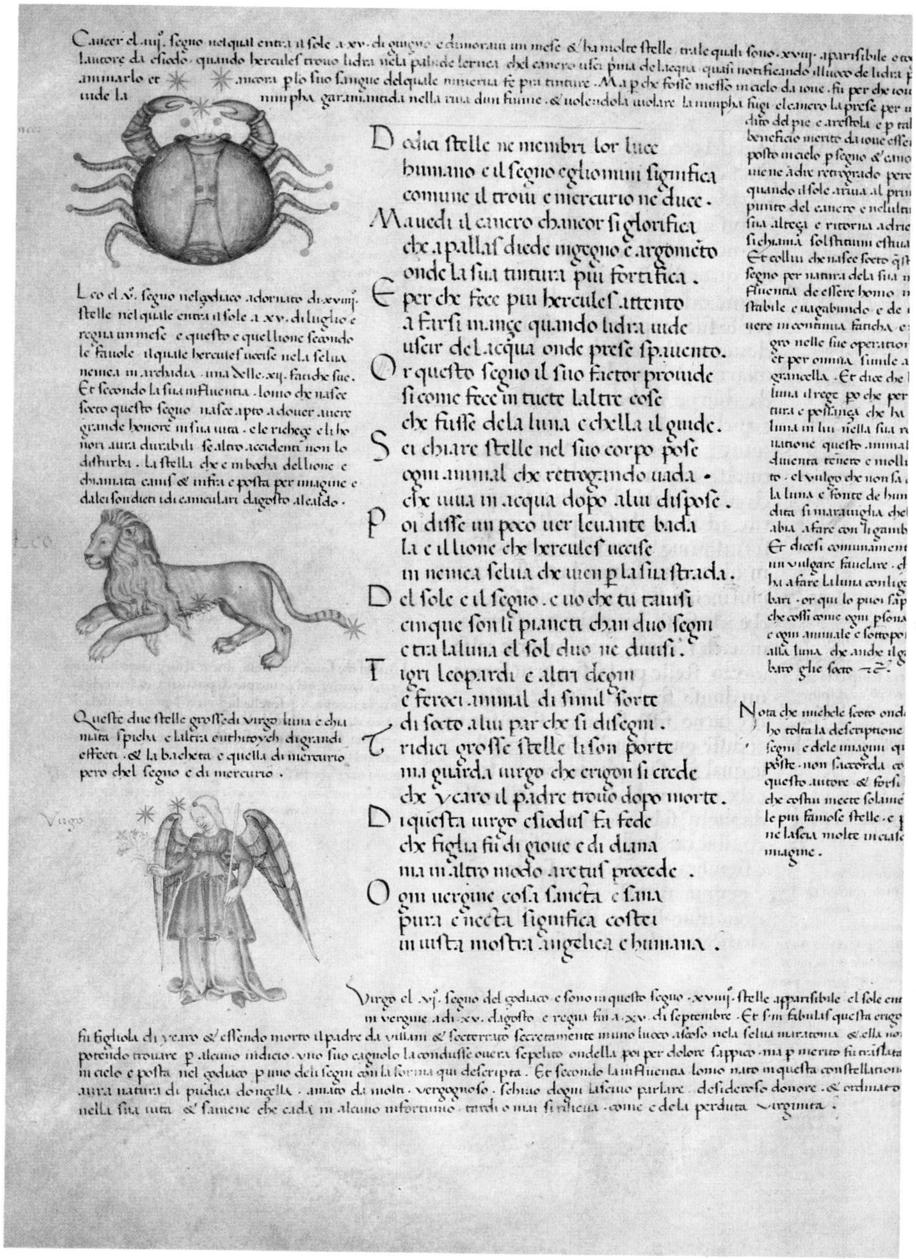

---

1. Many parallels have been redefined and suggested by André Barbault's excellent compilation, *Le Zodiaque* (The Zodiac), published by Editions Seuil.

127

the sacred beast of Mithra, the great Persian deity who ruled the elements and judged the dead? There was also a Gemini cult, and, in the history of religions, famous twins often appear (Jacob and Esau, the apostles John and James, etc.). Zodiacal symbols emerge in many rituals within every culture: they are part of our development, and they are engraved within the subconscious. Therefore, we are always receptive to these symbols, without being able to provide logical or rational explanations.

Thus, selection of symbolic forms did not occur by chance: the appearance and the role are meaningful. The pesent-day value of these symbols and the psychological associations which we establish with them represent a reduction in relation to former meanings.

There is also a seasonal origin: the attributes depend upon natural phenomena present at the time of birth, which we absorb.[1] Thus, zodiacal symbols link us to extremely specific terrestrial phenomena. It should not be forgotten, however, that the presence of the Sun within a sign of the Zodiac does not express the entire personality: it provides indications with respect to a person's ideals, or his manner of describing the world as he perceives it. This is even more obvious among artists who give

1. It is highly probable that it would be necessary to consider inversion of signs for the Southern Hemisphere.

us evidence of the manner in which they experience the world. The presence of the Sun within a Zodiacal sign often furnishes a synthesis of the goals which a person strives to attain, but the entire horoscope indicates the way in which he will pursue them. Although these observations concerning zodiacal symbols may be familiar to many persons, they are, nevertheless, insufficient for defining all of an individual's attributes.

In order to comprehend their identities, as well as their roles, I have mentioned the mythological deities governing each sign. Beyond the history of myths, there are ancestral laws, laws of nature which the Ancient World was only able to share with us through fables. The purpose of allusions to mythology in relation to psychological motivations, or my attempts to translate mythology into modern modes of expression, has been to restore contact between interested readers and a historical vision which is inaccessible because of its ancient origins, even though they relive it in their daily actions, their hopes, their joys, and their sadness.

In the same spirit, I have contemplated myths or legends — usually selected from sources other than Greek mythology — which may express the inner universe of zodiacal signs in another form. For Taurus, for example, I have considered Tristan and Iseult: this legend offers a close resemblance to the tendencies symbolically represented by Taurus. Thus, I leave this proposition for readers to ponder. Perhaps a new series of correlations can be uncovered. Of course, any suggestions along these lines cannot, in any sense, replace the symbolism of the Zodiac; they can only provide "poetic" counterparts.

The Zodiac is a universal symbolic language, and probably the oldest, for it constitutes a synthesis of all other symbols.

THE SOURCES

The Symbolic Image

♈ The ram is an animal with horns, symbolizing strength and fecundity.	♈ An Aries is a virile, strong and creative person.
♈ A ram is ready to leap.	♈ An Aries is impulsive and forceful.
♈ He runs forward with his head lowered, and nothing can stop him.	♈ He pursues his goals directly, with courage and audacity.
♈ The ram leads the herd.	♈ An Aries seeks to introduce innovative ideas. He is a precursor and a guide, with leadership instincts.

Mars: The Beginning of Spring

♈ The Spring equinox arrives: days and nights are of the same length.	♈ An Aries is divided between conscious daytime qualities and subconscious nocturnal ones; he is unsure of his own identity.
♈ Nevertheless, the days quickly become longer; there is more and more sunlight.	♈ His traits reflect subconscious drives: he is an active and impulsive person who does not always take time for contemplation.
♈ Winter comes to an end. Warmth triumphs over coldness, and the temperature of the Earth rises.	♈ Passion guides the actions of an Aries.
♈ The Sun becomes bright, and plants begin to sprout.	♈ An Aries is in a hurry to experience life. He is incapable of pretense, and he may tend to rush ahead unthinkingly.
♈ Nature provides nourishment; sap flows toward the buds.	♈ An Aries is full of generosity, and his vigor is abundant.
♈ When Spring begins, sprouts break through the ground, coming up practically everywhere.	♈ He may also be attracted by too many projects and use his time unwisely.
♈ Animals are mating.	♈ An Aries has survival instincts, along with an enormous capability for self-renewal.

Cardinal Spring

♈ Winter has ended. A new season is starting, and Spring is on the way.	♈ An Aries is always attracted by ventures which have just begun. He has competitive instincts and a strong need to be active.
Aries is a cardinal sign.	

Fire at its Source

Fire is the element represented by Aries: an element possessing vitality and intense energy. It is dynamic and produces transformations. Aries is associated with fire on account of its position within the zodiacal cycle. Among the triplicity of fire signs, Aries is the "original fire," the primordial fire, or the spark of life. It is followed by the steady fire of Leo (a controlled fire: the flame of the ego) and by the mutable fire of Sagittarius (a bright ember: the fire of the intellect).

With the cardinal fire of Aries (which is constantly being rekindled), feelings surge forth by leaps and bounds. An Aries is an intensely emotional person who immediately acts upon his feelings. His traits make him active and passionate, as well as strongly extroverted.

♈ Fire crackles, spurts, and erupts.	♈ An Aries is always highly motivated, and is constantly active.
♈ Flames spread in all directions.	♈ Introducing new ideas, an Aries seeks to inspire others and to lead them into action.
♈ Fire incessantly renews its strength.	♈ His eyes dart quickly; he has a stern voice; and his words flow rapidly.

Aries

MARCH 21 - APRIL 20

"A man's true worth can be measured by considering the degree and the manner in which he has succeeded in liberating himself from his own ego."

Einstein, *How I See the World*

Mars

Because he is ruled by Mars, the god of war and battles, an Aries struggles to maintain control over his own life.

♈ In mythology, an entire group of deities was associated with Mars: Audacity, Fearsomeness, Honor, Martial Bravery, and also Victory, Peace, and Serenity.

♈ An Aries feels impelled by contradictory forces. He is bold, and sometimes takes pleasure in intimidating others. He also has a sense of honor. Is his desire to reconcile victory, peace, and serenity a quest for the impossible?

♈ Mars' symbols are the lance, an instrument of warfare and death conveying authority, and the torch, a symbol of fire as a source of purification and enlightenment.

♈ An Aries goes into battle confidently, without fearing defeat. He is a person who is willing to face sacrifices for the truth.

♈ Mars also loved Venus passionately.

♈ An Aries has strong sexual instincts.

♈ His boldness and adventures provided amusement for the Gods. Once Venus' husband, Vulcan, trapped her in a net with Mars, and summoned the gods to witness their adultery. The gods laughed at Mars' predicament.

♈ It is difficult to comprehend the risks which he takes. He proceeds without foresight and is sometimes trapped by insurmountable difficulties. It is difficult to classify an Aries.

♈ Even this extremely humiliating experience (and there were others, too) failed to deter Mars. The gods decided that Mars "had no spirit or soul."

♈ Nothing stands in his way, and he is not afraid of humiliation. Impelled by his adventurous spirit, an Aries does not stop to explain his motives to others; he rushes onward.

♈ Mars brutally sought vengeance against one of Venus' lovers (Adonis), and the gods punished him by expelling him from Olympus.

♈ An Aries appears to be an outcast. Unable to find acceptance for his beliefs, he hunts for the meaning of life.

♈ Mars dealt harshly with his possessions and with his own holy places (the city of Thebes, which he devastated with wars), as well as with his beloved (Venus). He only seemed aware of his own turbulence.

♈ An Aries is capable of testing himself or destroying himself in pursuit of the source of his strengths. At the innermost level, an Aries is already convinced that the fire which rules him is inexhaustible and that it encompasses the meaning of life.

♈ When Mars was captured by the Alaudian giants and imprisoned in a bronze cage for thirteen months, Hermes, or Mercury (intelligence), helped him escape.

♈ Intrepidness often leads an Aries into situations which seem insurmountable, but, with faith in his intuitive intelligence, he is confident of finding solutions. An Aries is often surrounded by impossible situations.

♈ The goddess who dealt Mars his worst defeats was Athena, symbolizing wisdom. She guided the arm of Diomedes when he wounded Mars, who bellowed "like a thousand men" (Homer).

♈ An Aries may rashly ignore wise advice: the many dangers which he confronts are a form of trial by fire, allowing him to pursue self-awareness by taking risks. Does the arm raised against him represent his own arm, symbolizing the spirit of sacrifice which governs Aries? He is prepared to face sacrifices in order to provide an example for others.

The Head

♈ The head is the part of the body associated with Aries. An Aries often walks with his head held high and with an intent expression.

♈ An Aries prizes zealousness and strength. The urge to excel dominates him.

These sources provide the zodiacal formula for Aries: a vernal and cardinal sign, associated with fire and Mars. Aries is represented by the head.

Even though it is known that the position of the Sun in a person's horoscope does not offer a complete psychological portrait, but does suggest symbols associated with his goals and his way of pursuing them, attainment of these goals requires the aid of other planets or psychic forces.

The zodiacal formula of the Sun coinciding with Aries allows us to understand one of the principal behavioral attributes: exteriorization of the personality, which, in association with other elements of the horoscope, is manifested in a more or less recognizable form. The zodiacal formula, corroborated by examples, can be expressed as follows:

The Temperament of a Pioneer or a Leader
In search of adventures, an Aries "locks horns" with life. Obstacles do not deter him, and he zealously rushes into conflicts. Most of Napoleon's generals were born under this sign, as were Bismarck, Thiers, and Gambetta.

An Aries stubbornly and sometimes vehemently confronts his adversaries. We can think of Gambetta's campaign against clericalism, or Khrushchev's fist upon the podium at important international summits. An Aries sees himself as a trailblazer, and he seeks to lead others. People are "with him or against him," and he does not accept compromises: it is possible to consider Lenin or Napoleon III during their *coups d'etat*.

An Intuitive and Creative Spirit
An Aries possesses an audacious spirit which fosters innovation and renewal; he seeks to uplift the minds of others. For example, the celestial chart for Einstein, whose sign was Pisces, shows many planets (Mercury, Saturn, Venus) occupying the house of Aries. Einstein expressed many of Aries' characteristics by rejecting indeterminism and conventionally accepted laws, in order to discover relativity.

An Aries vigorously defends his beliefs: for example, there is Maurras, combatting the Third Republic and the entire philosophical outlook of the eighteenth century with a vehement logic which led to many conflicts. An Aries possesses creative drives which are also destructive. Thus, he may be the forerunner of new genres: for example, there is the originality of Chaplin's talents in satirizing society.

The way in which an Aries thinks can be compared to the sharp edge of a knife.

A Heart Struck by a Thunderbolt
An Aries is a passionate soul who falls in love spontaneously, and zealously pursues the target of his affections. Casanova does not fully express an Aries' type of love, but he does illustrate its passionate qualities. An Aries seeks love which can constantly renew his passions. For Saint Theresa of Avila, God represented this absolute form of love.

The Aries *ideogram* embodies the archetype: it is a gamma sign, representing the intersection of the ecliptic and the equator, which is the destination for the ascent of the Sun during the Spring. The Aries hieroglyph is also a stylized representation of the earliest sprouts as they break through the ground. Moreover, it can be compared with the "V" for victory.

Mars with his attributes. Mars rules Aries.

131

MODES OF EXPRESSION

Aries in Literature

Baudelaire's ardor: bursting with inspiration, he sought to shock his audience, awakening them to his suffering, but using art as an absolute means of doing so. Baudelaire was a pioneer of modern poetry. His work abounds with such Aries motifs as ecstasy, sorcery, Satanism, and mysticism, which are all exaggerated expressions of the most intense levels of his instincts.

As an Aries, Baudelaire expressed his rebelliousness in "St. Peter's Denial," where he challenged the established order, perhaps with the hope of creating a new order:

"Indeed, I for my part can gladly leave
a world where action is not akin to dreams.
I can use the sword and die by the sword!
St. Peter denied Jesus...and he did what was proper!"

"Hatred is holy (...) To hate is to love, to hate is to feel one's own warm and generous soul (...) Hatred exalts a person," Zola affirmed *(Mes Haines)*. Zola's works are full of conflict: In *L'Assommoir* or *La Bête humaine,* he describes lives burdened with misery, whereas his own life expressed a passionate faith in a better future: for Zola, the morality of the future should be based upon "Fecundity, Work, Truth, and Justice" (Cf. *J'accuse*). Are these not the typical attributes of an Aries?

"I sit in the sky like an inscrutable sphinx."
(Baudelaire, "La Beaute" (Beauty)). Portrait of the poet by Emile Deroy.

Aries in Art

The art of Gustave Moreau, which is unclassifiable because it heralded the future, was regarded as bizarre, symbolic, and eccentric.

"The strengths are so intense, and the defects so painstakingly calculated! This is a banquet for the fastidious person, dreamers, the disenchanted, or for anyone who considers nature insufficient and looks beyond it for more profound and more uncommon sensations..." (Theophile Gautier).

By abandoning the path of Impressionism, Moreau paved the way for Surrealism: because of the precision of his strokes and the themes which he evoked, Moreau's art is a passionate confrontation between the abstract and the concrete. He portrayed the forces of Good and Evil, as well as the conscious and unconscious minds, with women representing corruption and men embodying virtue. Moreau offers a seemingly virile form of art, where only the poetic effects, the fascination with esthetic exaggeration, and the luminous decors permit us to suspect that he had not yet triumphed over the "female ideal" within himself. Although this ideal is often expressed in a passive form, it appears to have exercised a spellbinding attraction upon the painter. Despite invocations to purity, this "female ideal" is the eternal temptress, also representing fate and death: in order to confront her, it was necessary to pursue divinity.

Like the deity Mars, Gustave Moreau sought to surmount and resolve the ethical problems associated with sensuality, justice, and courage. His quest was that of a mystic seeking to embrace the divine by exorcising his own fiery passions: "In this incarnation and with this holy exorcism, everything is transformed, purified, and idealized; immortality is attained, and the divine appears everywhere, so that all living things, despite their rough-hewn formlessness, can be released from their earthly bonds, to seek the true light (...) It is an ascent toward the uppermost spheres of the spirit, a journey toward divinity by cleansed and purified souls. Bodily death is a transition to immortality (...) Everything is transformed. It is a hymn to the divine." That is how Moreau described his *Jupiter and Semele.*

In addition to portraying mystical encounters between God and the human soul, symbolized by *Leda and the Swan* (as well as *Jupiter and Semele*), Moreau depicts the numerous obstacles to this union. The myth of Phaethon represents a theme which probably recurs frequently within the world of an Aries: Phaethon, throughout his youth, was unaware of his divine parentage, but, upon learning that he was the son of Helios, the Sun god, he wanted to reveal his origins to the rest of the world. His exaltation led to impetuous zeal. Phaethon asked his father if he could drive the sun-chariot, or the divine light, in order to reveal the truth to mankind. Because Phaethon lacked the experience for performing such a task, his father begged him to forego his wishes. Bound by his promise, however, Helios finally gave the chariot's reins to Phaethon who then ascended so high among the stars that Zeus slew him with a thunderbolt.

Moreau's painting depicts Phaethon vanquished by the forces he sought to surmount. As Phaethon tumbles back toward chaos, the wheel of the Zodiac, the wheel of life which he sought to transcend or to transform, is shown behind him. This painting could be an allegory of the rude awakenings which an Aries must often experience as a result of imprudence.

Exorcising the fiery passions associated with Aries, in order to enter the divine realm. (Detail from Gustave Moreau's "Jupiter and Semele.")

"My brain and my intellect seem ephemeral to me, and I am unsure of their reality. Only my innermost feelings seem eternal and indisputably real." Moreau, as an Aries who understood the essence of his own strengths, knew at the innermost level that a zest for life was the fire which inspired him.

Many painters born under Aries displayed inexhaustible creative drives: for example, Van Gogh communicated all of his "Aries energy" by repeatedly filling his canvases with evocations of the fire motif: the Sun or sunflowers.

Many of the *fauvistes* were born under Aries, and painters such as Odilon Redon or Vlaminck expressed a fascination for warm colors (red). The power of the sign was communicated through color by some artists, whereas others expressed it thematically: for example, Goya relied upon violence and exaggeration, seeking to transform the appearance of reality through his art, or there are the lines and forms of Max Ernst, whereby reality is altered so that only its shadow can be perceived.

Lastly, every Aries can take pride in knowing that Leonardo da Vinci, a ceaseless creator, was born under this sign!

Social satire in pursuit of greater justice (Charlie Chaplin in "City Lights").

Aries in Music

Likewise in music, composers born under Aries emphasized the originality and power of their feelings.

Has it not been observed that Rachmaninov's music is explosive? When we listen to it, personality seems to surge forth by leaps and bounds.

Mussorgsky was also an Aries, he gave some of his works solar titles, such as "Without Sunlight" and "Salammbo"[1] He never completed formal training as a musician, but his intuitions allowed him to discover skills which were not taught to him and to develop new forms of musical expression. The robustness and originality of his work is combined with a sometimes overpowering true-to-life quality, as in *Boris Godunov*.

The innovative style of Bela Bartok, who is regarded as possibly the greatest creator of our era, fully expressed the attributes of Aries. Throughout the vicissitudes of his life, Bartok never lost his creative drives. Because his work is so consistently innovative, it is difficult to classify it according to musical genres. Thus, Jean Hamon has cited "the exalting image of creative energy converted into a person, a perpetually erupting flow of energy which would outlast him..." Bartok disdained the easy success of composing for patrons, and he only allowed himself to be guided by the sincerity and honesty of his instincts. As a Hungarian, Bartok delved into the origins of his nation's folklore in order to rediscover artistic sources which permitted him to express his inspiration even more convincingly. Honegger has said: "Bartok truly represents a revolution in music."

If it were necessary to select a myth evoking the profound universe of Aries, Percival's quest for the Holy Grail would possibly be appropriate, for his myth reflects the ardent desire for a source, or a quest for the sacred fire representing this zodiacal archetype.

1. The Sun is said to be "exalted" when it coincides with Aries. In other words, its power is expressed with even greater intensity.

Taurus

APRIL 21 - MAY 20

"In the meadows, during the month of May, have you ever felt this scent which conveys to every living thing the rapture of mating?"

Balzac

THE SOURCES

The Symbolic Image

This symbol represents the bovine family: bulls, oxen, cows.

♉ The bull is a massive and powerful animal.	♉ A Taurus is endowed with a rugged constitution (a "bull neck," broad shoulders, stockiness).
♉ The bull lives in meadows.	♉ A Taurus is attracted to Nature.
♉ The bull's belly is a prominent feature.	♉ A Taurus is equipped for survival: robust health and great physical strength.
♉ The bull is a ruminant.	♉ A Taurus is a "mental ruminant": he reaches conclusions slowly. He digests the past and possesses a keen memory.
♉ The bull is a peaceful creature which seldom runs.	♉ Naturally calm, a Taurus has slow bodily rhythms.
♉ As a beast of burden, the ox is used to till less fertile ground.	♉ Working intently, a Taurus proceeds gradually, using his strength to overcome obstacles.
♉ The ox works steadily, without collapsing under the yoke.	♉ A Taurus can manage heavy responsibilities, but he does not know how to relax, and he can become a slave to his work.
♉ The cow is also associated with this symbol.	♉ A Taurus is prolific and productive.
♉ There is also the raging bull of the bullfight.	♉ When a Taurus learns that he has been deceived, he can be consumed with rage.

May: The Zenith of Spring

♉ The Sun heats the Earth as it continues to ascend within the sky.	♉ A Taurus is warm, amiable, and benevolent.
♉ The days grow longer: nights become shorter than days.	♉ The daily elements of reality prevail over the unconscious: a Taurus is unpretentious, stable, and confident.
♉ Plants are developing within the ground. They take root in order to obtain nourishment.	♉ A Taurus is rooted in life: he is instinctive and is directly in contact with nature; his senses are his guide.
♉ Grass, leaves, plants... Everything in Nature is beginning to flourish.	♉ A Taurus is an achiever: he represents reality and seeks accomplishment.
♉ Scents mingle, and a heady perfume spreads throughout Nature.	♉ A Taurus has a sensual side, with strong desires.

Spring Triumphs

♉ Halfway between the end of winter and the beginning of summer, spring prevails and comes to fruition.	♉ A Taurus is resolute, persistent, and patient. He is slow to act, but does not reverse his decisions. A Taurus is loyal in friendship and in love.

Taurus is a fixed sign.

The Bountiful Earth

Earth — a dense, solid, and firm element — is the element symbolizing the attributes of Taurus. It is linked to Taurus by the position of this sign within the zodiacal cycle.

Among the triplicity of earth signs, the fixed earth of Taurus is situated between the cardinal earth of Capricorn (the primordial earth; the cold ground where seeds are concealed) and the mutable earth of Virgo (the final form: the dry ground, when grain must be harvested).

Emotions form slowly and then take root within fixed earth (the ground is "being prepared"): the Bull facilitates the process.

♀ There is the rich, bountiful, and moist earth of springtime.	♀ A Taurus has a friendly voice and a benevolent expression.
♀ The earth is in a fully productive state, and it provides its greatest yield at the peak of the cycle.	♀ The actions of a Taurus are oriented toward productivity: he makes commitments when he is convinced that his efforts can bring results.

Venus

Venus, the goddess of the Morning and the Evening, who illuminates the path to the stars, is represented by various deities in mythology. There is Venus-Aphrodite, goddess of Love and Beauty, who governs Libra. There is also Venus-Astarte, the Phoenician fertility goddess, who rules Taurus. In Assyria, she was known as Ishtar, and in Greece, she became Cybele or Demeter, the Mother Goddess. The qualities evoked by the Cybele and Demeter archetypes are more understandable to us, because they are derived from Greek civilization.

♀ The cult of Cybele, the principal Phyrigian deity, spread to Greece, where she represented the incarnation of Rhea, mother of the gods and the Earth goddess. Cybele was worshipped as "the Great Mother," the *magna mater deum*.	♀ The vigor and strength of a Taurus seem to be unlimited and could be compared to primordial energy, emanating from the depths of the Earth. A Taurus identifies himself with natural energy.
♀ At a certain point, Cybele resolved to be eternally loyal to the young and handsome Attis.	♀ A Taurus has a steadfast temperament, and, when he falls in love, he is seeking lifelong ties.
♀ She made him the guardian of her temple.	♀ Affection is accompanied by complete confidence.
♀ Cybele imposed her terms upon Attis; she demanded that he remain a virgin.	♀ A Taurus is deeply possessive. Fearing a loss of loyalty, he may be impelled to dominate others.
♀ When Attis fell in love with a nymph, Cybele angrily drove him insane.	♀ A Taurus is jealous when he discovers deception. He may seek awe-inspiring forms of revenge.
♀ Like Cybele, Venus-Astarte was worshipped by an orgiastic cult.	♀ After long periods of stress and hard work, a Taurus feels a need to draw new strength from the elementary forces of life. Then his desires come to the fore with all their instinctive power.
♀ Demeter, a goddess of profound mysteries, rounds out the taurine psychological profile: she only lost her cheerful demeanor when her daughter, Persephone, was kidnapped by Pluto.	♀ Usually cheerful and easygoing, a Taurus may become despondent if he is deprived of his possessions.
♀ Demeter searched tirelessly for her daughter for nine days and nine nights.	♀ A Taurus stubbornly pursues his efforts until he attains his goals.
♀ Having learned that Zeus, conniving with Pluto, had lied to her, Demeter caused plants to stop growing; the Earth became barren, and mankind was in great peril.	♀ In accordance with his principles, a Taurus is honest and cannot tolerate failure to fulfill obligations: his anger can be violent.
♀ Demeter's tenacity led to adoption of a compromise: Persephone would spend three months of each year with Pluto in the nether world and nine months on earth with her mother. In return, Demeter withdrew her curse.	♀ As a pragmatic person, a Taurus is mainly interested in effectiveness: he cares less for perfect solutions than for tangible results.
♀ Upon returning to Olympus, Demeter gave a sheaf of wheat to Triptolemeus, so that he could teach men how to grow crops.	♀ A Taurus seeks to harvest what he has sown previously; he does not leave anything to chance.
♀ At Cadmus' wedding, Demeter fell in love with Iason, and made love to him in public, in a field which had been tilled three times.	♀ Love and work are derived from the same source in a Taurus.

The Mouth and the Throat

♀ The parts of the body which correspond to Taurus are the mouth and the throat, representing the sense of taste and absorption of nourishment.	♀ The Taurus' ideals are focused upon possession; he is governed by property. Historically, material possessions have been associated with the Bull symbol: the cult of the Golden Calf, or the Biblical episode of the seven fat cows and the seven lean cows.

From these sources, we obtain the zodiacal formula for Taurus: a vigorous, stable, earthy, and Venusian personality, symbolized by the mouth and the throat. This formula can also be defined in terms of:

A Forceful and Productive Temperament
Instinctive, stable, and slow-moving — that is how treatises on zodiacal physiognomy portray this temperament, which has been observed in Catherine de Medicis, Ella Fitzgerald, and Jean Gabin (who even acted in a film called *Under the Sign of Taurus*).

Concrete Thought
With his feet on the ground, a Taurus has a practical and realistic outlook: he is interested in concreteness, usefulness, and practical qualities. As a creature of instinct, he forms his beliefs through his senses, in contact with reality: he thinks with his hands. Thus, John Stuart Mill, who was a Taurus, formulated the ethics of "utilitarianism," while Karl Marx introduced historical materialism by defining the economic infrastructure as the root of social relations. Freud, who developed psychoanalysis by defining the libido as the source of human personality, was also a Taurus, as was Kant, the founder of "pure reason."

A Taurus' mode of thought could be symbolically compared to a plumb line.

Possessive Love
Sensual and down-to-earth, a Taurus is also tender and pleasure-loving: love and desire intermingle as a single emotion. A Taurus falls in love slowly, but becomes loyal and possessive; for example, there is the ardor of Balzac for Mme. Hanska, whom he married after having corresponded with her for eighteen years.

The Taurus *ideogram* could represent the actual head of a bull, a powerful and stubborn creature, or it could represent a vase adorned with a bull's horns. The vase bestows receptive and productive attributes, while the horns provide combative vigor.

Venus, the goddess of love and sensuality, rules Taurus.

MODES OF EXPRESSION

Taurus in Literature

Balzac's physique — thick-set, with a bull neck, ruddy cheeks, and thick lips — matched the Taurus archetype. His appetites were insatiable: he sought money, ostentation, women, glory, wine, and food... This taurine avidity, or this inexhaustible desire to possess, was it not the source of his literary output, or his *Human Comedy,* which was a study of how the mind seeks to possess the world?

Balzac devoted all of his strength and all of his persistence to this venture; at the age of fifty-one, after having been harnessed to his work for twelve hours a day during twenty years, he said: "My brain succumbed, like a run-down horse."

He was extraordinarily prolific: he wrote ninety-five novels comprising the *Human Comedy.* His novels, anchored in the realities of his era, reflect the material interests of the taurine world: power, financial ruin, business, and, in all instances, money as a force motivating people. In terms of form, the universe is mirrored by what is known as Balzacian realism: painstaking physical descriptions of the scenery and characters which emerge from his creative efforts. The characters themselves are heroic in their desires: there is the avarice of Grandet, Vautrin's lust for power, Rastignac's desire for glory, and the amorous ardor of Felix de Vandenesse...

In comparison with the Balzacian Taurus, Giono represents the elegiac type, exalting the senses, communion with nature, and rural life *(Le Chant du monde, Colline, Que ma joie demeure).*

Lastly, the image of Montherlant also evokes the Bull, which "needs to create just as one needs to eat, to caress, and just as one needs to drink."

Taurus in Painting

During the nineteenth century, Courbet's efforts characterize a Taurus painter. He was the pioneer of realism in painting; he was the first to reject "genre painting" and to draw upon ordinary social reality, which he portrayed without introducing picturesque touches, showing life in its true form: "I only paint what I see."

Courbet instinctively relied upon Nature for inspiration: "It always turns out well when one keeps his eyes on Nature." He introduced sensual aspects — undergrowth or meadows where cows were grazing — portraying tranquil scenes, as in the *Sieste pendant les foins,* or in the siesta of the *Demoiselles au bord de la Seine,* or voluptuous scenes, as in *Les Baigneuses,* which a scandalized Napoleon III assaulted with his riding-whip.

The Earth, the element associated with Taurus, is prominent in Courbet's paintings: the Earth must be worked, as in *Les Casseurs de pierre,* or shoveled away, as in *Enterrement à Ornans.* The Earth can also be represented by rows of cliffs. Finally, it is also present in the paint which Courbet spread with a knife.

Left: a sensual mouth expressing the oral drives associated with Taurus. (Gustave Courbet, "Self-portrait.")

Instinctive and forceful in his music, Brahms showed the same qualities in his writing patterns, as indicated by this original of the score of L'Intermezzo, **Opus 118, No. 1,** *for the piano.*

Taurus in Music

"We encounter nothing resembling the titanesque life of Beethoven, or the explosive life of Berlioz. This is the tranquil life of an artist who, day by day, slowly creates a masterpiece (...)." He obstinately pursues a straight path, without glancing to the right or left. His lack of intellectualism and his relatively rudimentary knowledge, acquired by diligent efforts, aided his endeavors," wrote Claude Rostand, the biographer of Brahms. Mild-mannered, persistent, and patient, the Taurus rhythm filled Brahms' life. Physically, he was a giant: thick-set, with a large head and a broad forehead. He had a generous, warm, and practical personality. As both a poet and a peasant, he embodied the taurine contrast. As an Epicurean, he was attracted by gustatory pleasures and habitually composed with a cigar in the corner of his mouth, thereby expressing the orality of a Taurus. As a nature-lover, he was a hiker who would rise at dawn in the summer in order to wander amidst the forests or along the banks of the Rhine.

"His entire work contains the scent or taste of this rugged Nordic soil, echoes of the peasants of Holstein, who were unrefined, but also dreamers, and the tones of their robust way of speech. (...) And this poetic milieu alongside the North Sea is always present." (Claude Rostand). Brahms, guided by his instincts, anchored his music in his "Nordic earth." This contact with reality is also expressed in his fascination with folklore: he wrote melodies for ballads, and composed Hungarian dances, rhapsodies, jigs, and waltzes for the piano. Brahms also produced monumental compositions for choirs and orchestras, such as the *German Requiem* and *Rinaldo,* which convey all of the power associated with Taurus.

Another musician born under Taurus was Massenet, whose creativity ensured his predominance in opera in France for twenty-six years: the sensual, voluptuous, and "Venusian" music of *Manon* embodies taurine love.

Does *Tristan and Iseult* echo the inner world of a Taurus? This myth, where two lovers possess one another on account of an unbreakable bond, reflects many symbols associated with Taurus. Furthermore, the two lovers transcend their surroundings orally by drinking a love-potion.

Gemini

MAY 21 - JUNE 21

"The man in whom one idea gives life to another strays from his goal, because one idea saps another's vigor."

Dante, *The Divine Comedy,* "Purgatory," Canto V

THE SOURCES

The Symbolic Image

♊ The symbol is represented by twins; they can be seen as two similar personalities, or the same personality within two people.

♊ Gemini may be a dual personality, or a single personality with two aspects: two can accomplish more than one. The Gemini archetype embodies great creativity.

♊ It is difficult to distinguish twins because they may be identical.

♊ A Gemini is playful.

♊ Twins are inseparable; one represents the essence of the other.

♊ A Gemini seeks brotherhood and friendship.

♊ The twin is both oneself and another person because he is present within and outside the self.

♊ The Gemini's dilemma consists of being himself and being other persons at the same time. He has an innate talent for expressing the feelings and thoughts of others, and others can see their own image reflected by a Gemini.

♊ These twins are young adolescents.

♊ "Young at heart," a Gemini is mischievous and may like to tease.

♊ This is the age of "fending for oneself."

♊ A Gemini possesses "D system" capabilities.

♊ This is the age of imbibing new ideas and seeking changes.

♊ A Gemini has a great need to remain abreast of the times, and may be unstable.

♊ The young twins may be naive in terms of knowing how to achieve their goals.

♊ A Gemini feels impelled by ideas which he seeks to implement rapidly.

May: The End of Spring

♊ Because the sap has flowed throughout the tree, its branches and leaves develop and grow.

♊ Inspired by an instinctive zest for life, a Gemini can undertake more than one project at a time.

♊ The leaves absorb air through their pores, rapidly converting it into chlorophyll.

♊ The many impressions which he receives from the external world sharpen his interest in developing generalizations.

♊ During the Spring, butterflies go from one flower to the next.

♊ A Gemini enjoys the company of others; he has a talent for making contacts.

♊ Living things are in harmony with Nature. It is a time for frolicking in the grass, and it is easy to adapt to all situations.

♊ A Gemini accommodates himself to any situation. He is an extremely adaptable person.

Mutable Spring

♊ With summer on the way, spring draws to an end. This is a transitional period. Gemini is a mutable sign.

♊ Full of plans which he is impatient to carry out, a Gemini is a fast-moving, restless person undergoing perpetual changes.

Air

Gemini is represented by air: the element of exchanges, mobility, and diffusion. It is specifically defined by the position of Gemini within the zodiacal cycle: among the triplicity of air signs, the mutable air of Gemini, causing an individual to feel deep emotions which fade rapidly, is situated between the cardinal air of Libra, representing sentimental ties, and the fixed air of Aquarius, representing spiritual ties.

♊ The air of Gemini resembles the wind rustling through the leaves.

♊ A Gemini can react to insignificant things.

♊ It also resembles the wind slamming the doors shut.

♊ As a highly emotional type, a Gemini cannot always control his excitable temperament.

♊ The leaves can still be heard, even after the doors are shut.

♊ A Gemini recognizes all forms of responses and feelings in others, and it is sometimes difficult for him to concentrate.

Mercury

Mercury has been identified as the planet which governs both Gemini and Virgo. The young Mercury corresponds to Gemini.

☿ Mercury's father was Jupiter, the ruler of Olympus and the god of Laws and enlightening Intuition. His mother was Maia, who personified the beginning of spring, symbolizing external expression of the self, or projection of the self upon the external world.	☿ Understanding the external world comes easily to a Gemini. His perceptions are instinctive.
☿ In his infancy, Mercury overturned his crib when his mother, Maia, was not watching, and he set forth to discover the vast world outside.	☿ A Gemini is curious about everything. He prefers adventures to tranquillity, and he may be unstable.
☿ Mercury decided to steal the heifers of Apollo. In order to conceal their tracks, he made sandals from the bark of trees and placed them on the heifers' hooves.	☿ Energetic and clever, a Gemini surprises others, especially when he amuses himself by flouting certain accepted rules. He overthrows or ridicules traditions, stripping away the dramatic content. He is attracted to controversy and parodies.
☿ Mercury killed two heifers and used their skins to make cords for a new instrument which he had invented: the lyre. With his lyre, Mercury was able to play extraordinary melodies.	☿ Usually, his aim is to introduce a new harmony, or to offer a new way of interpreting things.
☿ Apollo found Mercury in a cave and led him to Jupiter on Olympus. After having brilliantly defended his actions before the gods, Mercury confessed to everything. Won over by his charm, his liveliness, and his musical skills, the gods pardoned him.	☿ Impressionable and vulnerable, a Gemini finds it difficult to challenge others; he would prefer to be accepted. He is restless, and uses words and a talent for eloquence to win admiration. He is a seducer.
☿ "Give me the tortoise-shell lyre," Apollo said, "and I'll give you the heifers." In response, Mercury cut some reeds, and, in order to replace the lyre, he created a flute on which he played an entrancing solo.	☿ A Gemini is not possessive, and he does not seek to make others feel obligated to him. He cheerfully releases them from moral debts and constraints by rapidly reestablishing a basis for making exchanges. A Gemini prizes independence for others as well as for himself. He is a generous person.
☿ Jupiter welcomed Mercury to Olympus and appointed him the messenger of the gods. The symbols of his duties were a round helmet (a symbol of power) and winged sandals (a symbol of speed). Jupiter also gave him a special messenger's staff, adorned with white ribbons.	☿ A Gemini is capable of overcoming his intellectual diversity and of elevating his thought toward lofty ideals. He then expresses his understanding of the world to others. A Gemini can be a person who stimulates and enlightens.
☿ Mercury became the patron of merchants, jurists, intellectuals, and thieves.	☿ Willing to act in behalf of his own interests or those of others, a Gemini is seldom deterred by conventional morality: he solves problems ouside the realm of commonly accepted values. Reacting to the inspiration of a given moment, he pursues goals directly. "Living on the fringes of legality, they (Geminis) can be geniuses or master criminals" (Marcelle Senard).

The Lungs

☿ The pulmonary system is the part of the body associated with Gemini. The lungs are respiratory organs.	☿ The aspirations of human life are associated with Gemini.
☿ The lungs permit us to exchange air with our environment by inhaling and exhaling.	☿ The concepts of interchange, rhythm, and duality are also associated with Gemini.

These sources provide the zodiacal formula for Gemini: a youthful, mutable, volatile, and mercurial personality, associated with the lungs. These symbolic tendencies can be described in the following manner:

An Inclination to Seek Freedom
A Gemini is inspired by the energy of youth, which often propels him toward external accomplishments (for example, John Kennedy, the youngest president of the United States). He "needs breathing space," and must vary his pursuits during a given day. A

Gemini needs an occupation where he can express his desire for mobility: John Kennedy was initially a journalist, and his lifestyle was that of a "sportsman." He wanted to "make the current flow": in a highly symbolic sense, this is what the red telephone between Moscow and Washington represented. A Gemini is a person who extracts himself from scrapes easily; he improvises and tinkers with situations, like Gerard Philippe, who, in his many roles, always finds a way out of blind alleys.

A Lucid Mind Which Seeks to Resolve Contradictions
A Gemini is inspired and motivated by the many ideas which come to life within his mind. One idea collides with another, and it is difficult to establish harmony among all of them. Whereas other persons may be stymied by matters of logic or principle, a Gemini approaches problems as puzzles: he reconciles differences and contradictions by sleight-of-hand, devising third alternatives, just as Sherlock Holmes (whose creator Conan Doyle, was a Gemini) deftly overcame the difficulties of his profession and arrived at solutions which no one else had considered. A Gemini is often drawn toward lofty intellectualism, like Sartre, weighing the problem of freedom and responsibility.

A Fluttering Heart
Curious and perceptive, a Gemini tests and samples life, and then goes onward. He is aware of love, but he does not become dominated by passions which would restrict his freedom. Although one may believe that he has departed, the Gemini has a knack for appearing at the opportune moment. When someone else seeks to share love with him, he offers friendship, but, when friendship is the other person's aim, he may suddenly play the lyre of love. How can one be sure? Before the other person realizes it, a Gemini may already seem to be drawn in another direction. A Gemini does not poke fun, but, with an overly strong awareness of the liberty of others and himself, he perceives life as a series of experiences which must be enjoyed at the proper time, without being perpetuated in behalf of illusory certainties. A Gemini is a friend who knows how to become a lover, and he is also a troubadour, but one must know how to proceed carefully in his presence.

The Gemini *ideogram* is represented by the Roman numeral "II". It expresses duality, or bipolarity between the unconscious and conscious, masculinity and feminity and between subject and object. It also represents interchanges between two entities, generating movement and expressing activity: it promotes creativity.

Mercury rules both Gemini and Virgo.

MODES OF EXPRESSION

Gemini in Literature

Goethe, a Mercurian born under Virgo, is paired with Dante, a Mercurian born under Gemini, representing two of the loftiest intellects to express the deep contradictions of the human soul through literature. Dante pursued many fields of knowledge in order to develop an overview of the numerous impressions which he drew from his environment. He sought expertise in poetry, rhetoric, philology, dialectics, history, theology, astronomy, and zoology, devouring all of the knowledge which was available at the beginning of the fourteenth century. The world which he evoked in the *Divine Comedy* is, at the same time, a world of erudition, poetry, and mysticism. Dante's precision and warmth in describing animals, plants, or the heavens reveal a mind which was admirably capable of interweaving poetry and scientific curiosity.

Dante confronted the realm of logic with inspiration and vice versa. He sought to untangle the problems raised by philosophy and theology: whereas Virgil represented human knowledge permitting him to pass through Hell and Purgatory, it was impossible to reach Paradise without Beatrice, or mystical knowledge. Dante's reply to the religious and moral dualism underlying the *Divine Comedy* — "Providence has ordained two aspirations for Man: one is happiness in this world, and the other is happiness in Heaven" — appears to be that philosophy permits one level of happiness, whereas theology provides the second. Thus, he brings both perspectives into harmony, but, at the same time, he flouts Scholastic logic which consisted of rational comprehension of revealed truths. Whereas skill in logic is useful to the mind, it can also pervert the mind. Dante cleverly releases human thought from these restraints by letting Satan say: "Undoubtedly, you did not know that I was skilled in logic?" This was a highly ironic means for demolishing an intellectual tradition.

Although Dante accepted logic as a tool for obtaining knowledge, he did not consider it sufficient for discovering absolute truth. Divine revelation was also necessary. He dreamed of a "celestial Athens," where all methods of thought would be represented because he believed that each embodied portions of the truth. Nevertheless, Dante did not abandon his lucidity, and he warned of the danger of misuse of the mind when one wishes to explore "everything": "The man in whom one idea gives life to another strays from his goal, because one idea saps another's vigor." (*Purgatory,* Canto V.)

It is appropriate to reconsider the poet or the writer and to wonder how the *Divine Comedy* has been able to appeal to the most diverse proclivities. Why does this journey often give the impression of allowing us to rediscover ourselves, with our own questions, passions and dreams? A Gemini represents himself and others at the same time. In so marvelously revealing that which we could be, have been, or would like to become, Dante lovingly and subtly cultivated the various senses which a human being possesses: to compare and to describe the various spectacles of Hell, Purgatory, and Heaven, he interwove auditory sensations with olfactory perceptions, and also incorporated the sense of taste. Of course, Dante did not overlook carnal desires and pleasures. Although he was sometimes a bitter foe of gluttony, he was receptive to the lures of sensual pleasure. A realistic outlook was combined with imagination, and his eloquence did not prevent him from speaking lucidly.

In relation to the attributes symbolically associated with Gemini, it can be said that Dante, given his sense of harmony, was able to reconcile his diverse inclinations with a constant intensity and exceptional perspicacity.

Gemini in Painting

Although Jongkind and Dufy differed greatly, both were born under Gemini. Each, in his own way, is a painter who portrayed the atmosphere.

Toward the turn of the century, Jongkind, a precursor of Impressionism, captured elements of life without ever imposing an esthetic doctrine. By means of ships ready to embark upon choppy seas, or by means of far-away landscapes, his paintings reveal originality of feeling and a spontaneous spirit which flows through his brush-strokes. Jongkind's colors are fluid, and he was skilled in endowing his art with life.

"Oh, the power to dream, which sometimes takes us so far away from ourselves..." (Dante, **Divine Comedy**, *Canto XVII).*

The breeze billowing through drapes, the movements of an orchestra, or the turns of a merry-go-round embody the language of the wind within Dufy's work. Airiness abounds within paintings which we eagerly inhale instead of contemplating. His favorite color is blue, and the sky and its clouds are guided by measured and precise brush-strokes. The Gemini temperament is represented by the variety of subjects which Dufy offers: most of his paintings contain multiple scenes. Amidst the crowded streets, the peasant festivals, or the fairs, we encounter the notes of a fanfare, we overhear conversations, or imagine the excitement of a child. Dufy borrowed the emotions of other persons and transmitted them to us with spontaneity and originality. Painting was his way of communicating: "People hire me to paint a subject, but I give them the rest as part of the bargain."

Gemini in Music

The *Rite of Spring* constituted a revolution. Stravinsky, a Gemini, shattered all forms of tradition: nothing remained of the classical rules of harmony, grammar, and syntax. With alternating stresses and pauses, the *Rite,* by means of musical polytony, liberated music and gave it a new spirit in the spring of 1913. Amidst the uproar at the theatre on the Champs-Elysees, where the audience divided into "friends and foes," it appeared that a new theory of sound was emerging, but Stravinsky had not yet ceased to amaze audiences.

Earlier, with *The Firebird,* this musical magician had solved problems that had thwarted his contemporaries: in an enchanted milieu, where frenetic notes and harmonious intervals intermingle, *The Firebird* gave the art of ballet a new vigor: "I always prefer (...) to pursue my ideas and solve the problems which emerge during my work (...), without relying upon traditional methods which may, indeed, render my task easier, although I would be obliged to study them and then to remember them.[1]"

Ignoring accepted rules, Igor Stravinsky, in *Petrushka,* surprised audiences once again by his selection of a theme: "a puppet is suddenly turned loose, and, by cascades of diabolical arpeggios, he exasperates the patience of the orchestra, which responds to him with threatening fanfares.[2]" This is the author's way of evoking the origin of his inspiration. Parodying the *pathos* of the Romanticists, he staged a drama whose characters were puppets or marionnettes, thereby mocking the dramatic content of traditional musical compositions. Then, just as Mercury left the melodious lyre to others, Stravinsky, in his subsequent works, created more new sounds which no one, thus far, has been able to imitate.

Glinka, whose "airy and transparent orchestration" was admired by Stravinsky, was a Gemini. Wagner was likewise a Gemini. It is not possible to comprehend the full range of Wagner's genius solely in relation to symbols associated with Gemini. Whereas the multiple contradictions of his personality reveal his having been born under this sign, it is probable that his tenacity in overcoming all obstacles was derived from a Taurus ascendent. Lastly, his boundless confidence — "the world owes me what I need" — is attributable to the strong influence of the planet Uranus.

Wagner reflected the Gemini temperament by appearing to possess two personalities. Whereas some described him as a shameless manipulator (which he was in some ways), others emphasized his "bewitching gentleness" (Friedrich Nietzsche). A musician and a poet at the same time, he was slow to choose one art form or the other. After deciding upon music, he often composed two works at the same time, or, when one was barely completed, he had already planned another, hastening to write down the principal chords. His genius resided in an amalgam of contradictory talents: his sense of simultaneous perception was developed to the highest degree, and it was only matched by his ability to unify diverse elements. Wagner was also a master in combining poetry, music, symphonic qualities, and drama, to create a symbolic form of art which was uniquely his, but belonged to all mankind at the same time.

"If you look at me as I look at you, we both lower our eyes, and, without saying anything, we say everything." (Spanish copla, *"Narcissus Looking into His Mirror," Mocetto.)*

Is it not true that a Gemini projects the "images of his soul" amidst his environment, in order to discover its secrets? Does he not attempt, like Narcissus observing the stream reflecting his own image, to discover himself? It is quite possible that the myth of Narcissus is intertwined with the dualities of Gemini.

1. I. Stravinsky, *Chronique de ma vie* (Story of My Life), Paris, Denoel et Steele, 1935, Vol. 1, p. 32.
2. *Op. cit.,* Vol. 1, p. 70.

Cancer

JUNE 22 - JULY 22

"The older I become, the more I realize that dreams are something which do not fade."

Jean Cocteau

THE SOURCES

The Symbolic Image

🦀 The crab is an aquatic creature.

🦀 A Cancer, immersed in scattered perceptions, is a deeply sensitive person.

🦀 The crab is a crustacean who lives inside a protective shell.

🦀 Aware of his vulnerability, a Cancer seeks protection from the external environment: he is shy.

🦀 A crab has powerful claws.

🦀 A Cancer may obstinately pursue the goals which he adopts.

🦀 The crab clings to the rocks.

🦀 A Cancer may sometimes be dependent upon other people or things.

🦀 The crab is a lunar symbol: like the Moon, it can move forward or backward.

🦀 Thus, he often takes one step forward and one step backward. He seeks a corner where he can be at ease. He is indecisive.

🦀 In certain Zodiacs, Cancer is often represented by the image of a child (the Egyptian deity Horus).

🦀 Like a newborn child, he expresses innocence and purity; he is a person who does not understand evil intentions.

July: The Beginning of Summer

🦀 The Sun reaches its zenith, the highest point in the sky. The Summer solstice takes place.

🦀 A Cancer is a highly subjective person, possessing the highest degree of awareness of himself and his own privacy. He may be hypersensitive.

🦀 This is the point in the cycle of Nature where the days seem to last forever: these are the longest days of the year.

🦀 Intensely absorbed in his own inner world, a Cancer loses sight of passing time.

🦀 Temperatures rise, and it becomes extremely hot.

🦀 All sensations are amplified. A Cancer is a deeply sensual person.

🦀 Trees bear beautiful fruit.

🦀 A Cancer seeks pleasure and has many desires.

🦀 Animals bask in the Sun.

🦀 A Cancer is somewhat inclined toward indolence, and he shies away from confrontations when he feels that he is being attacked.

Cardinal Summer

🦀 Spring has ended, and Summer is beginning.

🦀 This is the sign of fascination with the imaginary.

Cancer is a cardinal sign.

A Fountain of Emotions

Cancer is the first water sign within the Zodiac. It represents cardinal water: the source, or emotivity. Then there is the fixed water of Scorpio (the marshes of the unconscious) and the mutable water of Pisces (the ocean of spirituality).

Within the cardinal water of Cancer, emotions appear "from the first gush," and they flow intensely through the personality. The first impressions of a Cancer are often accurate. He is a hypersensitive person, with a tranquil countenance, although a lingering fearfulness may also be present. In terms of his attributes, he is a phlegmatic and highly emotional type.

The water of Cancer is expressed in the following forms:

🦀 A bubbling spring, breaking through the ground.

🦀 A Cancer's emotions often go back to childhood. Their origins are remote and subconscious.

🦀 A spring which does not dry up.

🦀 A Cancer is closely attuned to his subconscious, which abounds with images. He is often a highly creative person.

🦀 Water from the spring flows rapidly from one stone to another, mingling with other elements.

🦀 A Cancer's emotions change in contact with other persons, and they vary according to the landscape. He is an imaginative wanderer and may be unstable.

The Moon is his Planet

Cancer is ruled by the Moon — the Moon which reflects the rays of the Sun, or the pole of conceptual and rational knowledge. The Moon is a source of intuitions.

The attributes of a Cancer are so closely associated with those of the Moon that we often speak of "lunar types," or whimsicality, when we attempt to understand persons born under this sign.

In Greek mythology, the Moon was represented by three deities corresponding to its different phases. The tendencies of Cancer can be more fully recognized by considering these three deities.

☽ The New Moon symbol: the lunar crescent facing either the heavens or the Earth was represented by Artemis, or Diana, the goddess of the hunt, who ran through the mountains and forests ceaselessly: she was the savage goddess of Nature.

☽ There are two types of Cancers: the "crescent pointing toward the heavens" type, who escapes from his inner world by pursuing images nomadically, or the "crescent pointing toward the Earth" type, who dominates his inner world, pursuing images in a sedentary fashion.

☽ One day, she said to Jupiter, "Oh, my father! Allow your daughter to remain a virgin forever!"

☽ A Cancer seeks purity. He cannot comprehend evil.

☽ From then on, Artemis was armed with arrows and a bow: "The queen of the forest, the impetuous huntress, had no pleasures other than pursuing and hunting her prey." (Mario Meunier)

☽ How would it be possible to understand the passive outward appearance of a Cancer without knowing that most of his energy is inwardly directed?

☽ Her bow is a symbol of virtue.

☽ Guided by a virtuous soul, a Cancer zealously pursues chimeras, beasts, or dark ideas within the subconscious. Could this be the source of his sufferings?

☽ Artemis was merciless in punishing adulterous women.

☽ A Cancer remains extremely devoted to the family and to traditions and customs. He cannot bear being deceived.

☽ Yet she protected pregnant women and was the goddess of Childbirth, to whom sacrifices and wild animals were offered.

☽ A Cancer is capable of making sacrifices for children. This is the most maternal sign.

☽ The Full Moon phase is symbolized by Selene-Helen. Helen's radiant beauty brought chaos to Europa because of her many admirers. Paris kidnapped Helen.

☽ A Cancer conveys a somewhat disquieting impression of "constant evolution," although he is unaware of it. He seems as difficult to grasp as a reflection, and he invites others to take possession of him.

☽ Hecate, the goddess of the Dead, who governs Hades and guides the souls of the dead, was associated with a sombre Moon on the darkest nights. Her symbols are daggers, serpents, and the keys to Hades.

☽ When a Cancer has betrayed his ideals, he is consumed with remorse, but these phases do not continue, for they are the prelude to regeneration. Like the Moon, the phases of a Cancer's personality are governed by a cycle of death and rebirth.

☽ In her journey through the shadows, Hecate appeared with a torch which gave off a hazy and ghostly light. Her name was invoked in sorcerers' rituals.

☽ A Cancer is bound to the world by irrational ties. He sees himself as a bearer of "indirect knowledge" (the Moon reflects the light of the Sun) which cannot be explained by logic. He is an intuitive person.

The Breasts and the Stomach

☽ The part of the body associated with Cancer is the maternal breast: a mother places her child close to her breast.

☽ The principal qualities of Cancer are the maternal ones of protection and warmth.

☽ The breast, representing fecundity and the milk which is our first nourishment, is also associated with images of intimacy, generosity, gifts and shelter.

☽ There are also the attributes of safety: a Cancer likes to provide protection and to be protected, to "nourish" and, at the same time, to find a shelter for his innermost feelings.

☽ The other bodily organ associated with Cancer is the stomach. It performs the digestive functions which relieve stress and often induce sleep.

☽ The maternal attributes are accompanied by dreaming, memories, and reminiscences.

These sources provide the zodiacal formula for Cancer: an estival, cardinal, aquatic, and lunar image, associated with the breasts and stomach. These symbolic qualities tend to be expressed by:

An Unstable and Obstinate Temperament

Although Francois II (the husband of Mary Stuart), Mazarin, and Henry VIII were three Cancers who appear to differ greatly, each, in his own way, embodied several qualities of this sign. Francois II, known as "the king without vices or virtues," represented the placid and indolent mode of his sign. His brother, Charles IX, who was also a Cancer, was haunted by the atrocities of the Night of Saint Bartholomew, which he had permitted. Both were sons of the domineering Catherine de Medici, and power actually lay in the hands of their mother.

Louis XIII's adviser, Mazarin, represented the attributes of this sign by pursuing policies intended to protect France from the rest of the world.

Lastly, Henry VIII displayed both the obstinacy of Cancer and its unpredictable qualities. Possibly inspired by Artemis, he was full of surprises; he defended traditions, but only those which he considered to be his own.

Among upholders of tradition, it is also appropriate to cite the deeply pious Ferdinand of Bohemia, who, in his devotion to Catholicism, persecuted the Protestants.

A Sensitive Mind

"I had feelings before I could think." Rousseau's ideals — simplicity, virtue, freedom — were inspired by his feelings, instead of by discursive logic. This entirely Cancerian way of perceiving the world influenced the *Declaration of the Rights of Man and of Citizens* in France, and, through the *Social Contract*, it inspired many revolutions in other countries. The fundamental concept rested upon the principle of the natural goodness of mankind, which required protection through suitable institutions. Throughout his life, Rousseau was devoted to defending traditional concepts of freedom.

Rousseau permitted his memory to return to childhood recollections which he sought to safeguard from the evils of civilization. In the *Confessions,* or in the *Meditations of a Solitary Wanderer,* he transmitted the echoes of his own innermost feelings.

The thought patterns of a Cancer represent thought filled with reflections, comparable to nights with a Full Moon, when lakes mirror the stars.

A Romantic Heart

This is the heart of a child seeking total devotion, as in the instance of Saint-Preux in love with Julie d'Etanges *(La Nouvelle Heloise).* The heart of a Cancer is not fickle: "Oh Julie, there are eternal impressions which time and the nights can never erase. The wound heals, but the scar remains."

A Cancer is a person whose heart never completely heals, and he lets the blood flow from the wounds inflicted by life.

The Cancer *ideogram* can be compared to a fetus curled up within the womb: a creature which is evolving. Symbolically, it embodies an encounter between polar opposites turning around one another within a closed circuit, in order to create something new: a Cancer is associated with fecundity.

Diana, the huntress, who is a personification of the Moon and a relentless goddess of Nature, is shown with her bow, a symbol of virtue.

MODES OF EXPRESSION

Cancer in Literature

Caught in the labyrinth of his own inner world, Franz Kafka did not cease his dialogue with himself. He travelled along the pathways of his own imagination, but was unable to discover a shelter for his solitary temperament. The themes of his largely unfinished novels could express the drama of a Cancer's life:

The Trial — an endless debate with himself; *The Castle* — the search for a place to take root and to uphold a tradition which may have been represented by a quest for origins with the aim of rendering his innermost self meaningful; *The Chinese Wall* — characters who appear to perform absurd labors by building a wall even though they have lost the initial blueprint: is this not a parable of an all-absorbing anguish which a person seeks to dispel?

The life of Proust strongly expressed both tendencies of a Cancer: initially, as he wandered amidst a worldly milieu, he wasted his time on futile things; then, in order to recapture his time and to relive it again with intensity, he began to write *The Remembrance of Things Past.*

Through his work, Proust draws us into the world of a Cancer, where everything is a pretext for reminiscences. "At the moment at which that sip mingled with cake crumbs touched my palate, I trembled with the awareness that something extraordinary was happening within me." The taste of a madeleine dipped into a cup of tea accounts for the presence of his memories. Perhaps we can surmise that the nutritive value of a madeleine permits him to "digest" his prior life again, while the water within the tea immerses him in scattered sensations.

"A child who did not finish being born (...) always returning to his mother's flesh," Alain Fournier wrote, in describing Proust. He was always attracted or even enslaved by his mother's breast. "My only consolation when I lay down to sleep was that my mother would come to hug me when I was in bed." Hemingway, the author of *To Have and Have Not* (a theme of indecision) was also a Cancer. His work reflected his life: he continued to tell his own story through his novels. Guy Dumur[1] wrote: "It is the image of childhood seeking emancipation through the imagination."

Lastly, there is Saint-Exupery's *Little Prince,* a children's tale intended for adults. "How can I find a friend?" the Little Prince asks, as he wanders from one planet to another, unable to end his spiritual solitude.

Mahler: a constantly evolving personality.

Cancer in Painting

In Chagall's paintings, is it not the evocation of an existence beyond conventional time which attracts our attention? Or is it simply his manner of knowing how to restore childhood images with all the nostalgia of adulthood? Chagall's paintings depict a past which is marvelously present, and the magical quality is possibly the result of this alteration of time: only the colors remind us that a dream is being evoked. There are blues, greens, and pinks which our dreams may have invented, returning to our minds in hazy awakenings. Why is it impossible for clocks to have wings, or for cows to be blue, if our inner thoughts perceive them in that form? Chagall created illustrations for the *fables* of La Fontaine, another Cancer, whose work is taught to us in childhood and remains with us as adults.

"No form of art ever issued such an urgent appeal to go beyond the visible in order to attain the invisible," René Huyghes has written with respect to Rembrandt, another Cancer. "The Philosopher in His Study," "Faustus" ... Rembrandt's subjects appear to bear a message imparted by a mysterious light: they are, indeed, lunar-

 1. Cited by André Barbault, *Cancer,* Seuil.

ized, and they appear to reflect the rays of the Moon. They invite other persons to ask questions, but their knowledge remains unarticulated, for this is an inner knowledge acquired over long periods of time. Their knowledge is not dominated by logic: it is the language of the soul. His subjects are in their later years and are perhaps ready to leave us, taking their secrets with them. Their expressions, directed toward us and into space, reveal an infinite tenderness and sadness: they are unfathomable. It can be recognized that these expressions reflect protracted spiritual journeys: Rembrandt's subjects do not appear to be affected by external reality, and they imperceptibly persuade us to contemplate ourselves. Nevertheless, we do not respond to their urgings, because we cannot pull ourselves away: they cast a spell upon us. Rembrandt was a Cancer.

Modigliani, who spent a nomadic life, carried the restlessness of a Cancer and his somnambulistic drunkenness from one cafe to the next. The contours of his subjects are fluid and frail. They appear to our senses, but their calmness and nonchalance render them incomprehensible: faces with "transparent expressions," with blue tones transmitting the echoes of an imaginary world. Modigliani's subjects, who appear to be astonished by their own existence, raise unarticulated questions which we are incapable of answering *(Fillette en bleu).*

Cancerians may feel that they possess indirect knowledge "Pierrot and the Moon."

Cancer in Music

"You love your mother, and you have looked for her in every other woman," were Freud's words to Mahler, who had sought his advice. Mahler, as a Cancer, displayed the characteristic symptoms of his sign: a mother fixation. He also had the typical physical features: a calm and contemplative expression. Mahler never felt truly accepted: "An intruder everywhere, not wanted anywhere,"[1] he said of himself. Thus, he travelled to many countries seeking a shelter for his inner solitude and suffering. His music is the music of a "salon composer," seeking to express his emotions and his feelings through *lieder* — German ballads or sentimental songs. Full of nostalgia, Mahler sought to recapture time in long symphonies which were often considered interminable. For him, music was the best bulwark against the external blows which he could not easily withstand: music permitted him to "build his own world," (a completely Cancerian expression) and this inner world was closely associated with the Summer: "I am a composer for the Summer." Indeed, most of Mahler's compositions were created during this season. "I am leaving my work behind unfinished, without having completed it as I had dreamed of doing. It is imperfect and incomplete: that is the fate of humanity." Like the perpetually evolving person that he was, Mahler created works containing points of suspension: both in the mode of expression, where certain portions appear to bring time to a standstill, and in their unfinished quality.

In the Preface to *The Little Prince,* Saint-Exupery said: "All adults were originally children (although few of them remember it), and I shall therefore amend my dedication: To Leon Werth, when he was a small boy." Perhaps the same can be said for the many Cancers who have understood the Little Prince so well...

"The Inner Silence" by Schwabe, who was born under Cancer, could be used to illustrate this concept from Proust: "The only thing which comes from us is drawn from the darkness within us and is unknown to others."

---

1. Cited by Marc Vignal, *Mahler,* Seuil, page 5.

Leo

JULY 23 - AUGUST 22

"From the sublime to the ridiculous, it only takes one step."

Napoleon to Msgr. Pradt, Archbishop of Malignes, in 1812, after the retreat from Russia.

THE SOURCES

The Symbolic Image

♌ The lion is the King of Beasts.	♌ A Leo is a person who possesses authority naturally.
♌ The lion is often depicted in a haughty pose, with his head held high.	♌ Conscious of his identity, a Leo is proud and has a sense of his own importance.
♌ He has a majestic mane.	♌ He is drawn to beauty and ostentation. He likes to make an impression and attract attention.
♌ The lion is a strong and vigorous animal.	♌ A Leo is courageous in the face of adversity.
♌ The lion is a beast of prey, with dangerous claws.	♌ He can be violent and cruel.
♌ The lion protects his family.	♌ A Leo is loyal to his social group and his family. He is generous. He can undergo sacrifices for his friends and protects those who are placed in his care.
♌ The lion defends his territory.	♌ A Leo has a combative spirit, and he does not permit others to intrude upon the realm of his desires and ambitions.
♌ The lion makes his presence known by his roar.	♌ A Leo has a strong flair for drama, and he is skillful in promoting the qualities which he represents.

August: Midsummer

♌ The Sun dominates the environment, and its rays touch everything.	♌ A Leo is an outgoing, dominant, and strong-willed person. His motto is "My will be done!"
♌ The day predominates; the light of the Sun is brilliant, and illuminates Nature.	♌ A Leo can be magnanimous, generous, and loyal. Guided by light, a Leo possesses a sense of fairness and can act as a conscience for other persons.
♌ This is the hottest time of the year.	♌ A Leo is an ardent and passionate person.
♌ Fruit ripens.	♌ He pursues each venture to its completion.
♌ Bright colors abound.	♌ A Leo is an idealist. He has lofty ambitions that cannot be concealed.
♌ Sometimes the brightness of the Sun damages crops.	♌ A Leo may not always take into account the effects of his actions upon other persons.

Fixed Summer

♌ This is the height of Summer, a period when Summer is present in a definitive form.	♌ A Leo has a great need for accomplishment and fulfilling his innermost desires.

Leo is a fixed sign.

Steady Fire

Fire, a dynamic and transforming element with great vitality and energy, is profoundly reflected by Leo. It is specifically associated with Leo's position within the zodiacal cycle: among the triplicity of fire signs, Leo is situated between the primordial fire of Aries (the spark of life) and the mutable fire of Sagittarius (the fire of the intellect). The stable fire of Leo permits control of the emotions. Its attributes produce an observably passionate personality.

♌ This is a blazing bonfire with steady flames.	♌ A Leo possesses considerable energy. He is radiantly alive.
♌ The logs which feed the flames are converted into bright red embers.	♌ The flame guiding a Leo is the "flame of the ego," but he is aware that expansion of this flame should permit him to change himself and others.
♌ The fire produces light.	♌ A Leo is self-confident. He is conscious of tasks which must be completed and possesses an exceptional sense of duty. A Leo has an intense gaze and a compelling voice.

The Sun

Leo is governed by the Sun, the source of heat, light and life. All of the other planets rotate around it. A Leo perceives himself as possessing a center of gravity, and compels others to fulfill his expectations. He seeks to influence society. The counterparts in Greek mythology are Helios or Apollo. The symbols associated with Apollo permit deeper understanding of this sign.

♌ Apollo is the son of Zeus. When he was only four days old, he asked for a bow and arrows to kill the dragon Python, the enemy of his mother (Leto).	♌ A Leo quickly feels a need to defend his family. He may be driven by vengeful instincts.
♌ In order to kill Python, Apollo boldly pursued him to the Delphic shrine. Zeus ordered him to go to the Vale of Tempe to atone for his misdeed, but Apollo disregarded Zeus and preferred to go to Aegialia to seek atonement.	♌ Nothing stands in a Leo's way when he is determined, but he can act rashly and has a tendency to disregard other persons' advice or orders. A Leo seeks freedom and mastery over his own conscience (Zeus is the king of Olympus). He is an individualist: he regards himself as the only person who knows how to achieve his goals.
♌ When he returned, Apollo persuaded Pan, through flattery, to teach him the art of prophecy. Pan represents the drives which we all seek to be "the god of All Life," symbolizing the generative or sexual energy of the universe.	♌ A Leo is receptive to flattery, and this would appear to be one of the techniques which must be used in order to discern his intentions. The deity Pan is merely one representation of his own desires. A Leo may express interest in "everything," and he may wish to possess all forms of energy.
♌ Apollo burned Marsyas alive for having dared to offend him by claiming that he played the flute more skillfully than Apollo.	♌ A Leo does not easily tolerate insinuations about his personal attributes, and he fears loss of self-confidence. He is strong-willed and does not accept shortcomings.
♌ Later, Apollo won a musical contest where Midas was the judge. He then became the God of Music, and he played the lyre with seven strings when he sang during the festivals of Mount Olympus.	♌ Is it true that a Leo is actually seeking a "music of the soul" which he would like to play for others? Whereas some persons hope to seize the celestial fire, a Leo seeks to master the harmonic laws of the universe, so that he may teach them to others. He is a warm and extroverted person, who delights in expressing what he knows.
♌ Apollo, who was renowned for his handsomeness, seduced many nymphs (Plithia, Thalia, Coronis, Aria, Cyrene), as well as many mortals. Although they bore him many children, he never married.	♌ A Leo is a prolific person (children), and, although he readily accepts assistance for accomplishing his aims, he is far less inclined to seek partnership. Within the domain of Love, he is perhaps too passionate to adapt to the daily obligations of marriage, or perhaps he fears losing control of his own passions.
♌ Apollo only incurred the wrath of Zeus on one occasion: when he killed the Cyclops, who were armorers for the monarch of Olympus. Apollo was sentenced to a year of hard labor, and he served his sentence with great humility. He profited from this lesson, because afterwards, he preached moderation in every aspect of life. He inspired the precepts of "Know thyself," and "Excess is a defect." These	♌ Perhaps this legend teaches us not to challenge certain laws: to seek to kill the powers or the demons of the unconscious (the Cyclops), which are part of the development of our lives, is to combat natural forces. A Leo pursues all types of power, and his efforts may be too violent to permit self-mastery, until he learns that victory over oneself is not always obtained through force, but through self-

maxims were engraved upon his temples in Greece.

awareness. Through his struggles, a Leo tends to gain control of his own strength, and, once he gains greater self-awareness, he is willing to share it.

The Heart

♌ The organ associated with Leo is the heart.	♌ A Leo's traits incorporate generosity. He "has a heart."
♌ The heart is the center of our bodily energy.	♌ A Leo also radiates confidence, because he seeks to be a center of gravity for others.
♌ It is the motor of our circulatory system.	♌ A Leo also seeks to be responsible. He has a sense of duty.
♌ The heart determines the rhythms of our lives.	♌ A Leo has a sense of continuity.

These sources provide the zodiacal formula for Leo: Summer, stability, fire, and the Sun, represented by the heart.

A Radiant Spirit — "Proud and Generous"

The Sun-King (Louis XIV), who actually was not a Leo (in fact, he was a Virgo), displayed the attributes of this sign, because the Sun appeared at its zenith in his horoscope: like a Leo, he was deeply influenced by solar symbolism. He proudly delighted in ostentation, and sought to represent the Sun for others: *"L'état, c'est moi"* (I am Authority).

Inspired by realistic ideals, Leo can evoke the earthly grandeur which is observable in the asolute monarchy of Louis XIV, in the conquests of Napoleon I, who was born under Leo, or in the territorial ambitions of Mussolini.

When a Leo is inspired by spiritual ideals, he seeks "celestial grandeur," represented by the lofty intellects of Petrarch or Lorenzo the Magnificent, who made Florence a center of intellectual pursuits and culture. Lorenzo only became "Magnificent" after he overcame a fear of being unattractive: indeed, because he was discontented with his physical appearance, he only wished to be surrounded by beautiful things in order to diminish the impact of an unappealing perception of himself. Bearing in mind the purity of the

In astrology, the Sun is a symbol of life, authority, and awareness.

Apollo, the Sun God, manages to reconcile the many contradictions within himself. The arrows he is holding symbolize the burning rays of the Sun.

Sun, he sought to reign with a burst of brilliance: thus, there is the luxury of Lorenzo the Magnificent, or the ostentation of Louis XIV. In many instances, a Leo actually becomes an inspiration to others by his generosity. At the bridge of Arcole, Bonaparte expressed a mood of honor and boldness. Indeed, in all of his battles, a sense of strategy, ardor, and resoluteness predominates. In literature, the same type of flame inspired Alexander Dumas to write more than 500 books.

A Lucid and Logical Mind
The "Napoleonic Code," or the cohesion and solidity of Napoleon's government, represents the highest expression of the far-reaching and assimilative approach which a Leo may adopt. He likes to solve sets of problems, establish correlations, and develop over-all solutions, but he does not concentrate upon details. Nevertheless, a Leo also possesses a lucid and keen mind which must quickly be put to use, as reflected by Rockefeller's sense of realities. With an excess of confidence, a Leo may sometimes consider himself infallible, and this is probably the source of Napoleon's errors at the end of his reign — for example the Russian campaign — or of Mussolini's tragic end.

If we proceed from the physical to the mental world, we encounter the ideas of Jung, who sought to reveal the full breadth of the unconscious: "My life is the story of an unconscious which achieved fulfillment."

The conductor of an orchestra — interpreting and expressing a composition, defining the role of each musician, directing by knowing how to emphasize the proper notes and how to permit each musician to exercise his greatest skill — could serve as a symbol for a Leo's mind.

Love: "Noblesse Oblige"
A Leo is a passionate soul who may be consumed by love for someone who appears to be extremely different from himself. In such instances, he feels torn between the heart and the role which he must play: if the Sun shifted from its center of gravity, what would become of the world? Without going to extremes, a Leo may sacrifice true love for the rank which he seeks. His egoism may thwart his love: Emily Bronte (a Leo) marvelously described this conflict in *Wuthering Heights,* where the heroine, Catherine, repudiates her love for Heathcliff, the servant, by marrying Edgar Linton, in order to preserve her social standing: "I would degrade myself if I married Heathcliff; thus, he must never know how much I love him." A Leo is inspired by exceptional qualities, and, in a situation comparable to Catherine's, he may overcome pride in order for "love triumphant" to emerge. The remainder of the novel recounts a transfiguration of this kind: Catherine's daughter marries Hareton, who is of a lower social rank; in this instance, love conquers.

The Leo *ideogram* is represented by a sign suggesting both a majestic flame and the tail of a lion, thereby representing expression of a certain degree of pride.

MODES OF EXPRESSION

Leo in Literature

Solar symbolism is echoed by the purity of emotions abundantly expressed within Petrarch's poetry: "If this is not Love, what is it that I feel?/ But if it is Love, then what could Love be?/ If it is good, why are its effects so bitter for mortals? If it is evil, why do these torments seem so sweet?" *(Canzoni).* Petrarch combined exceptionally vast humanistic knowledge with a worldly life. He was a loyal person who always pursued the truth and denounced the corruption of the Church, even though he was devout. In politics, he sought to transcend partisanship and dreamed of Italian unity triumphing over internal rivalries. He wrote historical treatises where he imparted his ethical and instructive aims. Thus, he explained the uselessness and mediocrity of vituperation in this way: "When a person condemns another, he condemns himself, because someone who delights in the misdeeds which he performs would have no reason to complain if he were, in turn, deceived by someone else." (*Il triunfo d'amore,* I.) The most striking aspect, however, is the somewhat manneristic virtuosity which Petrarch adopted to communicate the nobility, profoundness, sincerity, and spirituality of his feelings. "Unfortunate is he who lets his hopes rest on mortal foundations/ But who is strong enough not to put his trust in them?/ If we are deceived in the end, so much the worse for us." *(Il triunfo della morte.)*

Whereas Napoleon's *Memoirs* give evidence of his quest for light, Alexander Dumas, in the *Three Musketeers,* expresses a Leo's sense of honor, chivalric boldness, and interest in strategy.

The daily disappearance and reappearance of the Sun has inspired many religions, for it reflects death and rebirth in Nature; perhaps it can be assumed that this motif is strongly present within the subconscious minds of persons born under Leo and that it is a source for an innate sense of the theatrical, embodied by the dramatic talents which Alexander Dumas displayed.

Leo in Art

Both in his selection of lyrical themes and in his use of colors — copper and gold tones, deep reds or yellows — Rubens expressed a solar quality. The men or women whom he painted are distinguished by a leonine appearance; his men have a knightly demeanor, and his women are regally beautiful. *The Triumph of Truth,* the title of one of his paintings, embodies a typical Leonine theme. Even though Rubens was born in June, instead of August, the zodiacal house of Leo was prominent in his horoscope, and his life and work represent this circumstance in many ways.

Marcel Duchamp, who transformed modern painting, was born with a Sun-Leo conjunction. His behavior reflected his birth under

"Bellerophon astride Pegasus, killing the Chimera." In this painting, Rubens, whose horoscope revealed the importance of planets coinciding with the sign of Leo, displayed solar influences in terms of the colors and the theme which he chose.

Leo, for he displayed a combination of swagger and pride. Did he not incorporate the style of some of the Impressionists at the beginning of his career? He explained his "in the style of" paintings by saying, "This permits me to understand more fully how they did it." When Duchamp's fame began to fade, he lost interest in painting, because he always sought to avoid repetition.

Leo in Music

"To see a sunrise is more useful for a composer than listening to Beethoven's *Pastoral Symphony*." Claude Debussy was a Leo, and, like Apollo, he sought to comprehend the forces of Nature by observing and listening. Indeed, his final piano compositions were entitled "Invocations to Pan." Pan is the God of All Things, the god of primordial energy whom every Leo seeks to dominate. Debussy's style was derived from the purest traditions of French music: his work reflects an almost chauvinistic nationalism, but it won him international acclaim.

A Leo has a sense of purpose, and he expresses himself in relation to values which he wishes to defend. Debussy was deeply concerned with safeguarding French culture and with protecting it from foreign influences.[1] He could not understand why his work would be compared to that of other composers:

"The misled public! Are they incapable of listening to harmonies without asking to see an identity document and a list of characteristics? Where do they come from? Where are they going? Is it really necessary to know? Listen!"[2]

Lastly, I have yielded to the temptation to cite Debussy's replies to a young woman in 1889:

"What is your favorite virtue?"
"Pride."
"What is the most desirable characteristic in a man?"
"A strong will."
"What is the most desirable characteristic in a woman?"
"Charm."
"What is your principal characteristic?"
"My hair."
"What is your favorite motto?"
"Always go higher!"[3]

Debussy, or "Claude de France," as he liked to be known, codified a transformation of music initiated by others. Multiple influences, such as Wagner, Ravel, or Stravinsky, have been observed in his works, and, as Antoine d'Ormesson said, "Why not simply give unto Debussy what is Debussy's?"[4] Let us give unto Caesar what is Caesar's! Debussy was able to create music which appears to lack structural regularity: although sounds are given their independence, Debussy's music is actually governed by such vast harmonies that it is difficult for us to recognize them in the initial chords. His music seeks harmony with the universe, and perhaps we can compare it to the cosmos, which seems incoherent to ordinary minds because its structure can only be perceived or understood by souls who are sensitive to the thousand sounds of the universe. Debussy sought to create this synthesis, where each chord is simultaneously independent and "wholly interdependent," without our suspecting it. For this reason, his work remains inimitable: "I have created works which will only be understood by young children in the twentieth century."

Is it possible that the profound universe of Leo is associated with the legend of the Cid, which has acquired a mythological breadth? Do we not observe one of Leo's major traits when the Cid places himself above regional strife in order to lead the fight against the enemy of the entire nation, when he seeks to unify all Spanish Catholics and Moslems to defeat the common enemy, Ben Yusuf? The Cid is capable of being "non-partisan" in order to pursue a destiny without terrestrial boundaries. Anthony Mann's "Cid" has a destiny, and he seeks to fulfill it to the utmost: "Let me be subject to a higher judgment." With respect to honor, he says, "How can a man live without his honor?" The emblem of his native land, Castille, was the lion. Perhaps Corneille's *Le Cid* is one of the most intense portrayals of the profound universe of Leo: to unify the heart and the mind in striving to outdo oneself.

The Lion, the sign of Mark the Evangelist (Carolinian manuscript).

1. Emile Vuillermoz, *Histoire de la musique* (History of Music).
2. Cited by Jean Barraque, in *Debussy* (Seuil).
3. *Idem.*
4. Antoine d'Ormesson, *Initiation à la musique* (An Introduction to Music), Stock, 1980.

"In revolutions there are two types of people: those who make the revolution and those who profit from it," Napoleon wrote. David's painting shows Napoleon on Mount Saint-Bernard.

151

Virgo

AUGUST 23 - SEPTEMBER 22

"Only a man who masters himself can gain freedom from the forces which govern all living things."

Goethe, *The Mysteries*

THE SOURCES

The Symbolic Image

♍. The symbol represents a young woman.

♍ A Virgo seeks purity with a certain naiveté.

♍ She has wings (symbol of spirituality).

♍ A Virgo is a highly energetic person, especially in terms of mental activity.

♍ She is holding a sheaf of wheat or a cluster of flowers.

♍ This is a person who tends to make use of all talents.

♍ The origin of wheat is not known: according to tradition, it sprang from the marriage of Heaven and Earth.

♍ Efforts are made to reconcile intuition with logic.

♍ Wheat is subject to an unending cycle: the seed, fruit, and then the harvested kernels. Thereafter, it returns to the earth to grow again.

♍ A Virgo is aware of relationships between Man and Nature, cycles of death and rebirth, and the vicissitudes of life: a mature world-view predominates.

♍ The hand holding the wheat is the hand of a virgin.

♍ A Virgo is engaged in a quest for perfection.

August: The End of Summer

♍ The Earth has been heated by the Sun, and dryness pervades Nature. Like Nature itself, human beings are tired. They are overcome with too much heat and too much life.

♍ During this period of dryness, detachment from feelings is sought, and there is a desire to return to essential attributes. A Virgo relies upon the intellect, seeking a logical understanding of the world.

♍ The heat of Summer diminishes. The days imperceptibly shorten. The stalks have stopped growing, and the ripe wheat is ready to be harvested. Natural forces grow weaker.

♍ There is a sense of energy being lost, as well as the need for a secure framework. A Virgo seeks to evolve amidst standards, rules, prescriptions, and customs.

♍ Crops are being harvested, and the granaries are being filled.

♍ The Virgo is prudent, methodical, and meticulous. This is a person with a high level of practical sense and a keen awareness of realities.

♍ When the grain has been harvested, the Earth appears to be desolate.

♍ A Virgo is inclined toward anxiety and does not know how to emphasize the favorable.

Mutable Summer

♍ Summer is ending, and this is a period of transition.

♍ Characterized by considerable mental activity, a Virgo seeks to reconcile ethical values with the realities of life.

Virgo is a mutable sign.

Virgo: An Earth Sign

Earth, the element representing density, stability, and solidity, is associated with Virgo. It is specifically expressed by the zodiacal position of Virgo. Among the triplicity of earth signs, the mutable earth of Virgo, where the individual attempts to set aside feelings in order to act, follows the cardinal earth of Capricorn (sowing of crops, the conscience) and the fixed earth of Taurus (the flowering and fertile earth: a sense of realities and effectiveness).

Attributes include activity and impatience, without displaying of emotions. A Virgo has a lively and intelligent expression, a penetrating gaze, and a steady and premeditated way of speaking.

♍ The earth has been planted, tilled, and cultivated; harvesting has just been completed.

♍ A Virgo is aware of efforts and of all levels of suffering. A Virgo sympathizes with those who must perform difficult tasks.

♍ Freshly mown wheat is scattered upon the earth.	♍ A Virgo is motivated to fulfill obligations. This is a person with a strong sense of responsibility to others and to himself.
♍ The earth has been "drained." All of its resources have been depleted. The earth becomes dry and barren.	♍ A Virgo lacks spontaneity and is subdued and modest. There is a fear of sensitivity, and emotions are concealed.
♍ After the harvest, the earth possesses a new form. It is in a virgin and pure state, ready for planting of new crops.	♍ A Virgo verifies everything before proceeding. A Virgo analyzes and studies the facts before beginning projects.

Mercury

Mercury's role as an interpreter is shared by Gemini and Virgo.

Gemini is primarily associated with Mercury in his youth, as the messenger of the gods, symbolizing intelligence and communication. Virgo is associated with Mercury as an adult, when he has the caduceus, a symbol of profound intelligence.

Moreover, in many instances, Virgo has been traditionally linked to Demeter.

♍ Because of his agility and vivacity, Mercury won the admiration of Jupiter who gave him the role of a divine messenger.	♍ A Virgo has an excessive need for action (like Gemini, but within a different context), as well as for acquiring knowledge.
♍ In his new role, Mercury was responsible for facilitating contracts, promoting trade, and protecting roads. He became the patron of merchants, jurists, intellectuals, and thieves.	♍ A Virgo is an excellent intermediary, with a certain knack for managing people and situations in order to serve both personal interests and those of others.
♍ Mercury taught the gods how to make fire.	♍ A Virgo is capable of controlling and directing internal energy.
♍ Mercury helped the Three Fates to invent the alphabet, and he was the inventor of astronomy, which is associated with mathematics.	♍ A Virgo can contribute to qualitative knowledge in two ways: through pure knowledge (the alphabet) and through practical knowledge (mathematics). There is a strong motivation to gain greater knowledge and to apply existing knowledge.
♍ Mercury also invented written transcription of music according to staffs.	♍ A Virgo is skilled in conveying impressions, in rendering the irrational rational and in rendering the indefinite concrete: sounds are converted to music and images to poetry. In combining intuitions and the intellect, this is a realistic and concrete personality type.
♍ Mercury developed a system of weights and measures.	♍ A Virgo has a strong sense of proportions.
♍ He introduced cultivation of olive-trees.	♍ As well as a sense of organization and methods.
♍ He invented gymnastics.	♍ A Virgo is interested in body harmony and bodily functions. This is the sign of nutritionists and physicians.
♍ Pluto chose Mercury to guide dead souls to him. Thus, Mercury became an intermediary between sleep and wakefulness.	♍ A Virgo awakens the conscience.
♍ For this role, Mercury's emblem is the caduceus: a staff with two serpents coiled around it in opposite directions. The serpents embody a symbolic duality: one is benevolent, and the other is evil.	♍ A Virgo is simultaneously attracted by the forces of darkness and light. Thus, there is a quest for an equilibrium between good and evil. This aspiration explains the perpetual conflict within a Virgo.
♍ The serpents are coiled in a loop where one ascends and the other descends. This loop represents evolution.	♍ Two types of characteristics coexist: inhibition and compulsiveness, tradition and responsiveness. A Virgo is an ambivalent person who changes from one state to another: from evil to good, from benevolence to hatred. These changes bring awareness which permits growth.
♍ The staff of the caduceus represents the axis of the Earth. It reconciles opposite tendencies and symbolizes Peace.	♍ A Virgo seeks peace and serenity.

Along with Mercury who governs Virgo, this sign is also protected by Demeter, the mother-goddess who, as previously indicated, belongs to the symbolic context of Taurus. Nevertheless, a symbol may possess multiple aspects according to the mode of observation or the level of development. In relation to the sixth sign, for example, the myth of Demeter offers new levels of comprehension.

♍ Devastated by the loss of her daughter Persephone, who was kidnapped by Pluto, Demeter searched for nine days and nine nights without resting. The number nine, which frequently appears in mythology, represents perfection. It is a symbol of fulfillment.	♍ A Virgo seeks fruition, with an impression that there is always something lacking in terms of attaining complete fulfillment. Nevertheless, Demeter's lost daughter truly represents a portion of herself which discovers the profound mysteries of Pluto. A Virgo is drawn by the mysteries of life and death, at the spiritual and physical levels, and there is a strong desire to establish harmony.
♍ Demeter travelled throughout the known world without finding her daughter.	♍ A Virgo hopes to find the essence of life and even spiritual values through classification and analysis of physical reality.
♍ Moved by Demeter's desperation, Zeus sent Mercury into the underworld to take Persephone back to her mother. After their reunion, Demeter became the patron of the Eleusian mysteries.	♍ A Virgo may ultimately learn that the two worlds which are to be reconciled are only separated by appearance. To attain the hidden world, or the world of the subconscious or spirituality, it is necessary to "know" how to experience the world of apparent realities to the fullest — in other words, it must be fully accepted — this is the ethic which may guide a Virgo.

The Intestines

The intestines are the part of the body associated with Virgo.

♍ Their function is to sort out nutrients and choose those that are necessary.	♍ The attributes of selection, analysis, and activity are associated with Virgo.
♍ The intestines eliminate waste and assimilate food.	♍ A Virgo possesses the traits of rejection and assimilation.

These sources provide the zodiacal formula for Virgo: an aestival, mutable, terrestrial, and Mercurial temperament, associated with the intestines. The formula can be presented in the following manner:

Ambivalence
A Virgo feels torn between good and evil, and these two forces pull in opposite directions: a Virgo is perceived as being ambivalent. Greta Garbo, who sometimes played malevolent characters despite her virginal appearance, was able to express this duality. A Virgo is a responsible and efficient person who methodically overcomes difficulties in performing tasks. For example, groups whom France could not assimilate, Richelieu "eliminated," such as the Protestants, in order to ensure absolute monarchy in France. Another example is Colbert, who expressed a Virgo's talents for work and coordination.

Mercury as an adult is the ruler of Virgo, providing analytical, orderly, and methodical habits.

He worked zealously for sixteen hours a day, and sought to establish order at all levels of French society. Colbert drafted a Commercial Code, regulated manufacturing, promoted industry and agriculture, and established several academies (It is known that he excluded astrology as an area of instruction!). With an exceptionally strong sense of proportion, he sought to render Louis XIV aware of the senselessness of certain expenses: "I wish to inform His Highness that an unnecessary meal costing a thousand crowns causes me incredible grief."[1]

A Methodical Mind Which Always Seeks Evidence

As can be easily imagined, or, indeed, deduced, many scientists or persons who seek to investigate beyond outward appearances are born under Virgo. After determining the order which governs a given category, a Virgo scientist methodically classifies its components in order to render them logically comprehensible: thus, there is Lavoisier, the father of modern chemistry, who provided its system of nomenclature, or Cuvier, who developed a logical way of classifying animals.

A Virgo's thought patterns could be represented by a microscope or a clock.

Unsettled Love

What type of person can free a Virgo from the natural restlessness associated with this sign? Who can provide reassurance, or know how to display all of the sensitivity and tact which an introverted temperament does not dare to ask for? A Virgo is uninterested in superficial infatuation, and bonds are only established through sharing ideas: Love is seen as something which must be learned. A Virgo spends a great deal of time studying the person who may be destined to win his or her affection: "the heart of a Virgo" cannot be easily conquered. Furthermore, does a sense of transgression always remain if the veil of modesty is lifted? Not all Virgos are like Saint-Just, the harsh advocate of celibacy. Their ambivalent nature may suddenly awaken desires which are closely comparable to those attributed to Scorpio.

The Virgo *ideogram* is represented by an "M" with a slash through the last leg. This may be a simplified representation of the body and the wings of Virgo, with the extra stroke representing a seed-cluster, thereby suggesting a pure and productive character type. It is also possible, however, to associate the legs of the *M* with the intestines, representing selection and analysis.

---

1. Cited by (A.) Barbault, *La Vierge* (Virgo) (Seuil), p. 89.

Virgo seeks the inner purity which she already possesses.
(Rackham, "The Holy Grail".)

MODES OF EXPRESSION

Virgo in Literature

Goethe's having been born under the sign of Virgo is not the only factor permitting recognition of the ambivalence of his ideas, because Goethe's horoscope contained other indications of this tendency: the Moon in the house of Pisces, promoting sensitivity to multiple harmonies, was counteracted by the Sun in the house of Virgo, fostering a quest for order. In order to understand and maintain this dichotomy, the ascendant representing Goethe's "ego" was counterbalanced by the presence of Saturn in the house of Scorpio. Thus, Goethe was able to combine science and art. Indeed, he is more frequently recognized as a poet or as the author of *The Sufferings of Young Werther* or *Faust,* whereas his discovery of the intermaxillary bone or his theory of colors tend to be overlooked. Even in his youth, Goethe possessed a quality often associated with Virgo, namely an inclination to classify, collect and seek order, almost at the level of a mania. His entire life was guided by a quest for truth: "Throughout my life, I have sought to be loyal to myself and to others, and, wherever earthly disorder has been present, I have unceasingly lifted my eyes upward."[1] Whereas the emotions associated with the Moon in the house of Pisces were expressed during the first phase of his life, when he wrote the *Sufferings of Young Werther,* the Virgo pole gave Goethe the necessary strength for overcoming his unconscious during the second phase of his life. The Sun coinciding with Virgo represented his ideal, and it impelled him toward perfection and eternal wisdom, demanding constant efforts to overcome subjectivity. In the *Mysteries,* he wrote: "Only a man who masters himself can gain freedom from the forces which govern all living things." Goethe's constant inner restlessness drove him to seek an equilibrium and improve himself to an even greater degree. His pen frequently conveyed this type of tension: "My anxieties, my impatience, my efforts, my seeking, my thoughts, my hesitations. . ." He questioned his own talents or the value of his works: "I have written all sorts of things, but really not very much, and, in the end, nothing," he wrote after the first version of *Faust.* Before his thirtieth birthday, he recorded a noteworthy act of expiation in his *Journal:* he harshly weighed the value of all his work prior to that point, took note of the time which he regarded as wasted, and adopted resolutions for effectively allocating the remainder of his life. Until his final days, Goethe sought to maintain a clear and accurate estimate of his merits. He was never dazzled by success, and always remained extremely humble: "But if we wish to be loyal, what did I truly possess other than a capacity and an inclination to distinguish and to select?" He did not affirm anything without evidence, and, in his eyes, evidence could only be obtained through experience. Thus, knowledge was to be pursued through effort and hardship. Even with respect to the existence of God, Goethe was assailed by doubts when he tried to believe, and he sought to obtain confirmation by intellectual means. Always uncertain, he periodically questioned the approaches or conclusions which had emerged.

---

1. Cited by Jeanne Ancelet-Hustache, *Goethe* (Seuil), p. 69.

*"Who delivers
me . . ." from myself?
Artist F. Knopff was
a Virgo.*

155

He believed that everyone understands a portion of the truth, according to inclinations, occupations, and ages: "There are many rooms within my father's house." Indeed, the nature of religious belief mattered little; it could be polytheistic or pantheistic. Goethe's ethics encompassed a recognition of human limitations: "Men cannot be content until limits have been defined for their indeterminate powers." There was also a need for "dedication to an activity that becomes a duty for the individual and a benefit to society." *(The Dramatic Vocation of Wilhelm Meister).* Goethe was extremely aware of the difficulty of avoiding failure and withstanding the contradictory forces which baffle a person. A Virgo, to a greater degree than persons born under any other sign, is persistently aware of the conflict between good and evil: "(...) Alas! Two selves live within me." In *Faust,* with the intensity and perspicacity derived from a Scorpio ascendant, Goethe expressed the fundamental conflict represented by a Sun-Virgo conjunction, namely the eternal struggle between good and evil.

Virgo in Painting

The two great masters of nineteenth century classicism in France, David and Ingres, were both Virgos.

David was Napoleon's official artist, and he was asked to portray the principal phases of Napoleon's reign. Although he excelled in this capacity, there is a basis for believing that he may have lost a certain degree of individuality from an artistic viewpoint: his creations were intended to serve political aims, but they were dedicated to an empire which he admired. David selected themes from Roman history to express the moral virtues which his era honored. In one of his paintings, *Horace's Oration,* he fully reflected the ideals of his contemporaries, but it is also probable that these were his own values. The lines are precise, and the contours are bold; there is an observable self-control and a certain rigidity, from an artistic viewpoint and in terms of the emotions which are suppressed. In the background, women can be seen weeping, but the inflexible warriors ignore them; they are entirely absorbed in the destiny which they must serve. David was reproached for coldness or lack of emotion, but these criticisms did not matter to him. Furthermore, those who criticized David from this perspective probably did not share his world-view. It is unknown whether David lacked an impression of self-betrayal or of revealing himself. His image of the universe did not allow for emotional outpourings. In *The Assassination of Marat,* the artist showed somewhat less restraint, and the secret and often unexpressed aspirations of a Virgo's symbolic context emerged. Beyond the event of the murder, it is possible to discern an aspiration toward transcendence. The background of the painting is dark and uncertain, and it possesses a certain unfathomable depth. This painting combines the realities of life (through death) and the inaccessible, idealized in black, so that it radiates the ambivalence of a Virgo's personality.

Ingres was David's disciple, and he perpetuated the academic style of his mentor. He borrowed from earlier portraits in order to portray illustrious figures of his era. *La Grande Odalisque,* which was painted for Caroline Murat, Napoleon's sister, appears to have been taken from a daily newspaper. In another way, this painting also expresses the fundamental duality of Virgo: do the excessive detachment and the cold and distant stare create a certain air of excitement which the artist appeared to hold in disdain?

Painters born under Virgo did not limit themselves solely to classical modes of expression. Kaspar David Friedrich, one of the greatest German pre-Romantics, was a Virgo. His restless and tormented art possibly permits us to understand certain typical Virgo perspectives: "Art is presented as an intermediary between Nature and Man. The model is too extensive and too sublime to be recognized."[1] The monk in *Bord de la mer* (Seashore) — can he represent Man confronted by the inaccessible, or the human condition reduced to its limits, in contrast to the infinite? One question which appears to emerge is: does a human being have ways of making his own presence within the world coincide with eternity? How can these two dimensions be reconciled? Many Virgo personalities are inexorably attracted by the world of the subconscious. Yet how can it be attained without falling into chasms where we would lose our way? In the *Falaises de craie de l'île Rugen* (Chalk Cliffs on the Island of Rugen), three figures appear to represent three components of an answer: the first is a seated woman, whose left hand grips the roots of a tree, while her right hand points toward white stones and appears to question the infinite in vain. These intrusive stones, which are a virginal white, emerge between solid earth and dream-like blueness, or the sea of the unconscious. The second figure is a man in a prone position, only slightly resting upon his arms and hardly daring to observe the grandiose scene: is he capable, or is there too great a risk of abandoning the earth? Indeed, there is the risk that someone may encounter him, and his hat and cane, symbols of his role in society, are placed beside him. The third figure stands firmly, with his legs spread apart. He is rooted to the earth, and lacks the anxiety of the other two; perhaps he has attained serenity. These three figures may represent the three stages of life confronted by the unknown (which Friedrich often evoked in his paintings). Another painting, the *Femme devant le précipice* (Woman Facing a Precipice), represents a sense of destiny: a firmly rooted tree on the right expresses the world of beliefs, and an uprooted tree on the left expresses a person's death. In this way, the same symbol is used to express two opposite aspects of existence. A serpent symbolizing earthly temptations is staring at the woman,[2] who struggles to maintain her balance upon the trunk of a tree which shall permit her to cross the ravine of death. Her face expresses anxiety: she is not looking at the mountains beyond, which are situated in the background. She is abandoning earthly desires. Despite her uncertainty, she shows a certain level of courage in rejecting comforts which may have been attainable for her.

An extremely mature outlook is required to accept the destiny which Friedrich evokes: a path where one only encounters transitory beliefs, indubitably leading us toward death. Is destiny represented by these unattainable mountains of "eternal" truth?

1. Cited by René Huyghe, *Dialogue avec le visible* (Dialogue with the visible), Flammarion, p. 373.
2. Kaspar David Friedrich, *Tate Gallery Catalogue,* 1972.

*Burne-Jones'
illustration for the
"Roman de la Rose"
is an image of the
ideal and of the quest
for purity.*

Virgo in Music

Bruckner's work did not win public acclaim. This composer was a Virgo, and his natural timidity prevented him from seeking fame or even recognition.

Constantly dissatisfied with himself, Bruckner persistently reworked his compositions.

Encountering one disillusionment after another, he sublimated his suffering through art — an art which echoes his quest for God. The *Ninth Symphony,* which is unfinished, expresses his mystical aspirations.

Bruckner illustrated another aspect of Virgo: "the seed must grow in order to bear fruit." With a premonition of the true destiny of humanity, an individual can become detached from the physical world, elevating the sense of sacrifice to extreme prominence. Molded by pain and eternally vulnerable to doubts, Bruckner abandoned himself to his work while retaining exceptional humility. He prayed to the Virgin Mary to sustain him and grant him transcendence. Moreover, his life often reflected symbolic relationships with the month of August: this was the time of the year for publishing his works, or the time for seeking a spouse, but always without success.

Disenchanted with daily life, he remained wholly dedicated to his pupils, and persistently pursued his goals as a composer, continuing to support himself by serving as a church organist.

Bruckner's music expresses his love for divine ideals with an often incomparable sense of conflict.

In turn, Schonberg's dodecaphonism appears to echo the inclinations of the Virgo personality in another form: emotional overtones have been banished from his music, and his series of sounds and harmonies seldom express spontaneity. In order to understand his work at a deeper level, it is necessary to look beyond mere sounds and recognize the intellectual qualities of Schonberg's efforts as a composer: "I would rather compose as an intellectual than as an imbecile,"[1] he affirmed.

The myth of Isis seeking her dead husband abounds with meaningful symbols: Isis tries to gather the fragments of the body of Osiris, which had been scattered by Seth, the God of the Underworld. After accomplishing her task and bringing Osiris back to life, Isis discovers the importance of her son, Horus, whom she has carried within her womb. The Greek myth of Demeter is a counterpart. It appears to express[2] the quest for purity within the external world, followed by discovery of purity at an internal level. Is it not true that this myth illustrates the inner universe of a Virgo?

---

1. Cited by Antoine d'Ormesson, *Initiation à la musique* (Introduction to Music), Stock, p. 364.

2. As demonstrated by M. Senard in *Le zodiaque* (The Zodiac), Editions traditionnelles.

Libra

SEPTEMBER 23 - OCTOBER 22

"To cogitate" means: to stir up ideas and to make them dissolve, and "to discuss:" to strike in all directions; but to think means to weigh, and that is my task."

Lanza del Vasto, *Eclats de vie et Pointes de vérité* (Denoël), p. 33.

SOURCES

The Symbolic Image

⚖ The scale is a measuring device intended for weighing things.	⚖ Librans have a sense of proportion. This type of person develops in relation to accepted standards and measurements.
⚖ The beam wavers between two trays which tilt first to one side and then the other.	⚖ Librans seek equilibrium by alternating between spontaneity and reflection, attraction and distaste for life, and extroversion and introversion.
⚖ The slightest thing can make the beam of the scale waver.	⚖ A Libran feels the slightest vibrations and is an extremely sensitive person.
⚖ When the trays are balanced, their contents are interchangeable.	⚖ This is a person who readily sympathizes with and understands others. Librans are adaptable and sociable.
⚖ The beam can only tilt to one side at a time.	⚖ A Libran can accept reality and possesses a sense of sacrifice.
⚖ Another weight must be added to the opposite tray to restore equilibrium.	⚖ Librans need someone else as a counterpart to provide balance. They need an "I and Thou." They are attracted to partnerships.
⚖ The scale symbolizes justice: it represents weighing of human actions.	⚖ Librans pursue an equilibrium between fairness and the truth.

September: The Beginning of Autumn

⚖ The Autumn equinox arrives: days and nights are of equal length.	⚖ A Libran possesses two dispositions which balance one another: a youthful one (day) and that of an elderly person (night). A Libran possesses poise.
⚖ Nevertheless, nights gradually become longer than days.	⚖ Objectivity is overruled by subjective values. A Libran is sentimental.
⚖ Summer is ending, and, as heat diminishes, temperatures decline.	⚖ Librans do not tend to be passionate, and their actions may seem to reflect a certain detachment.
⚖ The Sun is descending, and the leaves begin to fall.	⚖ Librans have an anxious and restless temperament because of a sense of vulnerability.
⚖ The natural world is in a state of decline: trees lose their leaves, and the bare branches become visible.	⚖ Librans are attracted to spiritual values and genuine sincerity.
⚖ As Autumn begins, roses fall from the bush under the weakening rays of the Sun.	⚖ Librans are attracted to things which are fully developed, and seek to facilitate growth.
⚖ Animals go into their burrows, and prepare for cold weather.	⚖ Librans possess foresight.

Cardinal Autumn

⚖ Summer has ended and a new season is beginning. Autumn is at hand.	⚖ A Libran is sensitive to deep relationships and expression of feelings. A Libran seeks new acquaintances and feels a need to please others.

Libra is a cardinal sign.

Air

Air, the element of exchanges, mobility and diffusion, corresponds to Libra. It is specifically represented by Libra's position within the zodiacal cycle: the cardinal air of Libra, where natives tend to evaluate situations according to their feelings, is situated between the mutable air of Gemini (the wind, exchanging of ideas, bonds derived from friendship) and the fixed air of Aquarius (the limpid sky of Winter: psychic attachments, fraternal devotion). These traits produce a highly active person who can be cheerful or excitable (according to the particular situation, the cheerful type is extroverted, and the excitable type is introverted).

<table>
<tr><td>♎ The air of Libra resembles the air of a sky where the clouds are drawn toward one another as they are driven by the Autumn wind.</td><td>♎ A Libran feels an irresistible attraction toward others who may exercise an influence. The principal psychological function is feeling. A Libran has an amiable expression, as well as a pleasing and melodious voice.</td></tr>
<tr><td>♎ As the clouds mingle with one another, they regroup and separate under the power of the wind.</td><td>♎ Librans may lack the ability to judge carefully as a result of excessive adaptation to other persons or to their surroundings.</td></tr>
<tr><td>♎ The clouds are always in motion, and are molded by the breath of deities. Our imaginations perceive arabesques or all types of shapes.</td><td>♎ Librans' emotions are of esthetic nature. They are not guided by rigorous contemplation, but by the mood of a given moment.</td></tr>
</table>

Venus-Aphrodite

Libra is ruled by Venus-Aphrodite, representing the beauty, harmony, and love which inspire many artists.

<table>
<tr><td>♎ Venus-Aphrodite was born from the sea-foam which formed when Saturn threw the genitals of Uranus into the sea.</td><td>♎ Librans can cause order to emerge from chaos, because they are skilled at creating harmony, peace, and simplicity.</td></tr>
<tr><td>♎ Uranus is the father of the universe. Hence, Aphrodite is the daughter of the sky.</td><td>♎ Librans communicate through intuition instead of logic.</td></tr>
<tr><td>♎ Aphrodite emerged naked, astride a sea-shell, with the sea serving as her mirror.</td><td>♎ Librans show a certain fascination with natural beauty and they possess a unique capacity to reflect others' feelings. People feel at ease in their presence.</td></tr>
<tr><td>♎ Everyone said that she floated through the air, accompanied by doves and sparrows.</td><td>♎ Librans express an airy and fluid, or almost ethereal, image. Warmth and natural kindness are expressed with all living things, even animals, toward whom they may often display great affection.</td></tr>
<tr><td>♎ The Fates had chosen a unique divine duty for Aphrodite: to love</td><td>♎ Librans cannot live without warmth. This is a person who thrives on contact with others. Librans may be easily influenced by others.</td></tr>
<tr><td>♎ Aphrodite wore a magic sash which caused everyone to fall in love with her, but she seldom lent it to other goddesses.</td><td>♎ Librans defend prerogatives stubbornly. This is a restless and excitable personality, without great self-confidence.</td></tr>
<tr><td>♎ Aphrodite behaved in a rather fickle manner. She had many lovers: Dionysus, Poseidon, Mars, Mercury, Anchises, and Adonis.</td><td>♎ In terms of love, Librans' feelings are sincere although they may seem to waver. Their affections may stray because love is confused with immediate attraction. Fickleness may arise from adaptability, unawareness of differences, or a desire to conciliate.</td></tr>
<tr><td>♎ One of her lovers was Mercury, or Hermes, who symbolizes all types of relationships.</td><td>♎ It is not possible to remain angry, however, because a Libran is extremely skilled in overcoming difficulties. This is a person with exceptional tact.</td></tr>
<tr><td>♎ Their child was Hermaphroditus, who had the characteristics of both sexes.</td><td>♎ Librans promote peace and seek to create equitable relationships.</td></tr>
<tr><td>♎ Poseidon, or Neptune, was also one of Aphrodite's lovers. As the god of the seas, he represented the infinite and the limitless, the world of illusions or spiritual awareness.</td><td>♎ Because Librans possess the ability to gain knowledge through inner impressions, there is an inclination to dream and seek spiritual values.</td></tr>
</table>

The symbolism of Libra is derived from the beginning of Autumn.

♎ Her most long-lasting relationship was with Mars, the god of War, who symbolizes passion and violence, the antithesis of Aphrodite.

♎ Librans seek an ideal combination, a merging of opposites. Someone with different traits is needed to provide equilibrium.

♎ Eros, who inspired sexual attraction, was the child of Venus and Mars.

♎ Because a Libran inspires a desire for partnership, this is a person who is highly suited for marriage (a Libran places a high value upon conciliation).

♎ When Aphrodite complained that Eros had remained too childlike, Themis advised her to bear him a brother. This was Anteros.

♎ A Libran always feels a need to be compensated for his or her actions. Each act must be reciprocated. Alternation is necessary for equilibrium.

♎ Another lover of Aphrodite was Dionysus, the god of wine and revelry.

♎ A Libran likes to encourage joy and celebration so that everyone will attain satisfaction. A Libran promotes a festive atmosphere.

♎ Another lover of Aphrodite was Anchises, a mortal whom she defended against Jupiter's thunderbolts.

♎ Because Librans are emotional, they pour out their feelts to others, and defend the weak.

♎ Adonis, a symbol of male beauty, also shared Aphrodite's bed.

♎ Librans are attracted by beauty, and they possess esthetic instincts, as well as highly developed artistic inclinations.

The Kidneys

♎ The kidneys are the part of the body associated with Libra. Through excretion, the kidneys ensure a balance between the body and its environment.

♎ Balance and refinement are traits associated with Librans; their behavior and their appearance can reflect harmony between the inner person and the external world. Their gestures are precise, and they move gracefully.

These sources provide the zodiacal formula for Libra: an autumnal, cardinal, airy, and Venusian temperament, associated with the kidneys. These symbolic tendencies may be expressed in the following manner:

A Quest for a Balance between Introversion and Extroversion
Although Librans may be inclined toward spiritual values and introversion, they seek to share the benefits of their internal equilibrium with others. Their temperament is accompanied by a certain detachment, and there may be an inclination toward contemplativeness. Gandhi, Lanza del Vasto, or Virgil would exemplify this tendency. When Librans are inclined toward external values or extroversion, they communicate spontaneity and a zest for life; for example, there is Brigitte Bardot.

Notwithstanding specific modes of behavior, a Libran always seeks a suitable milieu for harmony and peace. For example, there is Gandhi's espousal of non-violence, or Erasmus' desire to reconcile Socrates and Jesus.

"Intelligence of the Heart" and the Just Mean
Weighing the pros and cons of ideas, Librans use intuitive thought processes, and display a certain independence in intellectual matters. The philosopher Bergson explored intuition, but refrained from making affirmations without evidence.

The beam wavers between the two trays. François Mauriac was a Libran who was inclined toward both intellectualism and sexuality.

When the beam reaches the midpoint, each tray bears the same weight; then the individual can put himself in another's place in order to understand. Gandhi possessed this type of instinctive intelligence.

In my opinion, the symbol of the scale is the truest symbol of this mode of thought.

An Amorous Esthetic and "A Fickle Heart"
Librans weigh pros and cons for long periods of time before making commitments. Thus, Madame Bovary reflects both credulity and frivolity, or there is Pauline Borghese' synthesis of marriage and free love.

Librans are most strongly inclined to repudiate extremes. Their thought processes may be externally represented by changing of partners or if they do not reveal their thoughts, they seem hesitant.

In one form or another, a Libran seeks an equilibrium between loving Beauty and loving Virtue, although it is sometimes difficult to reconcile these inclinations.

The Libra *ideogram* consists of two superimposed dashes: the first represents an interrupted equilibrium, and the second restoration of equilibrium. This ideogram corresponds to a person who quickly seeks compensation for excesses, with a strong instinctive drive to regain serenity. Libra embodies alternation.

MODES OF EXPRESSION

Libra in Literature

"One person is not here, and the whole world is barren." Is this not a cry for a companion to allow expansion of the self in its fullest form? Who, more than Lamartine, was able to convey shifts and fluctuations of the soul by the rhythms of poetry and his way of life? After a comtemplative youth, he promoted the struggle for democracy, always seeking to reconcile opposites. Libran symbolism is expressed by the titles of his works in terms of the season (Autumn), air (The Fall of an Angel), or the sign itself (Harmonies).

With Virgil, we observe an entirely air-inspired personality which is exceptional among the poets of his era when the same autumnal vigor guides his account of the deeds of Aeneas, a contemplative hero who brought harmony to the Trojans.

Although their subjects differed greatly, Oscar Wilde and Alain Fournier were closely comparable in their reverence for feelings, which each expressed in his own way. Oscar Wilde seemed to be fascinated with the sources of human emotions, whereas Alain Fournier, in *Le Grand Meaulnes,* evokes eternal adolescence, with a nostalgia for innocence and an abundance of intense protectiveness.

Libra in Art

Some Libran painters, such as Boucher, concentrated upon the ruler of this sign, namely Venus, portraying her life, her deeds, and her victories. Others, such as Watteau, sought to express "reality reduced to its lightest and most delicate forms" (René Huyghe), adopting a style which embodied an equilibrium between Classicism and Romanticism. The persons portrayed in *L'Assemblage dans un parc, L'Embarquement pour Cythère, L'Indifferent,* or *La Balançoire* possess facial expressions dominated by uncertainty and indecision. It almost seems that the artist himself cannot discern their true feelings. Bonnard displayed such a strong inclination for perfection that constantly altered his paintings in order to bring them to fruition. To the astonishment of the museum guards, he would even make changes in certain paintings already being exhibited in museums. Fernand Hazan[1] has said that, for Bonnard, "the air gives the artist a sensuality which he expresses through the world of objects," in paintings, prints, posters, or in sculpture. Is the actual subject important? It would seem that Bonnard was primarily interested in expressing the transparency emanating from a given decor.

———
1. Fernand Hazan, *Nouveau dictionnaire de la Peinture moderne* (New Dictionary of Modern Painting), Paris, edited by F. Hazan, 1963, p. 35.

A restless and elusive personality because of a sense of vulnerability. ("The Clown," by Watteau, who was a Libran.)

"Fleeing from time, without returning," (Virgil, "The Georgics"). Millet's "Gleaners."

Libra in Music

Saint-Saens, a Libran who detested Berlioz and Wagner because he considered them too grandiloquent and too violent in terms of his own auditory preferences, composed serenades and romances. Along with his own compositions, he also sought to provide "finishing touches" for Bach, Mozart, Haydn, Beethoven, Berlioz, and Wagner, because he produced arrangements or new versions for their works.

Although nineteenth century music was transformed by Wagner, Verdi's art established equilibrium among opposite forces. *Rigoletto, Il Trovatore, La Traviata,* or the *Vespri Siciliani* express profound human passions with simplicity and realism. With his lyrical talents, Verdi was able to appeal to all levels of feeling; emotions are expressed directly, and sentiments are sincere. Nevertheless, it would be misleading to define Verdi as a composer who typically represents the Libra symbol.

In music, Verdi was not one to "hesitate." At this point, it may be appropriate to clarify a slightly detrimental characteristic which is easily attributed to Librans. If Librans are sometimes hesitant, the reason is that they weigh matters carefully before adopting deci-

sions, often appearing to refrain from truly making choices. The horoscopes of some Librans embody too many contradictory forces, or a Martian counterbalance may be absent, for example. It should not be forgotten that Libra is a cardinal sign expressing a flow of energy. Indeed, the Libran Verdi said: "The artist who hesitates makes no progress." Thus, if a Libran appears to be changeable, the primary reason is a tendency to seek balanced relationships.

Like Venus emerging from the waves, Verdi's music entranced his contemporaries because it so strongly expressed the moods of his era. Nevertheless, this does not mean that Verdi's compositions are "genre pieces." The *Vespri Siciliani, Otello,* and *Aida* always appeal to our tastes, even though we have been influenced by many other famous composers: Verdi knew how to awaken feelings shared by all humanity.

Like Verdi himself, who inspired rivalries among his teachers, the charm of his music, which reflects the impulses and contradictions of our hearts with great simplicity and sensitivity, captivates us. From his earliest moments of fame, Verdi won widespread admiration, and it was difficult for him to chose among a thousand amorous invitations. Indeed, his affections alternated for a long time between two extremely different women: the aristocratic Strepponi and Appiani, the singer. After deep reflection, he chose Strepponi and married her several years after they met.

Another of Verdi's characteristics which distinguished him from many artists was his talent for reconciling creativity with financial acumen. Verdi carefully invested the money which he received, and he was able to obtain substantial profits.

Verdi was also noted for his constant awareness of public opinion: "When everything is carefully measured, weighed, and counted, *Macbeth* is a fiasco. Amen." These were his words after the failure of one of his operas. In contrast, after a performance of *Nabucco,* he wrote: "The theatre was overflowing (last night): this is the only true barometer for success."

Verdi sought to please others, and succeeded. In *Nabucco,* for example, he used the history of the Jews to evoke the patriotic spirit and desire for liberty which inspired the movement known as the *Risorgimento. Nabucco*'s success, in its own time and since then, is attributable to its having echoed not only the European desire for liberty in 1848, but the eternal values of mankind.

Verdi skillfully portrayed human passions in their purity and intensity, expressing contrasts between good and evil, strengths and weaknesses, vice and virtue, with his style providing a balance through alternation between choruses and the principal singer. Somewhat like Bonnard, he did not permit anyone else to complete the final touches for a given performance. He directly assumed responsibility for staging his own works up to the very last moment.

The need for a counterweight is most clearly expressed by *Il Trovatore* and by *La Traviata.* Although these two operas differ greatly, he wrote them at the same time, as if inspired by alternation. Whereas *Il Trovatore* proclaims passions vehemently, *La Traviata* (derived from the *Dame aux camélias*) appears to respond with tenderness. These two operas reflect the two sides of Romanticism. The differences in style are not readily understood, and Verdi appears to be self-contradictory, but it is possible that he had two different audiences in mind. Once, when Verdi was asked to indicate his favorite opera, he replied: "*Rigoletto* if I were a professional, but, if I were merely an opera-lover, I would admire *La Traviata* most of all." Verdi's preferences compensate one another. They are only unified through Beauty and Truth, and he did not hesitate to affirm: "In art, I admire everything that is beautiful (...) I like everything, if small things remain small, if large things remain large, and if cheerful things remain cheerful (...). In fact, everything has to be as it should be: it has to be real."

Correlations between Libra and Aries

Even though Aries and Libra are opposites in relation to the cycles of the Zodiac and the seasons, they are also complementary.

The circle of the Zodiac is a whole wherein the parts are not mutually exclusive. Instead, they are correlated with one another, and each is merely an expression of the same category of energy in a different symbolic form. It is only possible to understand each part in relation to the others, and this is especially true in terms of so-called "opposite" signs. Both Aries and Libra are cardinal signs because they begin seasons, and both are inspired by the same energy, namely the energy of life or forward motion:

♈ In Aries, fire converts this energy into action in the form of an attraction for new ventures.

♎ In Libra, air converts this energy into exchanges in the form of an attraction for new contacts.

Whereas the head for Aries symbolizes the drive to seek commitments, the kidneys for Libra symbolize the quest for equilibrium:

♈ Fire and Mars impel an Aries toward impulsive behavior which may sometimes be brutal.

♎ Air and Venus-Aphrodite endow a Libran with a talent for harmonious compromises.

The respective polar energies complement one another and are essential to the life cycle: whereas Aries penetrates and shatters, Libra restores the necessary equilibrium.

When a person finds affinities and echoes within a myth, the myth causes certain tones from an innermost world to be heard within the subconscious. Perhaps *The Beauty and the Beast,* a myth of the reconciliation of two dispositions or the conversion of ugliness into beauty, evokes multiple echoes within many Librans.

Lithograph by Pierre Bonnard. "The Little Laundress" appears to evoke a search for an equilibrium.

THE SOURCES

The Symbolic Image

The sign is represented by the scorpion and also an eagle.

♏ The scorpion is nocturnal; it avoids light and lives in crevices and tunnels, only coming out at night.	♏ Secretive and self-protective, a Scorpio seeks concealment; there is an air of mystery.
♏ The scorpion has a shell.	♏ This is a person interested in self-protection.
♏ With its exceptional capability to endure hunger and external conditions, the scorpion is one of the oldest species on our planet.	♏ A Scorpio is extremely tenacious and is well-prepared for the struggle to survive.
♏ Although the scorpion changes shells, it has survived for centuries without changing its form.	♏ Despite apparent metamorphoses, Scorpios do not change; they always resemble themselves.
♏ The scorpion has a poisonous stinger which inspires fear.	♏ Despite a peaceful appearance, a Scorpio is capable of great aggressiveness. A Scorpio does not seek to please others and may enjoy instilling fear. A Scorpio is not afraid to attack.
♏ If a scorpion is trapped by fire, it is the only animal which can commit suicide.	♏ Death is not alien to Scorpios; it is a natural companion for them.

In Antiquity, the symbol of the eagle was always associated with Scorpio.

♏ The eagle is the king of birds, because it is capable of flying above the clouds as it seeks the Sun.	♏ A Scorpio seeks perfection and has a strong sense of his own worth; a Scorpio disdains mediocrity.
♏ The eagle possesses keen eyesight, permitting him to see his prey.	♏ As an intuitive and lucid person, a Scorpio has confidence in his own judgment.
♏ The eagle has powerful talons.	♏ A Scorpio is tenacious.

November: The Middle of Autumn

♏ The Sun is losing strength rapidly, and the nights become longer than days.	♏ The every-day concerns of the real world are overshadowed by the nocturnal impulses of the unconscious. Scorpios are introverted.
♏ Silence and coldness pervade Nature, which appears motionless. The ice on ponds becomes firm.	♏ A Scorpio is a reserved and silent person who does not seem to be affected by the vicissitudes of life. He remains calm and silent, appearing to be indifferent.
♏ Dead leaves fall from trees and plants, and the bare trunks are visible.	♏ A Scorpio is not attracted by external qualities. He seeks the principle and the essence of everything.
♏ Leaves fall apart on the ground, and an odor of decomposition fills the air.	♏ A Scorpio is oriented toward destruction of that which exists.
♏ At the same time, decaying leaves produce humus, while decaying fruits and hulls provide seeds for the next cycle.	♏ A Scorpio is oriented toward rebirth: he restores, fertilizes, and facilitates.

Fixed Autumn

♏ Midway between the end of Summer and the beginning of Winter when Scorpio reigns, Autumn is at its peak.	♏ A Scorpio is headstrong and decisive, with a good memory.

Scorpio is a fixed sign.

Scorpio
OCTOBER 23 - NOVEMBER 22

"Within you who are also an angel, there lives an insect creating turmoil in your blood."

Dostoevsky

Deep Waters

Among the triplicity of water signs, the fixed water of Scorpio is situated between the cardinal water of Cancer (the original water, the source, expression of feelings) and the mutable water of Pisces (water in its final form, the ocean, spirituality).

The emotions are rapidly absorbed within fixed water (water which "acts"), and then they ferment slowly. The attributes of Scorpio produce a morose and somewhat phlegmatic person.

♏ Externally, the water seems to be the stagnant and murky water of a swamp.	♏ A Scorpio has a calm and impenetrable expression, as well as a voice which seems to come from deep inside.
♏ This seemingly tranquil water conceals an inner turbulence; sometimes it bursts forth like lava from the core of the earth.	♏ Scorpios draw their energy from internal compulsions, seeking to give them a concrete mode of expression.

Pluto and Mars

Scorpio is governed by Pluto, and Mars is another planet which rules this sign.

♏ Pluto, also known as the prince of darkness, governs the kingdom of the dead. To travel there, it is necessary to cross the Styx (abomination), the border of the nether world. Its tributaries are Lethe (forgetfulness), Acheron (misfortune), Cocytus (piercing sounds), and Phlegethon (a river of flame).	♏ A Scorpio has a tendency to see only the hidden side of life. He can easily see through the outer shells of others in order to identify their unexpressed instincts. A Scorpio displays a spellbinding magnetism which may attract and repel at the same time. This is a person who possesses a puzzling charm.
♏ Souls which are crossing the Styx must pay the miserly boatman Charon in order not to wait eternally beside the river forever.	♏ A Scorpio knows the "cost of living" and has strong financial talents.
♏ Not far from Tartarus, there is another river, the river of memory.	♏ A Scorpio possesses a good memory.
♏ When he ascends to our world, Pluto wears a helmet which renders him invisible.	♏ A Scorpio does not reveal his intentions. He is a clever tactician.
♏ Pluto judges the dead, sending souls to the pitch-black depths of Tartarus (Hell) or to the Elysian Fields (the realm of eternal happiness).	♏ Two contradictory forces, death and rebirth, are present. A Scorpio is a person characterized by metamorphoses: the depths of depression can readily be followed by a renewed zest for life.
♏ Because Pluto is aware of the invisible, he judges the dead according to their motivations instead of their actions.	♏ A Scorpio possesses great perspicacity and keen intuitions.
♏ Pluto rarely lets his prey escape: Persephone whom he kidnapped had to spend three months a year in the nether world despite the pleas of Demeter, her mother.	♏ A Scorpio is stubborn and persists to the end. He does not give way or change courses.
♏ Pluto was fearless. During the battle with his father, Saturn, he was the first to disarm his elder.	♏ A Scorpio is brave and combative.
♏ A noted lover, Pluto lustfully pursued the nymphs on Earth (Leucea and Menthea).	♏ A Scorpio possesses powerful sexual instincts and is attracted by innocence.
♏ Mars is the god of war, and his emblems are the lance and the sword.	♏ A Scorpio thrives on strife and does not fear risks.
♏ Mars never favors one city or one party over another: he initiates the battle.	♏ Scorpios are individualistic, and they do not like to follow norms. They also have a tendency to incite discord.
♏ Mars never takes the trouble of going to Olympus to justify his actions.	♏ Seldom affected by others' opinions, a Scorpio sets his own rules.

The Genitals and the Anus

Should it be surprising that the "secret" parts of the body correspond to the Scorpion (an animal whose home is the ground), which is governed by Pluto (the master of the underworld). The genitals and the anus, in this instance, are symbolic points of reference even more than anatomical features:

♏ The genitals represent reproductive capabilities and fertilization.	♏ A Scorpio is dominated by survival instincts: he tends to seek creativity and power.
♏ The anus represents decay and elimination.	♏ A Scorpio is governed by forces associated with death; he tends to be destructive and aggressive.

The genitals and the anus represent two poles, or the instinctive duality of a Scorpio, who is divided between the life-instinct and the death-instinct: Eros and Thanatos. A Scorpio simultaneously seeks creation and destruction and Heaven and Hell.

This ambivalence emerges:
— within the season: decomposition of the natural world in November is the source of the next cycle;
— within the liturgical calendar: All Saints' Day (glorification of spiritual life) is followed by the Day of the Dead;
— within the symbol itself: a scorpion buried in the ground (the secret life of subconscious instincts) and the eagle which ascends into the sky (nobility and an ability to exalt, associated with the transforming capabilities of this sign).

These sources provide the zodiacal formula for Scorpio: an autumnal, fixed, aquatic, Plutonic, and Martian temperament, associated with the genitals and the anus. The formula can be expressed in the following manner:

Ambivalence

The complex character of a Scorpio is derived from coexistence of intense creative and destructive instincts. The dialectic of these two poles produces torment, but also exceptional energy for living.

A Scorpio's physique often reflects ambivalence: although Scorpios do not usually appear to be robust, they possess great strength. Traditionally, the distinctive features of Scorpios embody an association with the eagle: an aquiline nose, an intent and penetrating gaze (which is observable among such Scorpios as Bernadotte, Paganini, Trotsky, Louis Jouvet, Clouzot, and Picasso). Strong physical magnetism is conveyed by this intent gaze, evoking the instinctive strengths associated with the sign.

Rooted in his own temperament, a Scorpio is fiercely individualistic: aggressiveness often produces conflict with the environment. A Scorpio stabilizes himself through contrasts and seeks expression through conflict, using it as a crucible or counterweight. Thus, Martin Luther, a Scorpio, resisted excommunication and began the Reformation by establishing the Lutheran Church. Another Scorpio, Blanqui, opposed capitalism and persevered in organizing the socialist movement, in spite of imprisonment.

DeGaulle, who was a Scorpio, renounced the armistice, refused to surrender, and established the Resistance, leading it in an underground struggle.

A Penetrating Mind

Along with ambivalence, Scorpios are characterized by sharp intuition, keen minds, and lucidity. With a strong sense of cause and effect, they enjoy untangling mysteries, as in the case of Mata Hari.

Attracted by inner depths, a Scorpio readily pursues the other side of reality: the hidden, the invisible, the occult, the mystical (Edgar Allan Poe, Barbey d'Aurevilly, Villiers de l'Isle Adam).

Capable of grasping multiple aspects of an issue, Scorpios possess a talent for observation: thus, Xavier Bichat defined the fundamental differences between animal and plant life.

An aggressive spirit often inspires critical faculties and intellectual rebellion (Camus' *The Rebel,* or Malraux's *The Victors*). The piercing eyes of the eagle strongly reflect a Scorpio's mode of thought.

Love as a Battle

Influenced by the two poles, Life and Death — Eros and Thanatos (Mata Hari) — a Scorpio's love is a passionate and intense form of love, often expressed as conflictive love, where bonds between two lovers are strengthened by the pain which they endure.

Rooted in sexuality, men and women born under this sign readily display their masculinity or feminity. In an extreme form, the Scorpio woman becomes a *femme fatale,* represented by the image of Carmen ("If I love you, watch out!") or by the myth of the vamp in films.

The Scorpio *ideogram* consists of a character whose first stroke is comparable to the scorpion's claws, whereas the final stroke suggests its tail. A scorpion clings with its claws and defends itself by means of its tail which can kill other creatures or even the scorpion itself. The ideogram is also the letter "M," with the last leg becoming an arrow, representing the stinger. The letter "M" represents water, the source of fertilization, and, in this instance, the arrow penetrates the depths. The Scorpio symbol may also express the mystery of redemption through the fecundity of water: death by means of the stinger represents renewal of life through water, resulting in rebirth.

MODES OF EXPRESSION

Scorpio in Literature

Like his protagonist Grigorovitch, whom he described in these terms: "His innate reserve, and his lack of any openness or any trust…" Dostoevsky had an intent, somber, and impenetrable demeanor suggesting the stationary water of Scorpio.

His life embodied the Scorpio cycle of destruction and rebirth. After winning fame with his first book, he was imprisoned and condemned to hang. Then he was pardoned on the eve of his execution and was sent into exile for four years, where he pursued a new career as a writer. He was a compulsive gambler, and, deeply in debt, he wrote *The Gambler* in twenty-nine days. He suffered from epileptic seizures, but he always renewed his strength. In his own words, he had "the energy of a cat." With Dostoevsky, the Scorpio dialectic assumed metaphysical proportions. The titles of his works could constitute a catalogue of Scorpio motifs: *Recollections of the House of the Dead, The Underground, Letter from the Underground, Crime and Punishment, The Demons.*

The scorpion itself appears within his works. In *The Idiot*, it haunts Hippolyte's dreams: "…it was already at the same level as my head, and it even grazed my hair with its tail, which turned and undulated with exceptional dexterity…" The theme of the scorpion also appears in *The Demons* and *The Brothers Karamazov.*

The knife is also present. There is Rogovin's knife in *The Idiot*, or Raskolnikov's hatchet in *Crime and Punishment*, or Troussotsky's razor in *The Eternal Husband.* This "blade" which suddenly emerges from the Dostoevskyan darkness, like a Scorpion's tail beneath the earth, has been a symbol of Martian aggressiveness since Antiquity, evoking the planetary deity Mars, who also rules Scorpio.

Nevertheless, the other pole of Scorpio, which is equally powerful and equally absolute, emerges to confront the "demons:" this is the longing for perfection. In *The Idiot*, Prince Myshkin says: "The essential purpose of my novel is to create an absolutely virtuous man, a Christ." In *Crime and Punishment*, the prostitute Sonia represents love, humility, and innocence. There are also all of the victims of illnesses, who are portrayed "with a compassion which has the intensity of a lifelong endeavor, just as his tendency to be unforgiving has the depth of a compulsion." (Dominique Arban).

The ambivalence of Scorpio is reflected by the presence of two poles: Prince Myshkin and Rogovin in *The Idiot*, or Sonia and Raskolnikov in *Crime and Punishment* — the bearer of the Cross and the bearer of the knife, Good and Evil, joined in a mysterious interweaving of energies.

With Raskolnikov, this ambivalence develops to the level of madness: unlimited pride, fierce individualism, scorn for social norms, and a thirst for power. He is an exaggerated Scorpio. He seeks to be "a strong man," but he travels to the depths of destruction by killing the moneylender. Subsequently, when he must give himself up, he accepts punishment in order to win redemption, guided by

This gigantic head, sculptured by Rodin, seems to reflect the values of a Scorpio: lucidity, thirst for the ideal, and rejection of mediocrity.

Sonia's love: thus, there is a rebirth, or a final renewal of the Scorpionic protagonist.

The duality of Scorpio is clearly revealed in *The Double:* "In all of my works, I have never pursued anything more important than this idea."

The recognizably somber and introverted image of a Scorpio personality evoked by Dostoevsky can be counterbalanced by those of Malraux and Camus, two Scorpios who, although they began with the same instinctive duality, respectively chose an epic mode of expression *(The Royal Road, The Human Condition, Hope)* and a quest for lucidity *(The Stranger, Sisyphus).*

Scorpio in Art

Picasso was "small, dark, energetic, restless, and disquieting, with deep, dark, piercing, and almost unmoving eyes" (Fernand Olivier). He possessed the magnetism of a Scorpio to the highest degree. He delighted in surprising and agitating others, but he remained unfathomable. Thus, there is "the Picasso mystery," which another noted Scorpio, G.H. Clouzot, sought to uncover.

Beneath their masks, Scorpios promote their own legends in order to acquire greater glory; they seek to be solitary eagles. Thus, Apollinaire wrote: "Picasso is one of those whom Michelangelo said should be called eagles because they surpass everyone else."

Picasso's initial objective was to demolish all prior forms of painting. He challenged all of the techniques of traditional portraiture, one after another. He did not hesitate to confront the most renowned works: Velasquez's *Las Meninas,* Manet's *Déjeuner sur l'herbe,* or Delacroix's *Femmes d'Alger.* Picasso seized these works …to transform them into his own creations: with the stubborn individualism of a Scorpio, he refused to adhere to predetermined rules and he defied norms, remaining loyal only to himself. This destructive power, however, reflects the energy of life at the same time: after demolishing everything, Picasso started with nothing, like Nature itself during the month of November, and, through his own efforts, he built the foundations of modern painting — introducing various forms of Cubism, use of collages and the use of print. It was "our era's most ambitious attempt to destroy and to create forms," (A. Malraux).

The pattern of destruction and creation set the rhythm of his work: Picasso ceaselessly changed techniques and renewed himself from one phase to the next (blue, pink, black hues). "He was a phoenix who constantly set himself on fire for the endless pleasure of arising from his own ashes," (René Huyghe). Nevertheless, through his series of metamorphoses and rebirths, Picasso always remained true to himself.

The source of his creativity was not the desire to possess (associated with Taurus), but the life-giving power of sexuality (associated with Scorpio). A perpetual creative eroticism produced the most important work in the history of painting: "there are paintings which become children," or "it is necessary for Nature to exist in order that we may defile it." This intense sexuality is also expressed by the centaurs, fauns, and satyrs which abound in Picasso's paintings.

His style reflects the ambivalence attributed to Scorpio: on one hand, he is a compassionate painter, *(Fillette aux pieds nus, Mère et Enfant au fichu, Le Vieux Guitariste)* and on the other, he is a remorseless painter who distorts bodies and twists faces *(Femmes en pleurs; l'Homme à la sucette).* Although Picasso was a relentless caricaturist, the purpose was not scorn: for him, caricatures were a means of expressing warmth, thereby revealing a Scorpio's relationship with the world. He painted both *The Dove* and *Guernica,* expressing the opposite forces contending within and the source of his creativity.

In sculpture, Rodin also represents the creative powers associated with Scorpio ("A genius is a creator of standards who does something new with Nature"). His work is a physical expression of the inner world of this sign.

Scorpio in Music

Carmen, the fatally alluring Carmen, is the heroine of Bizet's masterpiece, an opera of love and death. Bizet dramatized the two poles of a Scorpio's world, and Carmen represents the principal traits.

"Turmoil takes root deep within the heart.." (Goethe, "Faust"). Engraving by Peter Cornelius.

Possessing the power to attract men, she quickly captivates Don Jose, but her love for him also leads to destruction: she transforms him into a smuggler and a murderer. Carmen the gypsy has a deep loyalty to herself, which she cannot betray: as soon as she loses interest in her lover, she prefers to die instead of remaining with him. She defies him, and he stabs her, but she is not afraid to die.

The compositions of Borodine, who was also a Scorpio, evoke the atmosphere and landscapes of November. For example, there is *In the Steppes of Central Asia.* On the other hand, with Paganini, the individual himself existed as "the Scorpio virtuoso." No other violinist seduced his audiences to such an extent. Paganini exercised a true power of fascination, and his unsettling music mesmerized listeners. He said, "It is actually the Devil who guides my hand." His extraordinary talents appeared to spring from his deepest instincts. Posters for his concerts portrayed him as an alchemist, or as a phantom: he had a deep need to shroud himself in mystery.

Correlations between Taurus and Scorpio

Like other signs situated in a 180° relationship, Taurus and Scorpio, which face one another within the zodiacal circle, are complementary. Both are stationary signs, representing "fulfillment" of a season, and both are inspired by stubbornness and strength whereby:

♉ Earth, as the element associated with Taurus, is used for concrete and tangible accomplishments in life.	♏ Water, as the element associated with Scorpio, is used to express psychic attributes through a journey from the subsconscious to the realm of consciousness.

The forces of destruction and rebirth symbolized by the anus and the genitals in Scorpio correspond to the possessive drives symbolized by the mouth and the throat in Taurus:

♉ The Earth, along with Cybele and Demeter, give Taurus confidence in his empirical perspective.	♏ Water and Pluto endow a Scorpio with intuition, producing insightful subtleties.

These forms of energy are complementary and are essential within the life-cycle: the confidence of Taurus inspires and intensifies the doubts of Scorpio.

Beyond physiognomy and external manifestations of tendencies, which myth can permit us to enter the world of Scorpio? Is it not *Faust,* "between God and the Devil," where the protagonist exalts the perverse and perverts the sublime? Can Faust be an absolute representation of the Scorpio dialectic? Driven by a need for power and attracted by the goal of knowledge, Faust is torn between Mephistopheles, who seeks to reduce him to bestiality, and God, who gives him a means of gaining salvation.

Pluto and Proserpine, masters of hell. Ruler of Scorpio, Pluto is being encouraged to look at the face hidden by life.

Sagittarius

NOVEMBER 22 - DECEMBER 20

"We are born, so to speak, in a temporary form somewhere, and then, bit by bit, we create our birthplaces within us, in order to be reborn there each day, in a more definitive way."

Rilke, *Letters from Milan*, January 23, 1923

THE SOURCES

The Symbolic Image

↙ The symbol is represented by a centaur — half man and half horse.	↙ A Sagittarius is both instinctive and logical.
↙ This image is unique among the signs.	↙ A Sagittarius is independent.
↙ The centaur is bending a bow.	↙ He gains control of his own energies.
↙ The arrow is aimed toward the sky.	↙ He has vast ambitions and is adventuresome.
↙ The arrow is guided by the human half and propelled by brute strength.	↙ A Sagittarius views reality on a human scale and possesses great energy for communicating his perceptions. He seeks to excel.

November: The End of Autumn

↙ The Sun is descending further below the horizon. The leaves have fallen. The landscape does not clearly separate the sky and the earth. Quietness predominates.	↙ Sagittarians seek harmony, and reconciling aspirations with reality. They have a great capacity for awareness.
↙ In November, people prepare for the coldness of Winter.	↙ Sagittarians are contemplative, often philosophers.

Autumn in Transition

↙ Autumn is ending, and Winter is approaching. This is a period of transition.	↙ A Sagittarian wants action and transformation. He seeks to change things.
Sagittarius is a mutable sign.	

Spiritual Fire

Fire, the element of intense energy, dynamism, and change, is the element associated with Sagittarius. It is specifically represented by the position of Sagittarius within the zodiacal cycle: among the triplicity of fire signs, the mutable fire of Sagittarius, where a person enthusiastically converts his feelings into action, is situated between the cardinal fire of Aries (the spark of life) and the fixed fire of Leo (the flame of the ego). These factors produce a passionate, cheerful, and active person.

↙ The fire of Sagittarius is fire beneath the ashes: a red-hot ember which is not extinguished.	↙ Sagittarians are motivated by a constantly keen awareness which is always being renewed by an inner fire, or by the intellect.
↙ A blast of air can transform the ember into a flame.	↙ This is an enthusiastic person who may sometimes go to extremes.

Zeus-Jupiter

Sagittarius is governed by Zeus, or Jupiter.

↙ Zeus, or Jupiter, the ruler of Olympus, is the god of light, clear skies, and thunder. He dispenses good and evil, as well as administering the earth and the heavens. He governs the stars and everything on earth, appointing oracles and establishing laws. With his thunderbolt, he makes justice prevail.	↙ A Sagittarian seeks truth everywhere. He seeks to attain equilibrium, orderly progress, and abundance. He upholds hierarchies and possesses a sense of order.
↙ Although his father, Chronos (Saturn), devoured his offspring at birth, Zeus escaped the fate of his siblings, through the efforts of his mother, Rhea. To save her son, Rhea gave Saturn a	↙ With a sense of good fortune, a Sagittarian feels protected against adversities. He seeks to uphold fairness: he is confident and optimistic.

stone wrapped in swaddling clothes, and, believing that this was his son, he devoured the stone.

✓ Zeus was entrusted to the nymphs, who fed him milk and honey.	✓ Sagittarians like to develop their personalities in contact with pure ideas and gentle sentiments. They are not capable of bitterness.
✓ When he became an adult, Zeus decided to usurp Chronos' power, but he sought the advice of Methys (Prudence) beforehand. She gave Zeus a drug which he used to make Chronos disgorge all of his children (his suppressed desires) whom he had swallowed.	✓ A Sagittarian knows that he possesses a certain charm, but he uses it wisely to obtain favors. In winning power, his aim is to use it for enabling others to pursue their own wishes. A Sagittarian seeks to reconcile order and liberty.
✓ After a long battle, known as the Battle of the Titans, Zeus, with the help of the Cyclops (the forces of instinct and passion) whom he had freed from Tartarus, defeated Chronos and the Titans (ambition and the thirst for power). Then he expelled them from the heavens.	✓ He does not seek to gain power to satisfy his own ambitions (expulsion of the Titans). Instead, his efforts represent sublimation of instincts. A Sagittarian seeks greater justice and does not make concessions to mediocrity. A Sagittarian has a very favorable image of humanity.
✓ The giants were displeased, and, with the intention of avenging the Titans, they attacked Zeus. This struggle was known as the Battle of the Giants.	✓ A Sagittarian's intentions may outdistance his capabilities.
✓ To win this battle, Zeus had to seek the aid of a mortal, Hercules.	✓ In fact, ideals alone do not suffice: accomplishments are attained by an individual as a whole. A Sagittarian tends to unify his different tendencies: his purposes are both earthly and spiritual.
✓ The most difficult struggle was against Typhon, "the scourge of mortals," a partially human and partially animal creature. This monster symbolized the power of instincts at odds with wisdom.	✓ Nevertheless, it is difficult to overcome instincts (Typhon). Under the pressure of immediate needs, a Sagittarian may forget his aspirations for wisdom and become impatient.
✓ Zeus had many amorous conquests. Among them, it is possible to cite Themis, the goddess of laws. Their children were the "Hours": Discipline, Justice, and Peace, which ensure the survival of society, along with the *Moirae,* or the Fates, who represent destiny.	✓ A Sagittarian seeks order and discipline for maintaining social structures. Nevertheless, a monopoly on authority may make him a prisoner of his duties. Then he becomes a slave of himself through the destiny which he has pursued (the Fates).
✓ As the guardian of thunder, Zeus punished other gods or mortals who did not fulfill their duties.	✓ With knightly ideals, a Sagittarian takes action against all forms of injustice.

The Hips and the Thighs

✓ The parts of the body corresponding to Sagittarius are the hips and the thighs, which permit movement and facilitate access and contact.	✓ A Sagittarian is interested in social values: he seeks to be helpful to others.
✓ Together with the legs, the hips permit a person to run.	✓ Sagittarians are also associated with an active temperament. They are full of vim and vigor.

These sources provide the zodiacal formula for Sagittarius: an autumnal, mutable, fiery, and Jovian temperament, associated with the hips and the thighs. These symbolic tendencies may emerge in the following manner:

The Spirit of a Wise Man or an Adventurer
On the basis of information obtained from the rest of the individual's horoscope, we encounter a disposition which can be oriented toward either conformity or rebellion. Depending upon his temperament, a Sagittarian seeks to pursue the truth contained within his own soul. As a philosopher, priest, statesman, or businessman, he seeks to follow laws which he considers universal. During her reign, Catherine of Sweden, daughter of Gustavus Adolphus, flouted the conventions and rules defined by her role and rank. Freedom, or, more specifically, her own freedom had to prevail. Thus, when she was twenty-eight years old, she abdicated, in order "to be able to do that which seemed just." The Sagittarian family includes many adventurers, such as the famous pirate Surcouf, or Mermoz, the famous aviator, and these Sagittarians have travelled toward remote

horizons. The shadow of Nero is also situated within this sign: under the influence of specific planetary configurations, he inverted its attributes by directing the arrow of the ideal against his own personal aspirations. A Sagittarian seeks to arrive at a synthesis between the exalted nature of his ideals and the intensity of his energy, attempting to avoid excesses in one direction or another.

Universal Thought
When Zamenhof created Esperanto, a language which can be spoken by all of Europe's inhabitants, was it not his intention to permit communication among the greatest possible number of people, so that linguistic divisions would disappear? A Sagittarius attempts to grasp the world and reality by developing a broad overview, in order to express universal forms of thought which everyone can understand. As Rainer Maria Rilke wrote, "My true task is to see this world, not as a man, but as an angel." A Sagittarius is inclined toward lucid thought, which simultaneously encompasses Man's desires and his "celestial" aspirations. He seeks to establish a hierarchy of values which shall be universally acceptable. Thus, even though his ideas reflect human values, a Sagittarian may also be an extremely independent thinker. This factor can produce ambivalence. The Sagittarian mode of thought can be represented by a flash of lightning.

Fervent Love
Sensitive and idealistic, a Sagittarian hopes for a lover who embodies everything which he seeks in the skies. Thus, he may violate the laws of his social milieu and break ties with the group to which he belongs. It is difficult for him to maintain his perspicacity, so as to avoid confusing dreams with reality. The Sagittarian seeks absolute and eternal love, with an inextinguishable fervor. Like Alfred de Musset enamored of George Sand, he may seek exaltation for his loved one. Because a Sagittarius personifies ideals through his beloved, it may be difficult for him to accept reality and understand that he has envisioned qualities which are not present. There is also another type of Sagittarian who is no less fervent in love: he allows his beloved to be a guardian of his ideals. In both instances, love represents a means of striving to outdo oneself.

The Sagittarian *ideogram* is represented by an arrow, the symbol of speed, accuracy, and assurance: the arrow does not stray from its path, and it travels directly to the target. This is an arrow which joins the terrestrial and the celestial; it passes through "Space/Time," and expresses the breadth of a Sagittarian's ideas and personality.

Sagittarius is ruled by Jupiter, the god of light, clear skies, and thunder.

MODES OF EXPRESSION

Sagittarius in Literature

Gustave Flaubert, who described illusions so realistically, was a Sagittarian. "I am a barbarian...I possess...that kind of energy, obstinacy, and irascibility." Flaubert did not orient all of his energy toward the Romantic ideal; to the contrary, he portrayed the dangerous illusions engendered by Romanticism. Encountering a crisis of values, he sought to transform the novel into a pinnacle of Art, because he perceived Art as the only means for mankind to gain awareness and pursue excellence: "It is the only thing which does not deceive."

Thus, it was necessary for Art to be true and beautiful...as true as a scientific approach would be. The artist's duty was to disappear beneath reality, in order to communicate truth, instead of his own feelings. "In his creations, an author should be like God within the universe — present everywhere, but not visible anywhere," he wrote, in a letter to Louise Colet. Flaubert sought to create beauty through precise descriptions of his characters' attributes, because beauty alone conveys the universal language which can permit mankind to attain the absolute.

Driven by an inner fire which endowed with a legendary vitality and boldness, Flaubert spent six years writing *Madame Bovary,* while *Salammbô* required another five years. In seeking the true and the beautiful, he aimed his arrow toward the absolute. He wrote and rewrote individual sentences in order to attain perfection. With an individualistic outlook and style, he created a synthesis between the Romantic style and the Classical perspective. In pursuit of freedom, he disdained the admitted or concealed dependence of the bourgeoisie upon money, which prevented them from recognizing the role which human beings should develop. Artists and thinkers, the only persons seeking knowledge, had a duty, namely the duty of demonstrating the truth to mankind, in order to permit transformation of the hierarchy of values: "Is it not time for the concept of justice to be introduced into the Art? Then the impartiality of painting would attain the majesty of laws and the precision of science." For Flaubert, the novel itself was Jupiter's thunderbolt: by showing readers their true nature, he sought to convince them to change:

"Oh, I love the sea," said Monsieur Léon.

"And doesn't it seem to you," Madame Bovary replied, "that the soul wanders more freely on this unlimited expanse which elevates the soul and conveys ideas of the infinite and the ideal when one contemplates it?"

In *Madame Bovary,* Flaubert challenged these Romantic aspirations which he understood so well; he sought to show how harmful these illusions could be. Mme. Bovary, who perceived herself as the heroine of a novel, committed suicide because she could not face unpleasant realities. In this novel, Flaubert sought to instill an awareness of the dangers of poetic illusions for "ordinary souls." It is only possible to achieve greatness if a person's strength of will and energies are compatible with his aspirations.

Sagittarius in Art

Does a Sagittarius look at the world from another planet, or is he inviting us to discover a new world which, even though it belongs to us, he was the only person who understood it? Paul Klee was obliged to invent a new figurative language to express his perceptions: "Art does not reproduce the visible; it makes things visible." His script consisted of points, but also of lines extending into space: "the line is the source of all forms," he affirmed. In most of Klee's paintings, we encounter arrows, Sagittarian symbols, extending through the universe which he attempts to reveal to us.

The relationship between his personality and the world outdistanced visible reality, and, in order to draw us into Klee's domain, each painting is an image encapsulating a series of correlations. His thought bridges space and time, and his art evokes future horizons, modifying perceptions, penetrating transparent surfaces, and revealing fundamental formulas concealed from us by external appearances. Through signs and hieroglyphs, Klee distills his own intuitions about the world and permits us to rise to a higher level of awareness. "We learn the pre-history of the visible, but this is not yet art of a higher level. The mysterious begins at the higher level."

"I do not seek rest from my great duty, which is to show eternal worlds, and open Man's immortal eyes to worlds of poetry which capture eternity, always placing human imagination within the bosom of the divine." Like his poems, the engravings and paintings of the Sagittarius, William Blake must be "seen and heard."

During his youth, Blake believed that he was different from others; he perceived the invisible, and saw the impenetrable... He was often considered insane — "Mad Blake" — when he sought to express his visions. Unaffected by the scorn of his peers, he set out to "reproduce" the universe which was accessible to him.

"I entered this world hidden within a cloud," he said. His works portray the mysteries of death and the after-life, along with the forces of Good and Evil which he sought to transcend by expressing their essence. Blake rose above the terrestrial world, seeking "the marriage of Heaven and Earth," or the mingling of Man's energies.

Later, when he engraved the plates for "Blair's Tomb," Blake, instead of presenting a sad and macabre image of death, portrayed a serene and tranquil stage in the mystical journey of the human soul. Had "Mad Blake" achieved harmony between Heaven and Earth?

A Sagittarian often portrays a world which he himself cannot experience. Toulouse-Lautrec, whose growth was stunted by two childhood illnesses, retained the body of a child and was unable to participate in any sport; he was a dwarf and, in addition, was afflicted with a grotesque appearance. Nevertheless, he devoted all of his energy to portraying movements and rhythms which he could not experience. He painted legs which kick, run, and dance — the legs of acrobats, cyclists, jockeys, and dancers. Toulouse-Lautrec appears to have provided a marvelous iconography of the Sagittarian symbolic milieu: speed, the pursuit of something greater, with the hips or the legs as the source of energy.

Nevertheless, it is necessary to ask a painful question: was it not primarily on account of his affliction that he portrayed long and

As a Sagittarius, Blake sought to rise above the Earth, as shown within this painting, where God is creating the world ("The Ancient of Days").

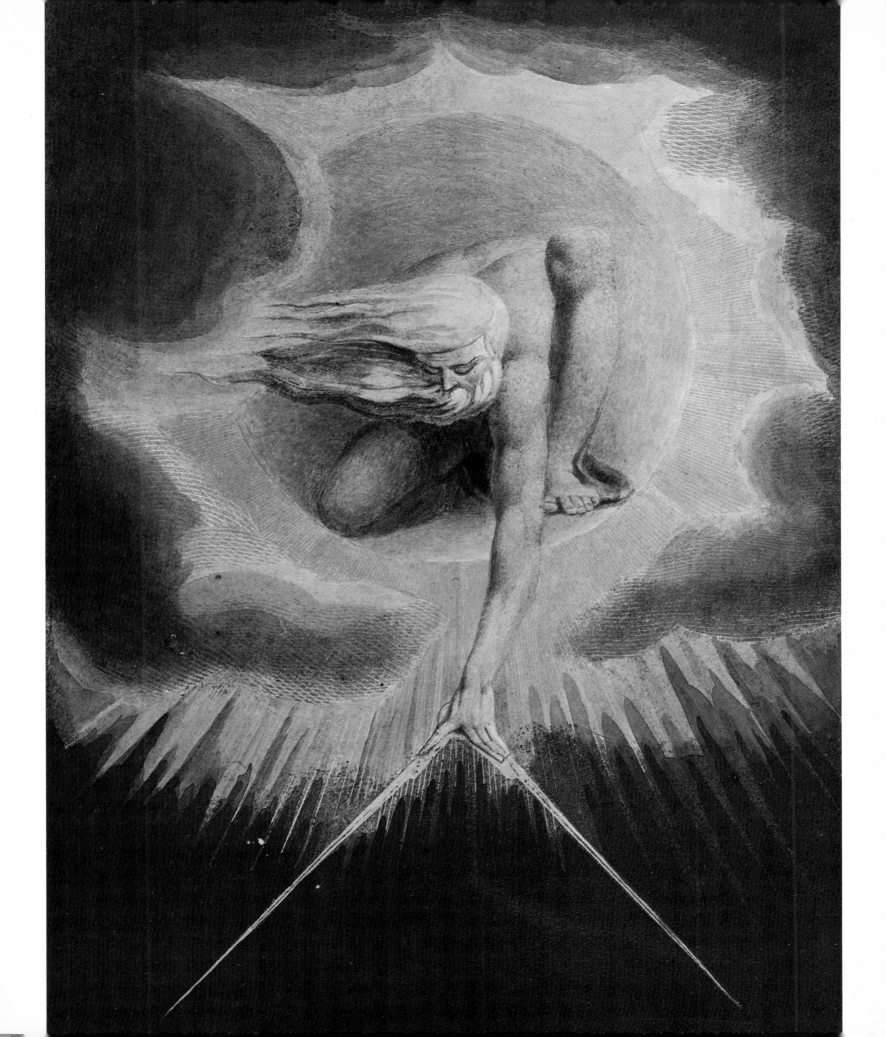

slender legs in muscular configurations which he could not achieve? It is difficult to affirm that his choice of subjects was influenced solely by his having been born under Sagittarius. In the end, it is necessary to ask how an artist with the same physical afflictions but with a different birth sign would have portrayed a world which was inaccessible to him. How would a Leo, a Capricorn, or a Scorpio have responded to similar conditions?

The Sagittarian talent is expressed to a much greater extent by his devoting energy to expressing that which he imagined and to outdoing himself in painting movements which were beyond his own capabilities, in order to attain inner harmony. Although his choice of subjects was influenced by his physical afflictions (it is also possible to ask why the legs, instead of some other part of the body, acquire such importance), his symbolic inclinations provided energy for selecting subjects and a style for portraying them. Toulouse-Lautrec was fascinated with lines because only lines are capable of expressing the vigor, the strength, and the energy of the horse which is present within a Sagittarian's world.

Sagittarius in Music

As the conqueror of the musical Olympus of the nineteenth century, Beethoven strongly influenced many later composers, even though some schools of criticism only recognize the excesses of Romanticism which his music reflected. His era was one where life was expected to resemble a novel, which the protagonist seeking to transcend life in search of the inaccessible and the mysterious. In spite of the fame which he earned, Beethoven did not need to envision a tragedy wherein he would be the protagonist. The stage had already been set: aside from impossible love relationships and insuperable family difficulties, Beethoven, at thirty years of age, became deaf. There was only one set of alternatives: either to forfeit his career, or to strive to excel. "For men who are more than ordinary men, strength is morality, and it is also my morality," he affirmed.

Immersed in contradictions, Beethoven was both a favorite of rulers and an opponent of submission to their power within our world: he praised moral rectitude and, at the same time, he showed no scruples in dealing with different publishers to whom he gave exclusive rights for a particular composition. Beethoven poured all of his energy into music, seeking to transcend his environment. For him, art was the means of winning the greatest victories against himself. Although he could no longer hear physical sounds, he listened even more closely to the echoes of his soul, which guided him to the path of spirituality. Thus, his spirit pursued a titanic struggle against physical reality: "I seek to forge a new path."

Imbued with lofty humanitarian ideals, he believed that his music accompanied the birth of a new era where privileges would be abolished. He became fascinated with Bonaparte, perceiving him as a champion of liberty, and dedicated the *Third Symphony* to him, until he discovered that his idol had been crowned as an emperor. Then he burst into violent rage and denounced Bonaparte for "trampling the rights of Man by only serving his own ambition to place himself above others." Beethoven tore out the dedicatory page of his completed work and renamed it "The Heroic Symphony."

Throughout his life, Beethoven overcame an array of disillusionments and obstacles (financial and amorous) cluttering the path to greatness which he had charted for himself: "Courage! Despite all of the betrayals of my body, my genius must triumph. It is necessary for this year to reveal a man who is satisfied and who has nothing more to do." It is difficult to determine whether his compositions express superhuman qualities which he sought to demonstrate, or the problems of being too human.

The Sagittarian Manuel de Falla directed all of his energy toward achieving a universal dimension in his work, drawn from Spanish sources. "Falla's entire being comes into play amidst the temperament of a reserved and silent child who is slightly mischievous and sometimes detached from reality."[1] During his childhood, Falla withdrew to his bedroom for hours at a time to create a personal universe which he called "Columbus." It is possible that, during this period, he formulated the new language which he sought to disseminate throughout the world. Falla hoped to develop opera in Spain, so that its art could travel beyond borders, instead of being confined to the Iberian Peninsula. He accomplished this goal with *La Vida Breve,* which expresses the quintessence of Spanish music and folk songs, but Falla's genius inspired even more ambitious creations which go beyond national themes. Falla led an extremely ascetic life, only permitting his inner fire to be expressed by such works as *El Amor brujo* and *The Three-Cornered Hat,* which radiate his fervent temperament and his inner warmth. "In Art, there is something far beyond public applause:" his bow was pointed toward the sky. Falla gradually withdrew from daily life to listen to the echoes of a mystical world which he sought to recreate for mankind. His lyricism burst forth *(El Concerto),* and developed a style embodying "abstract purity."

Falla spent the final years of his life in exile in Argentina, and, when it was suggested that he collect his royalties, he refused: "so long as other Spanish artists who chose exile as I did are not receiving their royalties."

In Argentina, he devoted his time to the *Atlántida,* which he regarded as his masterpiece. He spent seventeen years perfecting it, as if he could only finish it by reaching the lost continent. Falla died without having achieved his goal, and, although the *Atlántida* was finished by another author, it did not receive the acclaim which had been sought. Nevertheless, is it not true that the inscription which Falla chose for his grave reads "Honor and glory belong only to God?"

Correlations between Gemini and Sagittarius

As opposites within the zodiacal circle, Gemini and Sagittarius encompass complementary symbolic aspects.

Both are mutable, because they represent the end of a season and prepare the advent of a new season. Thus, there is a desire for change which:

♊ The air of Gemini is expressed in the form of multiple interchanges.	♐ The fire of Sagittarius is spread through passions and ideals.

1. Luis Campodicino, *Falla,* Seuil.

The qualities of life and inspiration which the lungs symbolize for Gemini can be compared with the aspects of social activity symbolized by the hips and the thighs for Sagittarius:

Ⅱ Air and Mercury inspire a Gemini to seek proliferation and diversity of ideas, or duality.

♐ Fire and Jupiter draw a Sagittarian toward hierarchies of values, as well as order and justice.

These attitudes are complementary and fundamental within the life cycle: the duality of Gemini is counterbalanced by the Sagittarian desire for unification.

Is it not true that a *guru* attempts to resolve the duality existing between Man and his environment, or between Man and God? Indeed, the *guru* may incarnate the symbolic goal of the Sagittarian psyche: to achieve harmony with the celestial and the terrestrial.

"Let us breathe the air of heroism---" ("Beethoven," Romain Rolland).
Portrait of Beethoven by Levy Dhurmer and excerpt from one of the great composer's scores.

Capricorn

DECEMBER 21 - JANUARY 19

"When one has arrived at certainty, he experiences one of the greatest joys which the human heart can feel."

Louis Pasteur, *Dedication Speech for the Institute,* November, 1888

THE SOURCES

The Symbolic Image

♑ A mountain goat is a horned animal.	♑ Capricornians are strong-willed, and know how to defend themselves.
♑ He lives amidst steep cliffs.	♑ A Capricornian confronts life's hardships.
♑ The mountain goat often leads a solitary life.	♑ He tends to be independent.
♑ He can easily climb the north side of a mountain.	♑ He does not take the easiest path, because he is not deterred by the impossible. He seeks to withstand difficulties.
♑ He climbs toward the peaks.	♑ He seeks to reach heights in life, and is a proud person.
♑ Always wary, he flees as soon as humans come near.	♑ Possessing keen awareness and reluctant to share secrets with anyone, Capricornians are difficult to understand.

December: The Beginning of the Winter

♑ The Sun is at its lowest point in the sky. The Winter Solstice takes place.	♑ A Capricornian is detached from the world, and seems to lack self-interest.
♑ Nights are longer, and days are shorter.	♑ He seeks solitude and security in order to attain the deepest level of concentration. He is extremely conscious of time.
♑ The ground seems exceptionally barren, but, beneath the surface, it is being prepared for planting of seeds.	♑ He uses his awareness of time to pursue his own aims.
♑ Temperatures drop, and it becomes extremely cold.	♑ Capricornians seem cold and unemotional. Their feelings are internalized.
♑ The trees merely seem to be dark skeletons.	♑ Often melancholy and sometimes somber, a Capricornian remains loyal to principles which have been tested.
♑ Animals hibernate, deep within their burrows.	♑ Capricornians are anxiety-prone, but realistic, and their foresight aids their survival.

Cardinal Winter

♑ Autumn is ending, and Winter is beginning.	♑ This is a sign representing a quest for greater awareness.
Capricorn is a cardinal sign.	

The Earth: Crystallization of Awareness

Capricorn marks the beginning of the zodiacal cycle for the Earth. It represents cardinal earth, where seeds lie buried — the seeds of awareness. Afterwards, there is the fixed earth of Taurus, namely the bountiful earth, embodying concrete realities, followed by the mutable earth of Virgo, or the earth as a source of purification or reason. Within cardinal earth, it is difficult for feelings to penetrate the conscience, but, when they do so, their effects are subterranean. A Capricorn has a silent demeanor and a calm voice. His words appear to be carefully measured: "Silence is golden, and words are of silver" would be an appropriate motto. This type of person tends to possess a wiry physique and to be somewhat unemotional.

♑ During Winter, the earth contains new seeds.	♑ A Capricornian possesses a sense of destiny, and feels that he is the only one capable of fulfilling his destiny.
♑ The earth initiates a slow process of growth.	♑ With little patience for uncertainties, a Capricornian erects a world where he can be sure of things. His friendships develop over long periods of time, and his plans are the result of protracted contemplation.
♑ The earth is hard and cold.	♑ This is a person who protects himself from futile distractions. He also protects himself from his passions and instincts.

Saturn: The Ruling Planet

Capricorn is ruled by Saturn, the most remote of the seven visible planets. When Uranus was discovered during the nineteenth century, it was recognized as another planet which rules Capricorn.

♑ Saturn overthrew his father Uranus by castrating him. Saturn was aided by his brothers the Titans (symbols of ambition and mental domination).	♑ Capricornians may allow their ambitions to take priority over feelings. With "their passions under control," they seek to define goals intellectually.
♑ He castrated his father with a weapon given to him by Rhea, his mother: it was a sickle made of flint (the blade of time).	♑ Knowing that time is on their side, Capricornians are persistent.
♑ When Saturn became king, he expelled the Cyclops (dark and instinctive forces), who could have been his rivals. He sent them to the depths of Tartarus (as his father, Uranus, had also done).	♑ Self-respect also requires careful choice of companions. A Capricornian demands as much of himself as he does of others. He can lack compassion for those who show weaknesses.
♑ When Uranus was dying, he predicted that Saturn would be overthrown by one of his children. Thus, Saturn devoured his children as soon as they were born.	♑ Capricornians are capable of foregoing the joys and pleasures which enhance life. They are capable of enduring self-restraint and austerity for long-term goals.
♑ In fact, Jupiter, one of Saturn's children who was rescued by Rhea, made him disgorge all of the others: Pluto, Neptune, Juno…	♑ They believe that, at some point, the plans which they have pursued will be fulfilled. Capricornians are secretive persons who only reveal their aims at the propitious time.
♑ Jupiter exiled Saturn to Italy, where Janus gave him a home. There, he introduced such widespread prosperity that his reign was remembered as "the Golden Age." The Romans celebrated this era each year at the end of December, with a festival known as "Saturnalia."	♑ External ambition is only one way of pursuing true wisdom: this is a Capricornian's secret knowledge. When a Capricornian has fulfilled his intentions, he is willing to share the spiritual and material fruits of his hardships. He can exercise a strong civilizing influence.

After Uranus was discovered, it was regarded as the second planet which rules Capricorn. Indeed, it is closely associated with the symbolic context of this sign:

♑ Uranus, the God of the Heavens, expresses the exalted awareness which Saturn seeks to acquire with his sickle (time). By dethroning Uranus, Saturn only displays an apparent thirst for power: he is actually seeking supreme awareness or control over his own fate, which he does not wish to entrust to anyone. When this goal is attained, the sickle acquires a new meaning: in addition to being a weapon for combatting time, it becomes a means of gaining benefits in the long run (a sickle is used to cut wheat).	♑ Behind his desire for prestige and power, there is the growth of awareness which the Capricornian seeks to promote, because external power is only a means of obtaining internal power and because obstacles and difficulties in life only represent a way of gaining greater self-control. A Capricornian weighs his motives carefully before expressing himself and before sharing his knowledge.

Perhaps a Capricornian's ethics can be summarized as follows: supreme awareness is only valuable when it can offer benefits for others.

The Bones, Skeleton, and Joints

The bones, skeleton, and joints are the parts of the body associated with Capricorn:

♑ Bones provide the basic structure of the body.	♑ Capricornians admire fortitude, endurance, and strength.
♑ The skeleton is the simplest expression of our anatomy.	♑ Simplicity and reducing things to the essential are combined with these values: Capricornians tend to be ascetic.
♑ With its "ironic smile," the skeleton symbolizes the knowledge of someone who has crossed the threshold of the unknown.	♑ Representing the benefits of knowledge, Capricornians are often encyclopedists.
♑ Lastly, the joints allow us to move and to initiate actions.	♑ Capricornians also include activity, work, and expression among their aims.

These sources provide the zodiacal formula for Capricorn: a wintry, cardinal, earthly, saturnine, and uranian disposition, associated with the skeleton, bones, and joints. These attributes can be more fully explained in the following form:

A Mountaineer's Temperament

His life embodies a struggle to ascend: Maurice Herzog, who climbed Annapurna, was a Capricornian who concretely expressed this feature — "to excel oneself in mountain-climbing." Konrad Adenauer was another Capricornian who steadily and courageously climbed from one level to another: he pursued his course inflexibly, without heeding criticism. Mao Tse-Tung, another Capricornian, tenaciously pursued a "long march" throughout his life.

An Encyclopedic Mind

Many scientists, particularly astronomers, have been born under Capricorn: Kepler, Newton, Tycho Brahe, as well as Louis Pasteur and Benjamin Franklin. Nevertheless, it would be somewhat inappropriate to conclude that a Capricornian passport is needed to become a scientist, because not all Capricornians have pursued this path. It can be recognized, however, that the tendencies associated with this sign produce a hunger for knowledge so that many of its natives become specialists.

A Capricornian's mode of thought can be symbolized by an encyclopedia.

A Tamed Heart

"Hidden suffering snows upon my heart," wrote the poet Henri de Regnier. A Capricornian's heart is constant, but difficulty in expressing feelings may lead to melancholy. There is a quest for perfection in loved ones, and a fear of not finding the desired qualities. Thus, a Capricornian controls his feelings or sometimes lets them flow, either charming or frightening his beloved. Love is regarded as a sacrament involving purity and conscience. Thus, Saint Therese de Lisieux and Joan of Arc sought marriage to God.

The Capricorn *ideogram* is a stroke which retrocedes toward itself, expressing the path of the conscious mind as it seeks to attain the infinite depths of the inner self. This is a convoluted graphic expression, evoking the tortuous self-scrutiny which Capricornians undergo: it is a symbol of introversion.

Capricorn is ruled by Saturn, the symbol of the intellect.

MODES OF EXPRESSION

Capricorn in Literature

"Lofty ambitions," "Faraway Dates," "The Respectable Robins," "The Fear of Love," "The Monk's Cell" — these were chapter headings chosen by the Capricornian Saint-Simon, who observed the court of Louis XIV and the Regency for thirty-two years (1691-1723). His *Memoirs* constitute a veritable encyclopedia of the customs of his era. Saint-Simon can be accused of a lack of impartiality, inasmuch as he sought to record history instead of producing literature. Moreover, he did not care for writers, "these begetters of books," because he prized truth above all: he sought to discern the hidden motives for individuals' actions, in relation to events. In order to convey a fuller understanding of the psychological traits of those whom he observed, he frequently departed from factual accuracy. Yet he did not overlook any significant details, and sometimes added details which he considered useful for describing inner qualities. Saint-Simon was a man of ideas: "My deepest and dearest passion is my dignity and my station." He detested the "appointed nobility," courtiers who comprised the lower echelons of Louis XIV's court. He only respected the hereditary nobility, which had not usurped its titles or its position.

Capricorn in Art

To be an artist, to paint — does not mean expressing the world as one perceives it? How does an artist born between December and January symbolize his own way of perceiving and experiencing Nature? How does he approach his environment in order to understand it and in order to be understood through his work?

In December, Nature is reduced to its simplest forms, and the Capricornian Cézanne, unlike his predecessors, did not seek to interpret Nature subjectively. Instead, he always sought to portray Nature according to the simplest levels of reality. He broke with the Impressionists, who, in his eyes, merely expressed confused feelings instead of creating works of art. Nevertheless, every work requires structure: even if one depicts Nature, it is necessary to reconstruct the order of the universe. "He sought to reconstruct Nature with cylinders, spheres, and cones, with everything placed in perspective, so that each side of an object or a surface is oriented toward a central plane."[1] Cézanne's art is the product of gradual growth, and it is possible to affirm that his painting symbolizes concentration: there is not a single dot or stroke attributable to bursts of imagination which may have arisen in a transitory moment. Everything is calculated: like the form or style, his themes embody an ascetic spirit. Cézanne did not choose his subjects randomly; he contemplated, studied, and observed them until he had captured the origin or essence, beneath the deceptive effects of light. Only then would he begin to paint. For Cézanne, everything in Nature contained a point (he would say "a zenith") or a center from which everything else emerged. We can think of a seed buried deep in the ground and invisible to the naked eye, although it can be a source of trees and flowers occupying the space captured by our field of vision. The artist's mission is to discover the "seeds" which others have failed to see, and to go beyond external appearances. Upon arriving at this center of gravity, it is then possible to develop an over-all "architecture," or to recreate the structure of objects.

Cézanne's art is a type of art which must be understood, instead of merely perceived, except by persons who view the world in the same way. His favorite subject was the *Montagne Sainte-Victoire* (Mount Sainte-Victoire). Is it not true that a mountain has always symbolized not only permanence but transcendance — something which one must climb in order to gain new heights? Indeed, a mountain appears to represent our innermost consciousness, and climbing to the top can symbolize attainment of a higher level of awareness. In an anecdotal sense, a mountain is a truly Capricornian symbol, and does it not also evoke Cézanne's personality?

Having owned Cézanne's *Trois Baigneuses* (Three Women Bathing) for thirty-seven years, Matisse said of this painting: "It has given me inspiration and perseverance." The Capricornian Matisse, enamored of bold expression, appears to be extremely unlike the taciturn Cézanne. Nevertheless, it can be recognized that both painters possessed the same ambition, even though they did not pursue it by identical means. Although the position of the Sun only indicates a symbol of a person's ideals, discovery of how an individual embodies, pursues, or rejects ideals requires knowledge of the forms of harmony provided by other psychological drives, expressed by the planets. In other words, it is necessary to know the aspects of planets in relation to the Sun at the time of birth. Merely by knowing that Cézanne was born under a January sky, whereas Matisse was born under a December sky, we would not be able to predict the precise ways in which their artistic talents were to be expressed, although it would be possible to determine what they would seek: "A work of art (. . .) is a creation of my soul," Matisse affirmed. He preferred solidity to lightness, conciseness and permanence to the ephemeral quality of form. As a methodical and strong-willed person, he always sought to achieve greater artistic simplicity in order to express his feelings more simply and more faithfully. "There is an inner truth which must be separated from the external appearance of the subject." Gradually, Matisse portrayed subjects in the simplest possible form, as if he had finally discovered their essence after protracted contemplation.

Capricorn in Music

Tosca, La Bohème, or *Madame Butterfly* may appear to be exceedingly remote from the realm of Capricorn, but, in certain aspects, Puccini's lyricism evokes the influence of his birth sign: "I prefer characters whose hearts are like ours (. . .), characters who can weep without shrieking, because they suffer from an entirely internal unhappiness." Instead of creating operatic symbols, Puccini selected themes which embodied an affinity to everyday life. His characters possessed dimensions which their creator knew to be authentic, and he depicted them with a realism which could only have been achieved through patient observation over long periods of time. Nevertheless, the dimensions gradually changed: in seemingly insignificant ways, Puccini's characters slowly reveal an unexpected majesty. Externally, or in terms of their ways of living, these characters seem superficial, but, internally, it is possible to perceive an ascent toward spirituality. An instructive inner alchemy emerges amidst the adver-

---

1. Cited by F. Hazan, *Histoire de la peinture moderne* (History of Modern Painting), Ed. F. Hazan, p. 51.

sities of life, and his characters display a fortitude which demands our admiration.

Although the compositions of Scriabin (1872-1918) have not gained widespread fame, they also draw us toward the typically Capricornian desire to ascend in a manner which some may consider exaggerated. Perceptions concerning the symbolism of zodiacal signs are influenced by the mood of a given era: today, the words "ambition" or "power" often reflect our concepts of this sign, but, in prior centuries, Capricorn symbolized an ascent toward spirituality. As we have observed through the myth of Saturn, Capricorn embodies ambition and power, although the role of power is to permit a transformation of the personality.

It is possible that our way of life does not permit us to perceive both qualities with the same intense awareness, whereby we are inclined to view power only in terms of the role which it usually possesses within the Capricornian symbolic framework. Nevertheless, Scriabin was a composer who wanted to express all of his spiritual breadth through his music: "I seek to merge with the cosmos through ecstasy." Deeply interested in philosophy, religion, and theosophy, Scriabin chose themes and an evocative style which illustrated his aspirations. He wrote three symphonies, including the *Poem of Ecstasy* and *Prometheus,* which expresses the qualities associated with Uranus, the other planet dominating Capricorn.

Frontispiece for Edgar Allan Poe's "The Raven," illustrated by Gustave Dore. Both Poe and Dore were Capricornians.

Correlations between Cancer and Capricorn

Although Cancer and Capricorn occupy opposite positions with the zodiacal circle, they are complementary signs: both are associated with an important stage in the journey of the Earth around the Sun. One sign incorporates the Summer solstice, and the other incorporates the Winter solstice. Under Cancer, the Sun is at its zenith in relation to the Earth; under Capricorn, the Sun is at its lowest point.

Both are cardinal signs because they introduce a season, and both reflect the same form of energy, representing the life-force or forward motion:

♋ A Cancer transports the energy of water to the imagination; there is a desire to seek the world of dreams.	♑ The earth of Capricorn carries this energy toward the conscience; there is a desire to seek the "higher realities" of life.

The maternal and protective traits which the breasts represent for Cancer are counterbalanced by the traits of endurance and deprivation symbolized by the bones and the skeleton for Capricorn:

♋ For Cancer, the Moon and water produce instability and dependency upon objects and other persons.	♑ The earth and Saturn inspire Capricornians to be stable persons who view their environments with detachment.

The polar energies of both signs are complementary and necessary within the life-cycle: Cancer's attributes render Capricorn's accomplishments possible.

It is my opinion that the image of the *alchemist* may express affinities with the innermost world of Capricornians. Beneath transformation of lead into gold (or beneath the appearance of power), "there is a true and everlasting science which can teach us to find the center of all things, known in the divine language as the soul of life," (Pierre-Jean Fabre, *Les Secrets alchimiques* [Secrets of Alchemy], 1636). The alchemist truly seeks a transmutation of his own soul.

⇌ The sign is an image of a mature man.	⇌ An Aquarian is an individual who seems to have acquired a certain understanding of life. He inspires trust.
⇌ He has an alert expression, but does not seem to direct his attention to a specific spot.	⇌ Nevertheless, he is seeking something different, which may not be consistent with conventional standards. He knows that he is different.
⇌ His body is extremely thin.	⇌ He often possesses a fragile appearance.
⇌ He is holding one or two amphoras in his hands.	⇌ His fragility is entirely relative. He possesses resources for surviving.
⇌ He is pouring water from an amphora. This is the water of knowledge.	⇌ An Aquarian disseminates new ideas and new sources of energy. He is interested in promoting knowledge.

February: the Middle of Winter

⇌ The Sun seldom appears.	⇌ An Aquarian is tactful.
⇌ The weather is cold.	⇌ An Aquarian does not readily express his feelings, and he appears to be detached from the world, or from reality itself. He has a contemplative and reserved demeanor.
⇌ Seeds are buried deep within the ground.	⇌ An Aquarian is not strongly interested in tangible realities, and he is detached from the realm of instinct.
⇌ The development of life is imperceptible to human eyes.	⇌ There is a strong interest in spiritual values. Aquarians are idealistic. They enjoy expressing ideas which are not fully developed, and they tend to be precursors.
⇌ But this is the point at which the germination process is beginning.	⇌ Although an Aquarian may sometimes seem unrealistic, he knows that he possesses awareness. He seeks authenticity.

Fixed Winter

⇌ This is the middle of Winter. Winter attains its fullest form.	⇌ An Aquarian is a resolute and persistent person who seeks to accomplish his goals. He can be obstinate.
Aquarius is a fixed sign.	

Air

Air, the element symbolizing interchange, mobility, and diffusion, is associated with Aquarius. It is specifically represented by Aquarius' position within the zodiacal cycle. Among the triplicity of air signs, the fixed air of Aquarius, embodying a tendency to perceive things intuitively instead of through logical deduction, with the result that its natives are confident about their opinions, is situated between the cardinal air of Libra, representing sentimental attachments, and the mutable air of Gemini, representing friendship. In terms of attributes, Aquarians are intuitive, expressive, and extremely sentimental or excitable.

⇌ The air of Aquarius is the pure air of Winter.	⇌ An Aquarian is motivated by a quest for moral perfection. His expression is serious and tranquil.
⇌ The air constitutes an invisible bond between Heaven and Earth.	⇌ He often pursues spiritual goals.
⇌ The sky is blue, and it has no impurities. Everyone can breathe its air.	⇌ An Aquarian may adopt human brotherhood as his highest ideal. He develops friendships easily.
⇌ A storm or rain can quickly appear within the Winter sky.	⇌ An Aquarian tends to reject conventional beliefs, and this may result in explosive anger.

Aquarius

JANUARY 22 - FEBRUARY 18

"When you learn that this world is unreal and ephemeral, you will cease to love it, your soul will be set free, you will reject worldly things, and you will be free from your desires."

Rama Krishna

THE SOURCES

The Symbolic Image

⇌ This is the only zodiacal symbol represented by one man. Gemini is represented by two men, and Virgo is represented by a woman.	⇌ When we reach the eleventh sign of the Zodiac, are we encountering an image of a fully developed human being?

Uranus and Saturn

Both Uranus and Saturn rule Aquarius.

≈ In the beginning, there was chaos — in other words, formlessness and mystery. Gaea, the Earth Mother, appeared and gave birth to Uranus.	≈ An Aquarian seeks to give a new meaning to life in order to untangle its riddles. His ideas are often intrepid and daring, but his way of thinking can clarify situations which seem perplexing to others.
≈ As the God of the Sky, Uranus, in order to create the world, impregnated his mother "by making a fertile rain fall upon her genitals."	≈ An Aquarian requires a vast amount of space, both physically and intellectually, because he is drawn toward the absolute. His fertile and imaginative mind motivates him to advance new ideas.
≈ Uranus and Gaea had many children, including the Cyclops and the Titans. Uranus exiled the Cyclops to Tartarus, one of the most remote locations on earth, and he deprived the Titans of their power.	≈ The Cyclops represent demons of the unconscious or primitive instincts, and the Titans represent ambition, or the opposite of spiritual qualities. This myth can be associated with the behavior of Aquarians, who tend to ignore or to disdain instincts in pursuing pure ideas, which they do not expect to assume a tangible form in the immediate future.
≈ Because Uranus ruled too strictly, Gaea encouraged the Titans to revolt against him.	≈ By pursuing his admiration for spiritual values too zealously, an Aquarian may feel misunderstood by others and may have a sense of being persecuted.
≈ Promethus, a grandson of Uranus, stole the celestial fire from Vulcan's forge in order to give it to mankind. Jupiter punished Prometheus by chaining him to Mount Caucasus, where an eagle devoured his liver each day.	≈ As a grandson of Uranus, Prometheus can be regarded as an extension of Uranus. An Aquarian is often tempted to play the role of a "sorcerer's apprentice." He seeks to learn more in order to bestow light and knowledge upon humanity, but he is disinclined to learn through experience. He is prone to take risks, and may become a victim of over-confidence.
≈ Prometheus was freed from his chains by Hercules, and Jupiter welcomed him among the deities.	≈ Nevertheless, an Aquarian is capable of overcoming weaknesses, and he can acquire self-control.
≈ Saturn is the other planet which rules Aquarius. Saturn dethroned his father with the sickle (a symbol of time) in order to avenge his brothers and sisters, the Titans. After ruling for a certain period of time, Saturn was overthrown and took refuge in Italy, where he bestowed all of the benefits of his experience.	≈ Whereas Aquarians seek to outdo themselves in mastering new ideas (stealing the heavenly fire), they are conscious of time, duties, and responsibilities. This aspect accounts for their ambivalence and for their difficulties in reconciling contradictory tendencies: they are externally expressive, but internally reserved. Aquarians are deeply humanitarian and altruistic.

The Circulatory System

≈ The bodily function associated with Aquarius is circulation of the blood. Blood is the source of life for the entire organism.	≈ Aquarian traits include diffusion, transmission, and circulation. An Aquarian disseminates life and warmth.

These sources provide the zodiacal formula for Aquarius: a personality representing Winter, stability, air, Uranus, and Saturn, as well as being associated with circulation of the blood. The symbolic qualities can be more fully described in the following form:

An Independent and Humanitarian Temperament
Under the influence of Uranus, Aquarians often show little respect for tradition and customs. They tend to eliminate considerations which they consider secondary, and they are spontaneous, but sometimes thoughtless. Their behavior is unpredictable because they are eternally youthful. The career and temperament of James Dean reflect this state of mind: he had an angelic appearance and "was driven to seek absolutes." Aquarians tend to promote their own individual rights and those of others. They possess strong humanitarian instincts, as in the instance of Abraham Lincoln in his fight against slavery. Calm and serene like the pure sky of January, Lincoln also reflected the influence of Uranus: he oriented the United States toward a quest for racial justice.

An Intuitive Mind
It is not surprising that many Aquarians have been brilliant scientists or inventors: Galileo and Darwin, for example, permitted us to envision a different "order" in our world, either on a macrocosmic scale (Galileo) or a microcosmic one (Darwin). Ampere, Edison, and the Montgolfier brothers provided advances in communication. Aquarians tend to be precursors, and to have scientific inclinations. Nevertheless, their quest for the ideal can also lead to mysticism: Eckhart and Saint Francis of Assisi were Aquarians. Will the sorcerer's apprentice be a victim of his failures (Prometheus), or can he master himself through experience (Saturn)? Will he be a person who directs his eyes toward the heavens in search of enlightenment? Only the rest of his horoscope, and especially relationships between the Sun and other heavenly bodies, or psychic forces, can suggest how an Aquarian may develop. An Aquarian's mode of thought can be symbolized by a mathematical equation or a musical stave.

The Heart
Aquarians combine love and freedom: they want to love and to be independent at the same time. It is necessary for them not to feel confined, because, in that instance, they become melancholy. Aquarians do not have a passionate disposition, even though they may express passion in a refined manner. They seek deeper relationships which go beyond passion. They are aware of the dangers of love, and may prefer what is known as platonic love. Aquarians seek someone who shares the same ideas and ideals. They do not evaluate other persons according to conventional criteria, such as physical attractiveness, but according to their ways of life. Because they do not measure trust according to presence and absence, they are willing to grant others the same freedom which they seek for themselves. Aquarians tend to regard true love as a communion of souls.

An Aquarian *ideogram* consists of two slightly slanted oscillating waves, symbolizing the flow of knowledge or the essense of energy. Hence, they can be compared to an electrical current: an Aquarian's perceptions are as rapid as lightning.

Fussli's "Women of Hastings." Goethe said of this painter: "He is a mortal endowed with divine powers." Fussli's style is integrated with the ideal which inspired him.

MODES OF EXPRESSION

Aquarius in Literature

Although he was a member of a noble family, Lord Byron did not uphold its traditions. When he spoke before the House of Lords and his peers wished to congratulate him, he only half-heartedly accepted their handshakes. He was later driven into exile for having defied convention and having stirred up scandals. In his youth, he had already shown signs of possessing unusual traits. He was regarded as being impetuous and was inclined to define the weak against the strong. His many passionate friendships were accompanied by an irreversible hatred for those who did not live up to his expectations. Byron was a man who loved humanity, but usually disliked human beings. It was often difficult to comprehend his unique personality, which frequently made him the target of gossip-mongers. He was simultaneously full of pride, generosity, disdain and lofty ideals.

He stood apart from his contemporaries, both in terms of his works and his character.

Enamored of travel, Byron recounted the various adventures in which he became involved, and, when he was at the peak of literary glory, he decided to translate his poetry into action. He left Italy, his home-in-exile, and went to Greece, in order to aid the Greek struggle for independence. He displayed heroism in battles but soon died of apoplexy. Both Britain and Greece claimed his remains, but, finally, this poet and martyr for freedom was returned to his native land, where he is buried today.

Aquarius in Art

Johann H. Fussli, a Romantic painter at the end of the eighteenth century, was born in the German-speaking region of Switzerland. At first, he was a Protestant theologian, but, after reading Rousseau, he rejected religion and adopted harmony between Man and society as an ideal, seeking reconciliation with the world and natural forces through an effort to transcend ordinary reality. His paintings, stressing eternal mythological themes, represent a quest for a new humanity within a new world.

Thus, the subjects which Fussli chose express the human content of eternal forces: Good or Evil, represented by angels and Satan. Gradually, these images acquired a spiritual transparency. G.C. Argan has written that "emotions do not convey pathos or feeling in Fussli's works; they are moral events." When Fussli produced illustrations for fairy tales, he dressed the sorcerers in the apparel of his own era. He also satirized the world in which he lived and sought to inculcate awareness of the false beliefs which portions of society still upheld, endowing his works with a certain sense of irony.

Nevertheless, he did not limit himself to mere portrayal: like Uranus exiling the Cyclops to the depths of Tartarus, Fussli urged men to free themselves from ignoble instincts. Although the young man in *Virtue Encouraging Youth to Forsake Vice* seems passive, the painter appears to be asking "What more would be necessary for him to understand?"

In other paintings, Satan disappears as soon as light emerges. Goethe said of Fussli, "he is a mortal who possesses the powers of the gods." In *Satan Fleeing the Blow from Ithurel's Lance,* the Devil departs with a feral leap which Fussli portrays by a shift in spatial perspective. His style was consistent with the ideals which inspired him: he possessed the power of a thunderbolt, and he was the herald of a revolution, or of a world which has not yet emerged, where passions and instincts would be ethereal. Thus, in *Romeo and Juliet,* the shapes and positions of human images surpass the realm of human passions.

Fussli's contours are not rigid; indeed, they appear to vibrate with something extra, extending beyond time and space. His paintings evoke fraternal and universal love.

Aquarius in Music

"This young boy's imaginative powers and his skills at reading music make him a prodigy. I never would have believed these things possible in a child who is so young. Your pupil, by his accomplishments, could be compared to the young Mozart."[1] These were Goethe's words to Zelter, the instructor of the young Felix Mendelssohn. Many persons compared the young prodigy's talents to those of Mozart, who was also an Aquarian.

When he was still a child, Felix Mendelssohn astonished others with his serious and serene demeanor. He sat at the piano and improvised unhesitatingly. He came from a wealthy German family, and was able to pursue his career at his own pace, without lacking anything which he needed for developing his musical talents. Thus, he was able to travel to France, Italy, and Britain in order to discover other modes of expression and to share his own artistic accomplishments. Mendelssohn gained numerous friends and corresponded with them prolifically.

He was born during the golden era of Beethoven and Schubert, whose fame soon diminished while new musicians appeared on the scene: Chopin, Schumann, Liszt, Wagner, and Verdi...

Nevertheless, the young Mendelssohn deeply influenced the art of his time with his own originality, by combining Classical forms with Romanticism, or by endowing Romanticism with a certain sense of form. Moreover, he was the forerunner of a new musical genre: a synthesis between symphonies and lyrical expression, namely the symphonic poem.

This is how Mendelssohn's sister Fanny interpreted his musical intentions in *Octuor Opus 20:* "...the tremolos, the trills, everything here is new and strange, but so ethereal that a light breeze appears to lift you into the world of spirits. One would be tempted to ride on a witch's broomstick in order to follow the flight of these airy creations more closely..."

In *A Midsummer Night's Dream,* which was his first success, Mendelssohn combined airiness with profound mastery of instrumental techniques. He was as skilled in writing music as in giving his orchestration a magical quality. *A Midsummer Night's Dream,* inspired by Shakespeare's play, is situated within a forest of dreams peopled with sylphs and fairies, where two souls encounter one another and pledge eternal love. The composer's genius created true musical sorcery which fills an intangible world with an inexpres-

---

1. Cited by Remi Jacob, *Mendelssohn* (Seuil).

sible poetry. After having heard a performance of *A Midsummer Night's Dream,* Robert Schumann wrote, "it is a stream of youthfulness."

Later, in *Paul* and *Elijah,* as in fifty other religious compositions, Mendelssohn expressed his religious beliefs. The prophet Elijah is torn between the urgings of God and the calls of his fellow men. This is a work representing Mendelssohn's maturity.

Correlations between Leo and Aquarius

Although they occupy opposite positions within the zodiacal cycle, Leo and Aquarius are complementary. Both are fixed signs because they represent "completion" of a season, and both are governed by persistency and an instinct for order:

♌ Inspired by fire, a Leo uses these attributes for self-fulfillment.

♒ Inspired by air, an Aquarian uses these attributes to provide fulfillment for others.

The role of the heart as a center of gravity for Leo is balanced by the role of the blood as a means of diffusion for Aquarius:

♌ Fire and Sun induce a Leo to be a passionate person who seeks centralization.

♒ Air and Uranus induce an Aquarian to be a person who seeks detachment from passions and decentralization.

Their respective forms of energy are complementary, as well as being necessary for the life cycle: whereas a Leo organizes the world around himself, an Aquarian distributes and disseminates energy to others.

Ganymede, a young shepherd, won the admiration of Zeus with his handsomeness and innocence. The rule of Olympus carried Ganymede away from the earth and made him the cup-bearer to the gods, so that he could serve ambrosia, the nectar of immortality. Through his innocence, Ganymede became an equal to the gods, as well as a source of life for them; to a certain extent, he came to represent the Truth, which bestows immortality... In many ways, this myth may evoke many echoes among Aquarians.

"Schubertiades," an engraving by the Aquarian Maurice von Schwind, a friend of Schubert (who was also an Aquarian), who was able to witness Schubert's musical improvisations.

The god Neptune.

Pisces

FEBRUARY 19 - MARCH 20

*"The God whom I worship placed my soul with a thousand voices, like a re-
sounding echo, at the center of everything."*

Victor Hugo, *Ce siècle avait deux ans*

THE SOURCES

The Symbolic Image

✕ The fish is an aquatic creature. It lives in water, which is essential to life.	✕ Pisceans live by means of their sensory perceptions and their feelings. They are deeply sensitive.
✕ It is difficult to grasp a fish.	✕ It is often difficult for others to know and to understand Pisceans.
✕ A fish swims with the current, without ever truly stopping.	✕ They seem to be in two places at once.
✕ Unable to defend itself, a fish prefers to go around obstacles.	✕ Pisceans feel defenseless in relation to others, and are elusive.
✕ A fish takes in water and draws its oxygen from the water.	✕ This is a person who adapts to his surroundings and absorbs all types of influences.
✕ A fish is a vertebrate whose bones are flexible, but delicate. A fish does not have very solid flesh.	✕ It is difficult for Pisceans to adopt objectives and pursue a definite path.
✕ The symbol consists of two fish touching one another.	✕ A Piscean has a talent for seeing both sides of an issue. He is a skilled mediator, but is also ambivalent.

February: The End of Winter

✕ After the harshness of Winter, people are tired of cold weather. The snow begins to melt and the Winter rains feed streams which become rivers, whose torrents wash away the soil.	✕ The conscience of a Piscean is molded by his surroundings. This is an extremely broad-minded person who is open to the influence of his environment, although he may lack a sense of direction and may appear to be irrational.
✕ Gradually, the temperature increases and days become longer. Nature imperceptibly comes alive once again, offering new scents, but nothing has acquired a definitive form.	✕ Pisceans feel flooded with many types of energy, and they let themselves be swept along easily. A Piscean develops in a formless and indeterminate manner, without adhering to norms.
✕ Seeds are not yet visible, and, even though we can guess that they are growing in this moist environment, we cannot recognize forms, because everything is dispersed. A new season is on its way.	✕ A Piscean lives in a hypothetical world, and it is difficult for him to choose among the many possibilities which may emerge. Pisceans often seem indecisive and vague; absorbed in their own worlds, they are unaware of practical consequences.

Mutable Winter

✕ Winter is ending, and this is a period of transition.	✕ This is a person who gives free rein to his unconscious, as he seeks forms of ecstasy which will link him to reality.

Pisces is a mutable sign.

The Ocean

Water is the element associated with Pisces, and symbolizes interchanges and expansiveness. It is specifically represented by the position of Pisces within the zodiacal cycle. Among the triplicity of water signs, the mutable water of Pisces follows the primordial water of Cancer (a spring, emotions) and the fixed water of Scorpio (a swamp, the unconscious).

This is a person who experiences multiple sensations, and his character type is considered sentimental and phlegmatic. Pisceans frequently have globulous eyes (like a fish), a detached expression which appears to be absent-minded, and a calm voice.

✕ The ocean extends infinitely; the further one travels, the more the horizon recedes.	✕ A Piscean's goals are not clearly defined, because there is an aspiration for the infinite or for spiritual values.
✕ In the distance, the sky and the water mingle.	✕ There are no boundaries between a Piscean and other persons. Pisceans are not individualists. They appear to be "everyone else," without ever truly being themselves. Attracted by groups, they can show great loyalty to others.
✕ At times, the depth of the ocean seems infinite.	✕ Pisceans' receptivity may render them vulnerable.
✕ The ocean comes into contact with all possible types of land.	✕ A Piscean is at ease everywhere and nowhere, because he feels all types of emotions.
✕ The ocean is affected by the perpetual motion of the tides.	✕ A Piscean's emotions produce a perpetual flow which renders him adaptable and tolerant.

Neptune and Jupiter

Pisces is ruled primarily by Neptune, but also by Jupiter.

✕ After Saturn was deposed, his sons drew lots to divide the world. Jupiter received the sky, Pluto the nether world, and Neptune the ocean.	✕ Zeus, or Jupiter, represents the spiritual domain; Pluto represents the domain of impulses; and Neptune represents the unfathomable subconscious. Pisceans are not at ease within the limited realm of the conscious mind and pure logic.
✕ Neptune made the bottom of the sea his home. He owned a herd of white horses symbolizing controlled and sublimated instincts (dark horses represent uncontrolled instincts). These horses had golden manes, symbolizing the quest for spirituality, and bronze shoes, symbolizing communication.	✕ Pisceans possess inner spiritual treasures. They can impart to others the meaning of universal correlations which they have identified intuitively. A Piscean can serve as a link among extremely different individuals. Other persons enjoy the presence of a Piscean, because a Piscean radiates calmness and serenity.
✕ The sea-god introduced horse racing.	✕ Nevertheless, the Piscean knows that this tranquil state may be disrupted. A Piscean is extremely susceptible to unconscious negative impulses.
✕ Neptune fell madly in love with Medusa, and seduced her in a temple dedicated to Athena (wisdom). Athena was outraged, and transformed Medusa into a monster. Medusa's hair became serpents writhing upon her head. Everyone who looked into her eyes was immediately transformed into a statue of stone.	✕ A Piscean may be the victim of dangerous illusions, especially when he is dominated by sensuality or sentimentality. Then he ignores the limits of reality and inverts scales of values. If a Piscean is unable to develop bonds with others, he may have a distorted concept of himself, which paralyzes him with horror. Then he becomes a victim of nightmares.
✕ Neptune is often portrayed amidst strange and monstrous sea creatures. Like all symbols, these creatures have both positive and negative aspects.	✕ A Piscean is inhabited by strange illusions emerging from his memory like forgotten ghosts, who disguise evil forces as virtues.
✕ The Chimera is one of the monsters accompanying Neptune. This is a hybrid creature possessing a goat's body as a symbol of perverse and capricious sexuality, a serpent's tail representing depravity and vanity, and a lion's head representing the drive to dominate.	✕ The sea creatures accompanying Neptune are products of the subconscious, or illusions. They only appear as monsters to those who fear that their inner personalities are filled with depraved, domineering, and vain instincts. A Piscean, who dwells in the world of the subconscious, may enable others to understand themselves.
✕ Another of Neptune's monsters was the Lernean Hydra, a serpent whose nine heads grew back whenever they were cut off.	✕ A Piscean may experience torments which give the impression that the only release is a deeper retreat into illusions.
✕ Cerberus, a monster with a hundred heads, symbolizes the terror of Death (he became Pluto's watchdog), or an inner Hell.	✕ A Piscean may become fearful of himself.
✕ There is also the Sphinx, a mysterious monster which posed riddles to its victims and devoured those who could not answer.	✕ A Piscean may represent a riddle to himself and others. His own intellect may not provide answers. A Piscean expresses and understands ideas at another level, namely at the subconscious level.

185

✕ Neptune was a prolific lover and seduced many nymphs.

✕ A Piscean does not like to be limited in love, and he may be drawn into many love relationships.

✕ Neptune was a great conqueror, and claimed the Greek provinces of Attica, Thrace, Aegina, Naxos, and Corinth. When the other gods refused to honor his claims, he sought vengeance by causing floods.

✕ A Piscean disregards limits and may be easily disillusioned. Insatiable desires may lead him to commit thoughtless acts and errors which are harmful to himself and his associates.

✕ Neptune's emblem is a trident symbolizing the three elements of the human personality: the body, the intellect, and the soul. It also represents the past, the present, and the future. The trident is the symbolic key which opens our eyes to the invisible and permits access to other worlds.

✕ A Piscean is a person who encompasses the past, the present, and the future within the same generalized and assimilative frame of reference. This type of world-view can lead him toward carnal desires (sensuality) toward intellectual skills (farsightedness), or toward the longings of the soul (spirituality). Harmony within a Piscean's deep inner world may produce an exceptionally powerful mystique.

✕ Neptune was the father of two horses: Pegasus, the winged horse, who made a spring emerge beneath his shoes, and Aerion, the wild horse.

✕ Piscean creativity can produce poetic inspiration (Pegasus) or the most chaotic fantasies. A Piscean can fluctuate between depravity and saintliness (or he can display both at the same time).

The other planet governing Pisces is Jupiter, which is shared with Sagittarius.

✕ Jupiter, the ruler of Olympus, had a paternal and benevolent personality. He imparted courage to tired heroes, and, with his thunderbolts, he maintained justice.

✕ A Piscean seeks membership in a community, and is desirous of comforting others. He has a sense of justice.

✕ Neptune, representing the unconscious, and Jupiter, representing the

✕ Self-fulfillment is sought through combining multiple tendencies. Under the

intellect, embody two kinds of mental powers, like the two fish in opposite positions, which express the forces governing Pisceans.

influence of Jupiter, a Piscean may achieve his Neptunian ideals: he is guided by an intuitive concept of justice, and seeks to unify all of his own capabilities in behalf of a purifying ideal.

The Lymphatic System

The lymphatic system is the part of the body associated with Pisces.

✕ Lymph is derived from transudation of the blood.

✕ A quest for spiritual ideals is attributed to Pisceans.

✕ Lymph is carried to all portions of the body through the transparent vessels.

✕ Dissoluteness and collective instincts are also attributed to Pisceans.

These sources provide the zodiacal formula for Pisces: a person associated with Winter, mutability, water, Neptune, and Jupiter, represented by the lymphatic system. This formula can be described in the following manner:

A Many-Faceted Character
Despite others' efforts to pin him down, a Piscean always escapes. He is real, of course, but he also appears to dissolve into thin air. He is with us and somewhere else at the same time. He appears to grasp everything which we feel and, perhaps, to understand our expectations for the future. A Piscean does not experience the solitary pain of a lone individual; he experiences pain on a collective plane, with a melancholy heart which reflects all human suffering. In the same way, however, a Piscean can express joy to the fullest extent. These inclinations spontaneously draw him toward universal principles, as in the instance of D'Annunzio. A Piscean can be fascinated by the absolute, which he may express through seeking new horizons, like the explorers Jacques Cartier and Henri de Montcalm, or the astronauts Gagarin and Tarashkova.

Cosmic or Spiritual Thought
Pisceans are not guided by logic, but by pure intuition. This is not the penetrating intuition of an Aries; it is a vision of vast generalities. Pisceans have a comprehensive mode of thought, which is more easily expressed by symbols or metaphors than by rational discourse. The collective unconscious is profoundly present, as if the entire memory of mankind had chosen the Piscean as its vessel.

The world above is more interesting than earthly things, and a certain degree of self-control is necessary if the Piscean is not to become detached from reality or spellbound by mirages. Many great astronomers were Pisceans who succeeded in giving their ideas a concrete form: Copernicus, Flammarion, Galileo, Le Terrier, Schoch. Nevertheless, spiritual instincts are sometimes so strong that there is a wholehearted devotion to religion, if the rest of the horoscope suggests these qualities: Clement VIII, Julius III, Leo XIII, Paul II, Pius XII, and many other Popes were Pisceans.

One figure from the beginning of this century who comes to mind is Rudolph Steiner, the father of a school of thought known as anthroposophy. He sought to establish a synthesis between Oriental and Western philosophies in order to attain universalism. Believing that cosmic thought or a universal reality capable of thought existed, Steiner investigated ways of gaining awareness in order to live in a more intimate relationship with the universe.[1] The Piscean mode of thought can be symbolized by a telescope pointing toward the absolute.

Sacrificial Love
Pisceans feel the sentiments and impressions of others so deeply that they run a risk of forgetting their own identity and, without realizing it, they may begin to act as if they share the situation of the beloved. A Piscean in love displays more of the other person's qualities than his own.

Because he is extremely impressionable, anything may affect him and have an impact upon his entire personality, just as a stone thrown into quiet water produces expanding ripples. It is difficult for a Piscean to express his feelings, however. Aware of his fragility, he sometimes avoids excessively strong emotions, in order to pursue another path. It is not always possible to understand a Piscean's attitude. In his eyes, human beings are not confined to limits or to a specific profile. The Piscean can become enamored of persons who are exceedingly different, just as Chopin fell in love with George Sand, and he can display surprising devotion.

The Pisces *ideogram* consists of two fish, joined by a cord, although they face in opposite directions. This ideogram can be interpreted as a combination of two ways of life or two modes of thought expressing the ambivalent qualities of a Piscean. The fish also express alternating motion, from above to below, and then from below to above: this evokes a person who, after having descended into the physical world, longs for the absolute. Nevertheless, motion between the two opposite poles does not cease; it resolves contradictions within the Piscean personality.

---

1. Rudolph Steiner, *Pensée humaine, Pensée cosmique (Human Thought, Cosmic Thought)*, Paris, La Science spirituelle, 1951.

Ambivalent and sensitive, a Piscean is often elusive.

MODES OF EXPRESSION

Pisces in Literature

Victor Hugo was born with the Sun and two planets occupying the house of Pisces. He was first and foremost a poet of the sea and the horizon: "Oh, leave me alone! This is the time when the horizon becomes misty ... the time when the giant star grows red and disappears." *(Reverie).* He let himself absorb people and things, in order to experience them internally, where "all the waves of the night are breaking within me." *(Toute la lyre.)* The poet responds to multiple emotions — "one feels weak and strong (...) like a wave within an ocean, or a soul in a storm," *(Contemplations),* and he dreams of remote horizons: "The feet here, the eyes elsewhere." *(Les Rayons et les Ombres)* (Sunlight and Shadows). After having witnessed the collapse of all philosophies and idolatries, "Philosophy dares to climb through the sky (...) like an ominous crag within an abyss," Hugo aspires to reach the absolute: "I shall go to the terrifying temple of the unknown (...) as far as the visionary gates of Heaven."

With an overflowing imagination, he did not express himself through logic; instead, he allowed the ebb and flow of his metaphors to predominate. Hugo's subjects became myths permitting him to gain access to all readers' minds through lyricism. Instead of expressing "a self," Victor Hugo expressed "selves," and his work became an echo of the collective unconscious.

In *La legende des siècles (The Legend of the Centuries),* he incorporated the successive stages of human existence and endowed his poem with a cosmic breadth. Through this work, Victor Hugo sought to portray "the flowering of mankind from one century to another (...) Man ascending from the shadows toward the ideal," where the triumph of Good over Evil would only take place beyond Time, within a divine future.

He was also a poet who advocated compassion for the downtrodden and the weak:

"Never curse the fallen woman!
Who can know the burden which crushes her tortured soul?"
(Les chants du crepuscule)   (Twilight Songs)

Victor Hugo gradually became the bard of all mankind, and in some instances, he even displayed prophetic insight with respect to future centuries. Possessing the symbolic attributes of a Piscean, he sought fulfillment within the broadest poetic dimension. His work probably permitted him to overcome one of its ambivalencies: egoism and vanity, in conflict with love for others. Indeed, two days before his death, Hugo wrote "To love is to seek action."

Closer to our era, another Piscean, André Breton, sought to transform human thought and the human condition at the same time, by freeing the forces of the subconscious. In the *Surrealist Manifesto,* Breton appealed to the imagination by condemning "absolute rationalism," which is only useful for "immediate purposes" and encloses human thought within a cage. Breton sought to liberate dreams, which possess their own continuity and reality within the human mind. When he called for combining "these two apparently

"Oh God, open the doors of the night," Victor Hugo. (Fortress drawn by the poet.)

contradictory states represented by dreams and reality into an absolute reality, or surreality," Breton appeared to resolve the ambivalency of the Piscean personality with a single sentence.

Pisces in Painting

The famous painter Michelangelo was a Piscean, and he developed a mystical concept of art, seeking consistently to imitate God Himself, as a creator in pursuit of artistic perfection. "The eye never looks at the Sun without becoming similar to the Sun." Understanding can only exist among similar entities. Michelangelo succeeded in his quest for divinity, and soon acquired the role of a demi-god. The fundamental motive was an esthetic quest, or an individual search for the eternal beauty associated with the divine. The ponderous bodies which Michelangelo created embody an attempt to express inner qualities, or the human soul, instead of external qualities. Beyond the outer forms of reality, his artistic goal was to achieve communion with the divine essence which he perceived in mankind. Michelangelo's statues and paintings reflect his sensitivity to the cosmos and to universal themes.

Closer to our own era, among the English symbolists of the late nineteenth century, there is Thomas Crane, a Piscean painter, whose ideal was to render art accessible to the masses. *The Horses of Neptune,* which can be compared to "a wave from the unconscious," permits us to understand the inner world of Pisceans more fully. Antoine Wiertz, who established a museum for his own works in Belgium, also expresses certain Piscean tendencies. First, there is the size of his canvasses, and Wiertz never found a large enough studio to complete certain works (such as the *Revolt of the Angels,* one of his greatest masterpieces). Second, one can consider his themes, derived from religion, mythology, and history, and, of course, there is the life of the artist himself, who sought to be an artistic missionary. His goal was to render his contemporaries aware of deep psychological and social problems — *Pensées et Hallucinations d'une guillotine* (Thoughts and Hallucinations from the Guillotine), or *Enfants orphelins* (Orphans). Wiertz also portrayed the emptiness of worldly success — *Une second après la mort* (One Second after Death), *les Consolations de la doctrine de l'imortalité* (The Consolations of the Doctrine of Immortality) and the virtues of brotherhood (*Partis devant le tribunal de Christ*).

Pisces in Music

Handel, the creator of the *Messiah,* was a Piscean, like Chopin and Ravel. He had written forty operas before he began to compose oratorios. Incessantly creative and endowed with a prodigious imagination, he initially dedicated his life to art, but later dedicated his art to God. Handel was born in Halle, and, after travelling widely, he chose to reside in England. He did not always win the acclaim which he hoped for. Despite disappointments, he fervently believed in the art which he was creating for his contemporaries, and he continued to compose unceasingly. His inspiration never faltered.

Before composing the *Messiah,* he had chosen heroic or Biblical themes for such operas as *Esther, Athalia, Saul,* or *Joshua.* In the *Messiah,* however, historical representation was no longer his intent; through the image of Christ, he sought to create composition

which places the gates of Heaven before our eyes. "When I wrote the Hallelujah Chorus, I think I did see all Heaven before me, and the great God Himself," he affirmed.[1] *The Messiah* is a work of redemption: prior to that point, Handel appeared to be "multifaceted" in his various works, where different themes emerge, but, with this oratorio, Handel expressed unity with God. In particular, he adopted the principal symbolic theme of Christianity, affirming redemption and access to eternal life. Handel expressed his hopes by means of a redeeming love, and he affirmed his belief in Christ: "I know that my Redeemer is alive."

Handel's contemporaries in England, who accused him of attempting to transform the theatres into churches, did not always respond favorably to the lofty aims of his work, but their objections did not seem to deter him, and, until his death, he continued to create music evoking his own spiritual ascent.

Correlations between Virgo and Pisces

Although Virgo and Pisces occupy opposite positions within the zodiacal cycle, they are also complementary. Both signs are mutable because they mark the end of one season and the beginning of another. Thus, there is a form of alternating motion produced by a sense of transformation or evolution, which:

♍ Earth, as the element of Virgo, renders concrete through logic.	♓ Water, as the element of Pisces, guides toward spiritual values.

The attributes of diffusion which lymph represents for Pisces are balanced by the attributes of filtration, symbolized by the intestines for Virgo:

♍ Earth and Mercury guide a Virgo toward analysis and interpretation of realities.	♓ Water and Neptune guide a Piscean toward intuition and dreams.

Where a Virgo lives within the confines of terrestrial reality, a Piscean tends to live within the unlimited vastness of the absolute. Their respective forms of energy are complementary and are necessary for the life cycle: Pisces dissolves that which Virgo classifies and coordinates.

Noah's Ark symbolizes the transition between two epochs: the period before the Flood, and a new period characterized by the various species which God permitted to take refuge in the Ark. The myth of a flood as a means of salvation for the world, heralding a new era, was shared by many civilizations. Does the realm of Pisces reflect the symbolism of Noah, as the zodiacal cycle comes to an end while also bringing hope for a better world?

Psyche: a personification of the immortal soul, by the Piscean Max Klinger.

---

1. Jean Gallois, *Handel.*

Conclusion

Astrology represents an accumulation of the psychological insights of the Ancient World which have been transmitted throughout history by the deep currents of the collective unconscious. I have attempted to describe its origins, its youth, and its maturity, as well as the shadows and bursts of light which astrology has produced, like any other human phenomenon. Many thinkers have already weighed the principles of astrology, and I do not pretend to be the source of all of the explanations which I have offered. Indeed, certain explanations, instead of being purely original, are derived from the ideas of my predecessors. I have also borrowed certain terms, because they express principles or ideas so effectively that they entered my own language and became a part of my own legacy, permitting fuller development of certain concepts.

In many instances, a contribution to knowledge consists of establishing a new order for truths which have been known for a long time or perhaps forgotten. Illuminated by a new beacon, these truths can return to our memories and revitalize concepts which appeared to be unknown.

I have attempted to approach astrology without being influenced by pre-established opinions, and my intentions would have been fulfilled if readers have been persuaded to investigate this subject more fully from the viewpoint of general knowledge, but also on the basis of personal contemplation. My intent has been not so much to convince the reader, but to identify what astrology represents on a human scale and to determine whether it can still contribute to our knowledge of the world and ourselves.

Thus, I have not wished to "promote" astrology by relying upon horoscopes, but to permit those who are interested in its "language" to explore historical, mythological, and scientific sources, in order to decide for themselves how much credence they may give to it.

Astrology may be a means of determining our capabilities, inasmuch as the natal horoscope expresses the grammar or structure of symbols living inside us, and it is valuable to uncover its secrets. Nevertheless, I suggest that we keep in mind a Chinese adage cited by Jung: "If a perverse man uses the proper method, the proper method is applied perversely."

Whatever the merits of a given method may be, the person who uses it is just as important, if not more important, than the method itself. Planetary symbols may become the "mother tongue" of the unconscious, permitting us to read the paragraphs allotted to us within the great book of the universe. Thus, we must be careful in determining who shall leaf through its pages.

Even though the process has not been precisely defined in scientific terms, it is probable that correlations with respect to energy exist between planetary symbols and the unconscious. It is gradually being recognized that we must take into account coincidences among heterogeneous events which are not causally related, although the respective forms of energy are similar and the same phases emerge: for example, DNA (deoxyribose nucleic acid) may possess a structure which is sensitive to the same force fields as the planets. Nevertheless, this circumstance does not imply that it is necessary to view planetary factors within a deterministic framework. Such an attitude would sever our natural bonds with the energy of the universe, and would detach us from the rhythms of the universe by confining us within an isolating causality.

Magritte's "Secret Agent."
Is it myself or someone else
who communicates with the
universe?

Although certain works in astrology express fatalistic views in order to prey upon a weakness which is inherent to human beings, they represent a quest for an illusory psychic superiority. These works disfigure the true wisdom of the Ancients, who affirmed, during the infancy of astrology, that greater knowledge of oneself permits one to live harmoniously within the cosmos. "Know yourself, and you can know the universe." In that way, our allotments of free will can be expanded.

The position of the Sun and the planets in our natal horoscopes is one of the many configurations created by a cosmic boom, or one of the many rays of light which we can reflect, in order to gain access to the heart of the cosmos.

A horoscope represents our own solar system within the universe; it is a "Sun-ideal," with our psychic attributes rotating around it. The horoscope can indicate the way in which we are attuned to the rest of the universe, or the cadence by which we shall absorb the eternal symbols of humanity. The true function of astrology should be to aid us in attaining harmony with these currents of energy, and our personal horoscopes should allow us to understand the rhythm governing our pulse, as it echoes the heartbeats of the universe. In this way, our conscious lives may become living echoes of the mysterious tones of the universal lyre.

To live in harmony with one's horoscope is to be aware of the notes played by each of our tendencies, like a musician within the orchestra of the cosmos, respecting the over-all harmony and knowing that one note may go unheard if another is played too loudly. Thus, an individual is no longer obliged to "endure" his horoscope, or to blame the planets for an infernal process which has dominated his life; instead, it is possible to "live" one's horoscope according to its rhythms and events. In other words, coinciding planetary movements and psychic or physical phenomena can be interwoven within the same fundamental experience. The horoscope can permit a person to establish conscious bonds between himself and his environment in order to become a reflection of the universe.

It may ultimately be possible for astrology to become a domain of human knowledge once again and to display its true merits by enhancing the most beautiful aspects of life: love and learning. Astrology would then be dedicated to understanding existence.

How to Prepare A Natal Horoscope

TERRESTRIAL SPHERE AND GEOGRAPHIC COORDINATES

When you entered the world, a specific planetary configuration illuminated the firmament and presided over your birth. This configuration embodies the same interrelations for every location on our planet, and consequently, for anyone whose time of birth is essentially identical to yours.

Nevertheless, the factor which distinguishes you from your counterparts is the way in which you individually perceive your planetary configuration. In order to identify this configuration, it is necessary to determine the proper terrestrial coordinates (four cardinal points) for the time of your birth, and to project these coordinates onto the ecliptic, in order to discover how the cosmic space around you should be polarized, or to learn how you will achieve harmony with the universal consciousness and express the planetary symbols situated therein.

Two steps are involved in preparing a natal horoscope:
(1) Computing Greenwich Mean Time (GMT) and planetary positions.
(2) Determining the ascendant and the terrestrial coordinates (according to local time and sidereal time); and casting the horoscope.

Phase 1
Determining Greenwich Mean Time

Greenwich Mean Time (GMT) at the time of your birth permits you to locate planetary positions within your celestial chart. Then it can be used during the second set of computations to compute local time (which is necessary for determining sidereal time), in order to project your terrestrial coordinates onto the ecliptic. The most well-known coordinate is the ascendant.

The basic method will be explained in a form whereby it will be possible to cast a horoscope for any location on our planet, if official birth records are available. In this instance, all of the necessary principles for determining the ascendant for persons born in the United States will be explained.

The time recorded on your birth certificate is the applicable *official* time for the zone where you were born. It is not always equivalent to Greenwich Mean Time (GMT), except in the instance of countries close to the Greenwich meridian, and during certain periods. Therefore, it is necessary at the outset to consult documents indicating the type of official time for your zone when you were born, in order to determine the time correction (TC) which you must subsequently apply (with a + or − sign) to the official time, in order to determine Greenwich Mean Time (GMT).

Example 1 (Standard Time)

West of Greenwich
GMT: Official Time + TC
Example: It is 8:18 A.M. in Wisconsin (the zone time[1] is six hours west of Greenwich). What is the corresponding GMT time?
GMT = 8:18 + 6 hours = 2:18 P.M.

East of Greenwich
GMT: Official Time − TC
Example: It is 3:45 P.M. in eastern China (the zone time[1] is eight hours east of Greenwich). What is the corresponding GMT time?
GMT = 3:45 − 8 hours = 7:45 A.M.

Example 2 (Daylight Saving Time)

Several countries, during certain seasons, have set the clock ahead by one or two hours in relation to normal time. Hence, in order to determine GMT, it is necessary to make an adjustment for this change:

West of Greenwich
(1 hour ahead during the summer)
GMT = Official time + TC − 1 hour
Example: GMT = 8:18 A.M. + 6 hours − 1 hour = 1:18 P.M.

East of Greenwich
(1 hour ahead during the summer)
GMT = Official time − TC − 1 hour
Example: GMT = 3:45 P.M. − 8 hours − 1 hour = 6:45 A.M.

Calculations of GMT

Standard Time

9:23 AM in New York. New York is five hours west of Greenwich.
GMT = 9:23 AM + 5 hours = 2:23 PM

5:42 AM in Chicago. Chicago is six hours west of Greenwich
GMT = 5:24 + 6 hours = 11:24 AM

7:22 AM in Denver. Denver is seven hours west of Greenwich
GMT = 7:22 AM + 7 hours = 2:22 PM

2:03 AM in Los Angeles. Los Angeles is eight hours west of Greenwich
GMT = 2:03 AM + 8 hours = 10:03 AM

N.B.: The above examples are for AM births. PM births are the same plus 12 hours. Sometimes when a person is born late in the day in the U.S., it is already the next day in Greenwich, England.

E.G. 5:15 PM in Los Angeles
5:15 = 12 hours (for PM birth) = 17:15 hours past midnight local time

17:15 + 8 hours (west of Greenwich) = 25:15 GMT
There are only 24 hours in a day. Thus the person was born 1:15 hours into the next day.

---

1. "Zone time": the Earth is divided into 24 "sectors," with each representing 15 longitudinal degrees corresponding to one hour apiece. It is sufficient to consult an atlas in order to determine the time zone for a locality when you want to determine its coordinates.

Daylight Saving Time

Daylight Saving Time means that an hour was subtracted from standard time. When calculating the GMT, add the time of birth to the zone time plus one hour for Daylight Saving Time.

E.G. A person born July 1, 1954 at 3:22 AM in New York City would have a GMT of 3:22 (local time) + 5 hours (zone time) + 1 hour (Daylight Saving Time) or 9:22 AM

Daylight Saving Time generally runs from the last Sunday in April to the last Sunday in October and changes at 2:00 AM on those days. In the U.S., during World War II, Daylight Saving Time was observed year round from February 2, 1942 to September 30, 1945.

For those born before 1945, prior to the standardization of Daylight Saving Time, check with your local state or town or see *Time Changes in the U.S.A.* by Doris Chase Doane published by the American Federation of Astrologers, Inc., Tempe, Arizona, 1981.

Positions of Planets According to the Ecliptic

Now it should be possible for you to determine Greenwich time for your birth, no matter where you may have been born, provided that you have allowed for the time correction and for daylight saving time.

At this point, it shall be possible to determine positions of planets in relation to the ecliptic by consulting ephemerides (tables indicating positions of planets).

In fact, these positions are independent of the terrestrial point for which a horoscope is being cast. They only depend upon the time of the event, expressed in GMT.

Ephemerides which you may consult indicate the ecliptic coordinates once each day, at 12:00 A.M. GMT (Some use 12:00 P.M. GMT), for bodies within our solar system: the Sun, the Moon, the planets (with phases of the Moon in some instances).

In order to be more accurate, we should take into account the period elapsing between the time of birth (GMT time) and the GMT hour (12:00 A.M. or 12:00 P.M.) for which a given ephemeris indicates planetary positions. Therefore, it shall be necessary to introduce corrections for the Moon, for the Sun, and even for Venus. For slower planets, from Mars to Pluto, where there is a smaller change of position each day, interpolations can be completed when it is considered necessary to do so.

What is the precise position of the Sun for a person born at 3:00 P.M. on November 23, 1960?

GMT = 3:15 P.M. + 1 hour = 2:15 P.M.

(1) It is necessary to determine movement of the Sun during twenty-four hours: between November 23, 1960 and November 24, 1960.

Position of the Sun at 12:00 A.M. on November 24	1°43′12″
Position of the Sun at 12:00 A.M. on November 23	0°42′30″ from Sagittarius
	1°00′42″ (Movement of the Sun during 24 hours)

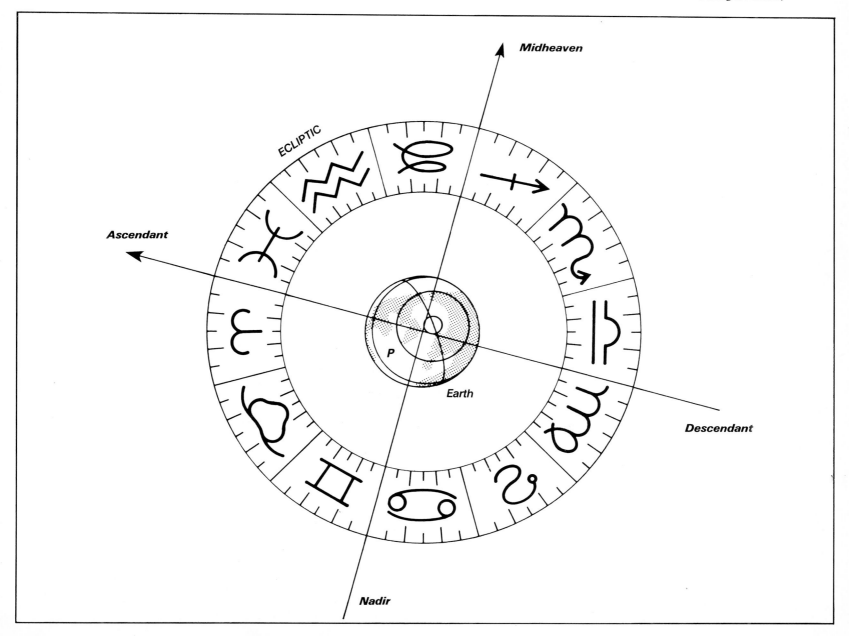

(2) By a simple rule of three, it can be determined that the Sun had advanced by 35°25' by 2:15 P.M.

Hence, the position of the Sun at 2:15 P.M., on November 23, 1960 can be defined in the following manner:

Position of the Sun at 12:00 A.M. on November 24	0°42'30"
Movement of the Sun by 2:15 P.M.	35'25"
Position of the Sun at 2:15 P.M.	1°17'55" within Sagittarius

For all of the heavenly bodies which travel rapidly, it is possible to perform the same interpolation. The following table indicating average trajectories (movement) constitutes an example:

	24 hrs.	1 hr.	15 mins.	5 mins.	1 min.
Venus Mercury The Sun	60'	2'30"	37"	12"	2"25'
The Moon	13'	32"	8"	2"42'	32'
Mars	30'	1'15"	19"	6"	1"25'

Phase 2
Computing the Ascendant and Terrestrial Coordinates According to Local Time and Sidereal Time

During this phase, it is necessary to determine the ascendant and subsequently, the descendant, the midheaven, and the nadir (which are indicated in a "table of houses"[1]).

The ascendant is the horizontal plane intersecting with your birthplace and meeting the ecliptic (path of the Zodiac) in the East. As we have seen, it is the first location which is rising at the time of birth, so as to merge with the cosmos. According to the sign which it occupies, the ascendant permits a person to understand his inner personality more fully, in the form in which it may tend to be expressed during his or her life (with its potential in terms of physical forces, or its tendencies). Whereas the position of the Sun within a sign of the Zodiac reflects development of individual characteristics, namely the ways whereby a person may attempt to fulfill inner ideals (symbolism for individual signs, as described earlier), permits a person to define his or her psychological tendencies at various levels). When the ascendant and the Sun occupy signs representing the same element, such as fire, this situation may facilitate fulfillment of ideals, if other planets do not interfere in a countervailing form.

In order to determine the ascendant (3), it is necessary to compute the parameter known as *local sidereal time* (LST) (3), which defines the position of the celestial sphere in relation to the meridian (see the diagram) for a particular time and place. To determine local sidereal time, one must initially identify local time (1), namely the actual time at one's birthplace, with the geographic longitude taken into account. The geographic longitude expresses the precise differences between Greenwich time computed during Phase 1 and the local meridian time for a person's birthplace.

---

1. Having arrived at the sidereal time for the time and place of birth, look up the number in a table of houses to get the midheaven and ascendant. The intermediate house cusps will be there as well. The most popular table of houses is Dalton's published by Macoy Publishing and Masonic Supply Company, Richmond, Virginia.

(1) Computing Local Time

West of Greenwich
Local time: GMT: − Longitude
Example: Kenosha, Wisconsin
Western Time Zone — Add 6 hours
Longitude: − 5 hours, 51 minutes West;
thus, if the official time is 8:18 A.M., or 2:18 P.M. GMT, the local time is: 2:18 P.M. *minus* 5 hours, 51 minutes, or 8:27 A.M.

East of Greenwich
Local time: GMT + Longitude
Example: Peking (China)
Eastern Time Zone — Add 8 hours
Longitude: + 7 hours, 45 minutes, 53 seconds East;
thus, if the official time is 3:45 P.M., or 7:45 A.M., GMT, the local time is:
7:45 A.M. *plus* 7 hours, 45 minutes, and 53 seconds, or 3:30'53" P.M.

N.B.: Usually, longitude is indicated according to degrees. Thus, it can easily be found in an atlas. In order to convert longitude to time, you can use the following table, which provides the principal angle/time equivalencies:

Angle	Time	Angle	Time
1°	4 minutes	15"	1 minute
5°	20 minutes	1'	4 minutes
15°	1 hour	5'	20 minutes
60°	4 hours	15'	1 hour
180°	12 hours		
360°	24 hours		

Days	Jan.	Feb.	March	April	May	June	July	Aug.	Sept.	Oct.	Nov.	Dec.
1	6 34	8 38	10 33	12 36	14 33	16 35	18 34	20 37	22 39	0 37	2 39	4 38
2	6 40	8 42	10 37	12 40	14 37	16 39	18 38	20 41	22 43	0 41	2 43	4 42
3	6 44	8 46	10 40	12 44	14 41	16 43	18 42	20 45	22 47	0 45	2 47	4 46
4	6 48	8 50	10 44	12 48	14 45	16 47	18 46	20 49	22 51	0 49	2 51	4 50
5	6 52	8 54	10 48	12 52	14 49	16 51	18 50	20 53	22 55	0 53	2 55	4 54
6	6 56	8 58	10 52	12 55	14 53	16 55	18 54	20 57	22 59	0 57	2 59	4 57
7	7	9 02	10 56	12 58	14 57	16 59	18 58	21	23 03	1 01	3 03	5 01
8	7 04	9 06	11	13 02	15 01	17 03	19 02	21 04	23 07	1 05	3 07	5 05
9	7 08	9 10	11 04	13 06	15 05	17 07	19 06	21 08	23 11	1 09	3 11	5 09
10	7 12	9 14	11 08	13 10	15 09	17 11	19 10	21 12	23 14	1 13	3 15	5 13
11	7 15	9 18	11 12	13 14	15 13	17 15	19 14	21 16	23 18	1 17	3 19	5 17
12	7 19	9 22	11 16	13 18	15 17	17 19	19 18	21 20	23 22	1 21	3 23	5 21
13	7 23	9 26	11 20	13 22	15 21	17 23	19 22	21 24	23 26	1 25	3 27	5 25
14	7 27	9 30	11 24	13 26	15 24	17 27	19 26	21 28	23 30	1 29	3 31	5 29
15	7 31	9 33	11 28	13 30	15 28	17 31	19 30	21 32	23 34	1 32	3 35	5 33
16	7 35	9 37	11 32	13 34	15 32	17 34	19 34	21 36	23 38	1 36	3 39	5 37
17	7 39	9 41	11 36	13 38	15 36	17 38	19 38	21 40	23 42	1 40	3 43	5 41
18	7 43	9 45	11 40	13 42	15 40	17 42	19 42	21 44	23 46	1 44	3 47	5 45
19	7 47	9 49	11 44	13 46	15 44	17 46	19 46	21 48	23 50	1 48	3 50	5 49
20	7 51	9 53	11 48	13 50	15 48	17 50	19 49	21 52	23 54	1 52	3 55	5 53
21	7 55	9 57	11 52	13 54	15 52	17 54	19 53	21 56	23 58	1 56	3 58	5 57
22	7 59	10 01	11 55	13 58	15 56	17 58	19 57	22	0 02	2	4 02	6 01
23	8 03	10 05	11 58	14 02	16	18 02	20 02	22 04	0 06	2 04	4 06	6 05
24	8 07	10 09	12 02	14 06	16 04	18 06	20 06	22 08	0 10	2 06	4 10	6 09
25	8 11	10 13	12 06	14 10	16 08	18 10	20 10	22 12	0 14	2 12	4 14	6 13
26	8 15	10 17	12 10	14 14	16 12	18 14	20 14	22 16	0 18	2 16	4 18	6 17
27	8 19	10 21	12 14	14 18	16 16	18 18	20 18	22 20	0 23	2 20	4 22	6 21
28	8 23	10 25	12 18	14 22	16 20	18 22	20 22	22 24	0 26	2 24	4 26	6 24
29	8 26	10 29	12 22	14 26	16 24	18 26	20 26	22 27	0 30	2 28	4 30	6 28
30	8 30		12 26	14 29	16 28	18 30	20 30	22 31	0 34	2 32	4 34	6 32
31	8 34		12 30		16 32		20 33	22 35		2 36		6 36

Table of Longitudes and Latitudes of the Principal Cities of North America

Atlantic Standard Time
4 hours west of Greenwich

Canada

Halifax, Nova Scotia	63°W 35	44°N 38
Charlotteville, Prince Edward Island	63°W 07	46°N 14
Fredericton, New Brunswick	66°W 39	45°N 05

Eastern Standard Time
5 hours west of Greenwich

Augusta, ME	69°W 46.7	44°N 18.8
Portland, ME	70°W 15.7	43°N 39.2
Concord, NH	71°W 32.2	43°N 12.3
Montpelier, VT	72°W 34.7	44°N 15.7
Brattleboro, VT	72°W 33.8	42°N 51.1
Burlington, VT	73°W 12.4	44°N 28.5
Boston, MA	71°W 3.5	42°N 21.7
Providence, RI	71°W 24.4	41°N 49.0
Hartford, CT	72°W 40.5	41°N 46.0
New Haven, CT	72°W 54.6	41°N 18.1
Albany, NY	73°W 45.4	42°N 39.0
New York, NY	74°W 0.0	40°N 42.5
Syracuse, NY	76°W 9.0	43°N 3.1
Buffalo, NY	78°W 52.5	42°N 53.2
Trenton, NJ	74°W 46.0	40°N 13.5
Philadelphia, PA	75°W 9.8	39°N 57.0

City	Longitude	Latitude
Harrisburg, PA	76°W 53.0	40°N 15.8
Pittsburgh, PA	80°W 0.5	40°N 26.2
Dover, DE	75°W 31.9	39°N 9.6
Baltimore, MD	76°W 37.0	39°N 17.3
Annapolis, MD	76°W 29.7	38°N 58.6
Washington, DC	77°W 0.6	38°N 53.3
Richmond, VA	77°W 26.9	37°N 32.5
Roanoke, VA	79°W 56.2	37°N 16.4
Charleston, WV	81°W 37.9	38°N 20.9
Raleigh, NC	78°W 38.0	35°N 46.3
Charlotte, NC	80°W 50.8	35°N 13.1
Greensboro, NC	79°W 47.6	36°N 4.4
Columbia, SC	81°W 2.7	33°N 59.6
Charleston, SC	79°W 55.8	32°N 45.8
Spartenburg, SC	81°W 56.6	34°N 56.4
Atlanta, GA	84°W 23.2	33°N 45.0
Augusta, GA	81°W 58.0	33°N 28.2
Savannah, GA	81°W 5.6	32°N 4.6
Tallahassee, FL	84°W 16.9	30°N 26.7
Tampa, FL	82°W 27.0	27°N 57.1
Miami, FL	80°W 11.4	25°N 46.5
Jacksonville, FL	81°W 39.4	30°N 19.8
Lansing, MI	84°W 32.6	42°N 44.0
Detroit, MI	83°W 3.0	42°N 20.0
Frankfort, KY	84°W 51.7	38°N 12.0
Louisville, KY	85°W 45.7	38°N 14.8
Knoxville, TN	83°W 55.1	35°N 58.1
Chattanooga, TN	85°W 18.6	35°N 2.6
Nashville, TN	86°W 46.7	36°N 9.8
Indianapolis, IN	86°W 9.3	39°N 46.3
Ft. Wayne, IN	85°W 8.5	41°N 4.3

Canada

City	Longitude	Latitude
Quebec, Quebec	71°W 13	46°N 48
Montreal, Quebec	73°W 34	45°N 32
Ottawa, Ontario	75°W 42	45°N 25
Toronto, Ontario	79°W 22	43°N 39
Saulte Ste. Marie, Ontario	84°W 21	46°N 21

Central Standard Time
6 hours west of Greenwich

City	Longitude	Latitude
Montgomery, AL	86°W 18.5	32°N 22.9
Mobile, AL	88°W 2.6	30°N 41.3
Birmingham, AL	86°W 48.4	33°N 30.7
Jackson, MS	90°W 11.5	32°N 17.9
Baton Rouge, LA	91°W 11.1	30°N 27.0
New Orleans, LA	90°W 3.8	29°N 57.8
Shreveport, LA	93°W 45.0	32°N 30.5

City	Longitude	Latitude
Memphis, TN	90°W 3.4	35°N 7.5
Little Rock, AR	92°W 16.7	34°N 44.8
El Dorado, AR	92°W 40.0	33°N 12.4
Fayetteville, AR	94°W 9.6	36°N 4.0
Gary, IN	87°W 20.0	41°N 36.0
Jefferson City, MO	92°W 10.1	38°N 34.4
St. Louis, MO	90°W 11.6	38°N 37.0
Springfield, MO	93°W 17.4	37°N 13.2
Springfield, IL	89°W 38.9	39°N 48.0
Chicago, IL	87°W 37.5	41°N 53.0
St. Paul, MN	93°W 5.7	44°N 56.8
Duluth, MN	92°W 6.8	46°N 47.0
Madison, WI	89°W 23.6	43°N 4.2
Milwaukee, WI	87°W 54.8	43°N 2.3
Superior, WI	92°W 6.1	46°N 44.1
Bismarck, ND	100°W 48	46°N 50
Fargo, ND	96°W 47.8	46°N 52.5
Pierre, SD	100°W 20.9	44°N 22.3
Sioux Falls, SD	96°W 44.0	43°N 32.5
Lincoln, NB	96°W 41.1	40°N 49.4
Omaha, NB	96°W 0.5	41°N 17.0
Grand Island, NB	98°W 21.1	40°N 55.3
Topeka, KN	95°W 40.2	39°N 3.1
Kansas City, KN	94°W 37.5	39°N 7.1
Wichita, KN	97°W 20.2	37°N 41.5
Oklahoma City, OK	97°W 30.2	35°N 29.6
Tulsa, OK	95°W 54.5	36°N 9.6
Austin, TX	97°W 44.5	30°N 16.9
Dallas, TX	96°W 48.7	32°N 46.6
Houston, TX	95°W 21.7	29°N 45.8
San Antonio, TX	98°W 29.7	29°N 25.4
Corpus Christi, TX	97°W 23.9	27°N 46.8
El Paso, TX	106°W 28.8	31°N 45.3

Canada

City	Longitude	Latitude
Winnipeg, Manitoba	97°W 09	49°N 53

Mountain Standard Time
7 hours west of Greenwich

City	Longitude	Latitude
Helena, MT	112°W 1.6	46°N 35.7
Butte, MT	112°W 31.6	46°N 0.2
Billings, MT	108°W 30.3	45°N 46.8
Cheyenne, WY	104°W 48.8	41°N 8.3
Casper, WY	106°W 18.8	42°N 50.8
Jackson, WY	110°W 45.7	43°N 28.7
Denver, CO	104°W 59.3	39°N 44.4
Pueblo, CO	104°W 36.3	38°N 14.4
Crested Butte, CO	106°W 59.1	38°N 52.1

City	Longitude	Latitude
Sante Fe, NM	105°W 56.7	35°N 40.8
Albuquerque, NM	106°W 39.0	35°N .0
Phoenix, AR	112°W 4.4	33°N 27.3
Tucson, AR	110°W 58.1	32°N 13.0
Salt Lake City, UT	111°W 52.9	40°N 45.3
Boise, ID	116°W 13.1	43°N 36.8
Idaho Falls, ID	112°W 2.0	43°N 29.5

Mexico

City	Longitude	Latitude
Chihuahua	106°W 05	26°N 38

Canada

City	Longitude	Latitude
Calgary, Alberta	114°W 04	51°N 03
Edmonton, Alberta	113°W 20	53°N 32

Pacific Standard Time
8 hours west of Greenwich

City	Longitude	Latitude
Olympia, WA	122°W 53.4	47°N 2.7
Seattle, WA	122°W 19.8	47°N 35.8
Spokane, WA	117°W 24.3	47°N 40.3
Salem, OR	123°W 2.0	44°N 56.4
Portland, OR	122°W 37.2	45°N 32.1
Eugene, OR	123°W 4.3	44°N .9
Sacramento, CA	121°W 29.4	38°N 35.1
San Francisco, CA	122°W 25.0	37°N 46.5
Los Angeles, CA	118°W 15.0	34°N 3.5
Eureka, CA	124°W 9.4	40°N 46.9
Fresno, CA	119°W 47.0	36°N 43.9
San Diego, CA	117°W 9.2	32°N 42.8
Carson City, NV	119°W 46.0	39°N 10.0
Las Vegas, NV	115°W 8.8	36°N 10.3
Reno, NV	119°W 48.4	39°N 31.4

Mexico

City	Longitude	Latitude
Tijuana	117°W 02	32°N 32
Ensenada	116°W 37	31°N 52

Alaska Standard Time
10 hours west of Greenwich

City	Longitude	Latitude
Juneau, AL	134°W 24.5	58°N 18.2
Ankorage, AL	149°W 53.5	61°N 13.1
Fairbanks, AL	147°W 43.2	64°N 50.8

Hawaii Standard Time
until 1947 then Alaska Standard Time
10.5 hours west of Greenwich
then 10 hours west of Greenwich

City	Longitude	Latitude
Honolulu	157°W 51.8	21°N 18.8

Below are listed computer services which will calculate your chart for you. Please include your date of birth, time of birth, and place of birth.

AGS, Inc.
Box 28
Orleans, Massachusetts 02653

Astro Computing Services
Box 16430
San Diego, California 92116

To find an astrologer in your area who can interpret your horoscope, as well as to calculate it refer to the agencies listed below.

American Federation of Astrologers
P.O. Box 22040
Tempe, Arizona 85282

National Council of Geocosmic Research, Inc.
P.O. Box 16430
San Diego, California 92116-9987

NCGR, Inc.
Charles Emerson, Director
436 West 22nd Street
New York, New York 10011

Jane Graham, M.A.F.A.
7 Gay Road
Watertown, Massachusetts 02172

Contents

Acknowledgments

Translated by Lawrence Lockwood of Somerville, Massachusetts.
English edition edited and typeset at Arts & Letters, Inc., Brookline, Massachusetts.
Astrological consultant: Jane Graham, Watertown, Massachusetts.